This book is due for return on or before the last date shown below.

13. JUN 2000

23. APR. 2001

-9. MAY 2001

-6 JUN 2001

26. JUN 2001

03 JUL 2015

Don Gresswell Ltd., London, N21   Cat. No. 1207   DG 02242/71

BOYS WILL BE MEN

RAISING OUR SONS for COURAGE, CARING and COMMUNITY

Paul Kivel

NEW SOCIETY PUBLISHERS

Cataloguing in Publication Data:
A catalog record for this publication is available from the National Library of
Canada and the Library of Congress.

Cover design by John Nedwidek; page design by Miriam MacPhail.

Printed in Canada on acid-free, partially recycled (20 percent post-
consumer) paper using soy-based inks by Transcontinental/Best Book
Manufacturers.

Paperback ISBN: 0-86571-395-2

Inquiries regarding requests to reprint all or part of *Boys Will Be Men* should be
addressed to New Society Publishers at the address below.

The Act Like a Man Box, Men Stand Up Exercise, Women Stand Up Exercise,
and The Power Chart are reprinted with permission from: *Helping Teens Stop
Violence* © 1990, 1992 by Allan Creighton, Battered Women's Alternatives, and
Oakland Men's Project.

To order directly from the publishers, please add $4.00 shipping to the price of
the first copy, and $1.00 for each additional copy (plus GST in Canada). Send
check or money order to:

New Society Publishers
P.O. Box 189, Gabriola Island, B.C. V0R 1X0, Canada

New Society Publishers aims to publish books for fundamental social change
through nonviolent action. We focus especially on sustainable living, progressive leadership, and educational and parenting resources. Our full list of books
can be browsed on the worldwide web at: http://www.newsociety.com

NEW SOCIETY PUBLISHERS
Gabriola Island B.C., Canada

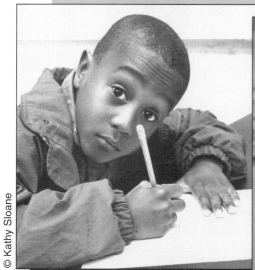

DEDICATION

*This book is dedicated to all of our sons,
and to our daughters*

Table of Contents

PART 3: RELATIONSHIPS

PART 4: PUBLIC ACTION

Acknowledgments

I find it hard to know where to begin acknowledging all those whose lives, struggles, courage, critical thinking, caring, and encouragement have nurtured and sustained me.

Certainly in my own lifetime the civil rights movement, women's movement, and many other individual and collective actions to build a more just society have drawn me in and inspired me. These movements have been led by concerned individuals — including young people, people of color, women in all groups, lesbians, gays, and bisexuals, people with disabilities, and Jews — who have greatly challenged my behavior and expanded my thinking.

My Jewish foreparents and traditions have taught me much about survival, about social justice, and about *tikun olam* – our responsibility to help repair the fabric of the world.

I have been inspired and challenged by many feminists who have written about parenting and childraising in the last thirty years including Pauline Bart, Phyllis Chesler, Nancy Chodorow, Marita Golden, Selma Greenberg, Audre Lorde, Cherrie Moraga, Robin Morgan, Letty Pogrebin, Adrienne Rich, and Alice Walker.

I have been fortunate to know many wonderful parents who are raising sons in new and exciting ways. I would thank Robert Allen, Heru-Nefera Amen, Chris Anderegg, Bob Boardman, Jim Coates, Hari Dillon, Steve Falk, Joe Foster, David Lee, David Kim, Terry Kupers, David Landes, Victor Lewis, Walter Riley, Barry Shapiro, Richard Speigleman, and Hugh Vasquez for being models for me of men who have responded to the challenges of raising children with thoughtfulness and creativity.

I have great appreciation for the network of friends, family, and colleagues who sustain me and inspire my work. Some of them read early drafts of the book and contributed valuable feedback. All of them have supported my efforts to write about raising sons. I want to particularly mention Bill Aal, Margo Adair, Robert Allen, Heru-Nefera Amen, Cathy Cade, Janet Carter, Allan Creighton, Isoke Femi, Luz Guerra, Lakota Harden, Wendy Horikoshi, Ellen Kahler, Beth Kivel, Kesa Kivel, David Lee, Amy Levine, Aurora Levins-Morales, Victor Lewis, Peggy McIntosh, Daphne Muse, Nell Myhand, Kiran Rana, Penny Rosenwaser, Ilana Schatz, Jackie Shonerd, John Tucker, Naomi Tucker, Hugh Vasquez, and Patty Wipfler. I also want to acknowledge three fallen warriors of my community — Martin

Cano, Ricky Sherover-Marcuse, and Harrison Sims. I miss each of them.

I want to thank John Stoltenberg for encouraging an early article about raising sons, and the editors at *On the Issues* magazine for publishing it.

I want to thank my publishers Chris and Judith Plant at New Society for their enthusiasm and support for this project. Their entire book list speaks to their vision and commitment to building a better society. Chris was particularly attentive to this project; Audrey McClellen did a fine job of editing; the cover design by John Nedwidek is beautiful; the interior design is by Miriam MacPhail & Sue Custance; Lisa Garbutt's enthusiasm for the book and her marketing skill will undoubtedly make it a success; and Gail Leondar-Wright has added her talents to the publicity efforts.

I greatly appreciate the wonderful ability of Kathy Sloane and Cathy Cade to capture the magic of boys' lives and their partnership with me in this project. Thanks also to Khalil Jacobs-Fantauzzi who contributed photos to the book.

I could not have written this book without a wonderful life partnership with Micki with whom I've co-parented our children. Her love, commitment, passion, insight, challenge, and sense of justice continue to nurture and inspire me.

And most of all, my appreciation goes to my children, Ariel, Shandra, and Ryan, for their loving, their courage, their creativity, and their passion for justice. And to all the other young people whom I've been blessed to know and work with over these years.

Preface

As I sit down to write this preface, our two youngest children, Shandra (15) and Ryan (11), are just coming home from school. The house is filling up with their energy, their friends, homework assignments, endless questions, music, and afternoon snacks. They each come into my small study off the living room to tell me about their day and to discuss homework, dinner, and other details of family life.

I have just received a notice from Ryan's school that one of the boys was suspended for fighting, so I ask him about what happened. He also reminds me that this Friday night there is a dance at his school — his first dance — and I can see the excitement and trepidation in his eyes as he tells me that he will need a ride.

Shandra tells me about how her school is coping with the death of one of her classmates the week before. A girl, a friend of hers, died of a cerebral hemorrhage in front of a group of students. Shandra is still visibly shaken by it. She also tells me about the booth for an upcoming school fair that is being put together by a club she has joined — Gay and Lesbian Awareness Group.

The news I have for them is that the articles of impeachment for President Clinton have been passed and will be voted on soon.

Our discussions about violence, sexuality, dating, death, sexual identity, and politics remind me why the task of raising children is so important. Their interruptions also remind me that it is getting late and I have to stop writing soon and go shopping for dinner. Parenting is like that — a complex mix of loving, caring, joy, hope, connection, large issues, and small, everyday details. Sometimes the everyday detail seems so consistently demanding that it is hard to hold on to the other feelings.

I remember our hopes when we had Ariel, our oldest son, some twenty years ago. We thought we would just incorporate him into our lives, take him with us wherever we went, instill our values in him, and create a new man. It seemed relatively easy — until his birth. After that it seemed like we were flying on our own. How do you raise boys who will be able to take care of themselves and those around them, who will be involved in building a better community, and who will work to end injustice? There seemed to be few guides.

As Ariel entered adolescence in the early 1990s, boys and young men became more embattled, faced more violence, greater cutbacks in education, more blame for social problems. As Shandra became a teenager in the mid 1990s, girls began to receive more attention and as a society we began to recognize that we needed to drastically rethink our responses to girls if we were to create a society that was not based on gender inequality. Now, as Ryan becomes a teen at the beginning of the twenty-first century, society is beginning to pay attention to the plight of boys. But I still can't find books that would have helped me as a parent raise sons who are the involved members of the community that we need them to be.

This book grows out of twenty years of raising children, working at the Oakland Men's Project with men and boys, community education, training, writing, and activism all focused on one overriding question: How can we live and work together to sustain community, nurture each individual, and create a multicultural society based on love, caring, interdependence with all living things, and justice?

I still don't know the answer to that question. But I feel more strongly than ever before that the challenge that question poses is the most important one we face in the world today. I have used that question to guide me in writing this book — the book that I was looking for twenty years ago when Ariel was born. I hope this book will help guide your efforts to raise our sons for courage, caring, and community.

Introduction

I imagine a world in which boys are successful in school, active participants in the life of their families, and responsible members of the community. A world in which boys are strong and powerful, but also gentle and caring. I see them as not only able to get by, but also to get ahead; not only able to get ahead, but also able to get together with others to work to improve our society. I imagine this for *all* of our sons. Can you imagine this as not being at the expense of our daughters?

WHAT KIND OF BOYS DO YOU WANT TO RAISE?

To create this better world we would have to raise boys who feel connected to the environment so that they will help take care of it. We would have to raise boys who are able to express a wide variety of feelings so that they can empathize with the situations of others and reach out to them with caring. We would want them to be able to take care of themselves physically and emotionally so they would not expect others, especially women, to take care of them. And finally, we would want them to understand the social, political, and economic systems they live within so that they could work to

© Kathy Sloane

1

change the conditions that presently produce too many boys who are either destructive or self-destructive, fearsome or fearful, dependent or adamantly independent.

I want our boys to be men who will treat women as human beings and participate in the struggle to end violence against women. I want them to treat others with fairness and respect, and to intervene when others are being discriminated against or treated disrespectfully. I want them to help the poor, the sick, the hungry, and the homeless, *and* I want them to join with others to change the social conditions that produce poverty, homelessness, inadequate medical care, and lack of opportunity.

The question "What kind of boys do you want to raise?" leads to another question: "What kind of world do you want to create?" My vision is of a society in which every person is cared for and valued regardless of gender, race, cultural background, sexual identity, ability or disability, or access to money. This society would provide adequate shelter, food, education, recreation, health care, security, and well-paying jobs for all. The land would be respected and sustained, and justice and equal opportunity would prevail. Such a society would value cooperation over competition, community development over individual achievement, democratic participation over hierarchy and control, and interdependence over either dependence or independence. If our sons are to help us build such a world, we will need to raise them in new ways.

WHY BOYS?

During the 1970s and 1980s many feminists questioned traditional roles, patriarchal values, and the limits placed on what women could achieve. As part of this struggle they discussed how to raise daughters who would be strong, self-assured, and successful. They had a clear sense of how they wanted girls to be but were less clear about how they wanted boys to be different. One couple, committed activists, admitted to me in the early 1980s that they almost wished they had a daughter instead of a son because they had a much better idea how to raise a feminist daughter than a feminist son.

Feminists knew that they wanted to raise boys who would not be violent and abusive to women and who would share in the housework and childcare, but many were less clear about what else would be required to raise boys who would participate in community struggles for gender equity and social justice. The sphere of discussion was primarily the family; the prescriptions were for interpersonal and family relationships. There hardly seems to be less uncertainty today, as reflected by a 1993 *Ms.* magazine cover article, "It's a boy! Now What?" or the much more arrogant 1998 *Newsweek* cover story, "How to Build a Better BOY."

In the 1990s there has been a spate of books about raising sons.[1] Although there is much that is useful in some of these books and it is refreshing to see critical thinking applied to the subject of raising boys, I find a significant gap between the methods proposed by these books and what is needed.

The authors of these books do not talk about the need for social change and the role that can be played in creating it by men who challenge social injustice and traditional definitions of masculinity. They do not talk about men as citizens, social actors, or people with social values. They do talk about how to raise sons who will survive, avoid violence, and escape the pitfalls of adolescence, but they don't discuss how to help young men become part of the community struggling to end violence and exploitation that claim the lives of so many young people.

As I see it, Boys are being raised, have always been raised, to participate in and thereby to enforce the current social, political, and economic structure; to drop out and thereby to fail by its standards; or to collude with it by accepting their role as its beneficiaries.

- Young men enforce the status quo when they become police, soldiers, security guards, deans, probation officers, prison guards, or even just the fathers in families where they teach their sons to "Grow up and act like a man."
- They drop out when they drop out of school, drop out of community life, drop out of families, drop out of political action.
- They collude by accepting inequality and injustice; by working in jobs that placate and pacify people; by enjoying the benefits of being men — or white, or heterosexual, or well-off — without protesting the inequality upon which those benefits are based.

Boys Will Be Men is a different kind of book about raising boys. It goes beyond the basics and asks deeper questions, calls for a more profound response, and invites you to take on the urgent task of raising sons who will join those of us working to transform our society so that children can become healthy, productive, and politically active adults. These boys will become men who do not enforce or drop out or collude with injustice, but who resist, challenge, and organize against it.

WHAT DO MEN STAND FOR?

On April 22, 1998, more than 2000 middle- and high-school students from over fifteen schools around the San Francisco Bay Area participated in a school walk-out and rally to protest deteriorating conditions in the schools and recent attacks on immigrant rights, affirmative action, and bilingual education. The rally took place in front of the new police station in Concord. The station's $20 million price tag symbolized our society's priorities: prisons over youth and education. The students gathered in Concord and marched to the police station where they held a peaceful rally with hip-hop music, speakers, and lots of spontaneous comments from participants. The multiracial demonstrators cleaned up after themselves and left no litter.[2]

The rally was planned months in advance by a multiracial coalition with both young women and young men in leadership positions. The participants demonstrated knowledge of political and economic issues, sensitivity to gender and race politics, dedication to making their community better, respect for the environment, and a commitment to full inclusion and democratic processes. Although the youth had adult mentors and support, they were clearly in charge. Adults have much to learn from their insights and much hope to gain from their efforts — but newspapers and radio and TV stations, which have no trouble covering youth crime, gave little attention to youth taking leadership. The Bay Area media scarcely covered the event and many adults I talked with in the area were not even aware that it had occurred.

I mention this event because it is indicative of the kind of critical thinking, commitment to social justice, and leadership that young men, working in partnership with young women, are capable of. I want this book to provoke that kind of questioning and activism, which is much more far-reaching than most of us are used to envisioning. This book is not just a call to get our sons to become men who vote or who vote for a certain party or platform. Nor is this book an appeal to raise boys who will volunteer for community groups or mentor younger men or give to their local charity or battered women's shelter, as important as these actions are. All of these are things that men do, but they do not say what they stand for.

If men don't stand for equality, democracy, and equal opportunity, and if they don't know how to participate in efforts to achieve those goals, then their actions will not link them to the struggle for social justice.

It is important to note that I am not talking about training our sons to go out and fight for democracy or to fight on behalf of women. Our notion of men who are warriors or fighters for justice is based on male roles that exclude women or define them as dependent on men's protection or rescue. Our stories of warriors tell of men who battle dragons, attack demons, or tilt at windmills. This insistence that men be warriors comes out of a tradition of men standing alone, pursuing individual dreams and goals, being strong, independent, and ultimately unaccountable only to another man if to anyone. Although the call to be a warrior in our society occasionally leads to community leadership, it more often leads men to fight for the power, status, money, and other goods rewarded to the best and the brightest.

The struggle for social justice is a collective effort — the collective action of communities of people for political power and participation. I see a need to ask our sons who are becoming men not only what they stand for, but who they stand with. I hope to help them stand with the poor and exploited in efforts to achieve economic democracy, regardless of their own economic status. And, will they stand with women in collective action for gender justice and an end to male violence? Whether they are white, of mixed heritage, or boys of color, will they stand with people of color[3] for an end to racial discrimination and violence?

Injustice, discrimination, inequality, and violence are all too present in our lives and have a devastating impact on our communities. In the struggle for social justice and equality, each of us is potentially an actor. Our children will be actors. Their actions will be influenced by how we raise them. Of course children raised by progressive parents sometimes grow up to be conservative. Progressive adults sometimes grow up in conservative households. The times, the issues, and the culture influence what kind of political lives adults will have. Even so, we can have a tremendous impact on our children's lives. We have the opportunity to give our sons tools and guidance in becoming progressive, anti-racist, feminist, political activists.

I think we can do this most successfully not through lectures, abstract discussion, or arbitrary authority but by simply offering sons and daughters the support, nourishment, critical thinking skills, challenges, and experience that will lead them towards values and actions that contribute to community efforts for social justice.

You might be thinking at this point that a focus on social justice is all fine and good but many of our sons are in trouble. They are dying. They need survival skills. They need job skills. They need to read, write, and do math. They need to be able to avoid violence.

I agree. But what do they need these things for? And will the motivation to gain these skills come simply from their sense of self-preservation? Simply from their desire to get ahead, at whoever's expense?

Survival is not enough. Yes, our sons need jobs and job skills. But there are not enough jobs for everyone. At whose expense will they obtain jobs? They need education, but there are not enough good schools, not enough funding for education, not enough seats in our universities for everyone who wants a college education. At whose expense will our sons become educated?

The acquisition of living and work skills are crucial to our young men, particularly to our most threatened youth. But I am convinced that we will only be able to reach most of them when those skills are attached to values that speak to young people's need for connection, participation, respect, creativity, and social justice.

OUR JOURNEY

I will use two questions to guide us throughout this book. What will our sons stand for? Who will they stand with? This book is about how to raise sons who answer those questions in ways you and they can be proud of.

I will start off in Part One by looking at the big picture — gender differences, some current issues that face youth, and the pressures on our sons to "Act Like a Man" and to get ahead or at least to get by, but not to get together with others to make a difference. Then I suggest ways of thinking about what you bring to parenting or your work with boys so that these personal issues will not get in the way of providing what boys need. From there I will examine the role that homophobia plays in enforcing the training boys receive to be tough, aggressive, and in control, and the difference that racism makes in how boys are able to cope with the pressure to act in socially prescribed ways.

In Part Two, I suggest ways to help boys connect to the natural world, guidelines to help them learn to take care of themselves physically and emotionally, and some thoughts about teaching them to value family and youth culture, including ideas to help them find creative outlets through the arts for their feelings and thoughts. The following chapters look first at family and then at school, with guidelines for introducing cooperation and democratic practice into interactions with boys. More specific topics follow, including chapters on sports, disability, violence, guns, and drugs.

Part Three of the book is about relationships and how to help boys create intimacy and respectful, satisfying relationships, sexual and nonsexual, with both women and men.

Part Four looks at consumerism, public policy issues, programs that build the leadership of young people, and ways our sons can become involved in community action.

QUESTION EVERYTHING

In this book I hope to provide some ideas and suggestions to make raising boys less overwhelming and less isolating and to help you prepare boys to deal effectively with the complex challenges they face. I offer these ideas cautiously. There is a long history of male experts — primarily white male professionals — giving parents (usually assumed to be mothers) arbitrary and constantly shifting advice about how to raise children.[4] Such advice is supposed to override common sense, practical experience, and the words of other parents because of its male authority and "scientific" basis.

I also offer these words cautiously because there are few generalizations that will apply to everyone. Generalizations about boys are just as problematic as generalizations about girls or any other group of great diversity. Any broad prescription needs to be modified by attention to the particularities of the boys you are raising or otherwise nurturing.

You, the reader, are right to question everything I suggest. Take anything I say (or that any other "expert" says), reflect on it critically, and sift it through your own experience and personal situation. I hope you will be open to my ideas and suggestions, will adapt what you find useful, and will reject anything not appropriate to your situation and needs.

1 Male Socialization

HOW DIFFERENT ARE BOYS AND GIRLS?

I believe that boys and girls are fundamentally not very different. Babies are born with a personality that does not fit into a category of girl or boy. Controlled studies show that, when a baby's sex is not visible, adults, including the biological parents, cannot tell what sex a baby is even after playing or otherwise interacting with it.

It is equally clear that an adult's interaction with a baby will be strikingly different depending on which sex he or she thinks the baby is. Take a set of babies in a nursery and put blue blankets on them. Doctors, nurses, and parents will come by, pat the baby on the back, and make comments about the physical activity and health of the baby. A few hours later put pink blankets on the same babies. Adults will come by, stroke the baby, and, in softer voices, comment on the prettiness of the child's hair or eyes. The same experiment conducted at six months or three years (using pink and blue unisex snowsuits) will produce similar gender-stereotyped behavior from adults, even from those sensitive to gender issues. They will describe the identical behavior differently based on whether they think a girl or a boy performed it.[1]

There are some visible biological differences between boys and girls (although there are thousands of babies not easily described as either male or female), but there is no correlation between these differences and any specific kind of behavior. I think it is very misleading to call these gender differences, because the behavior of girls and boys overlaps so much. Differences in behavior among boys and among girls are much greater than the differences between boys and girls. To use a biological analogy in an example we are all familiar with, men on average are taller than women. However, there is huge variation within the group "men" and within the group "women." There are millions of women who are taller than millions of men in the world. A diagram might make this clearer. (See next page).

In other words, if you saw a person of indistinguishable gender at a distance, you could not tell their gender from their height.[2] Similar diagrams for any physical or behavioral quality — such as aggression, nurturing, large motor activity, or fine motor activity — would show a correspondingly large overlap between genders.[3]

Because rigid ideas about gender difference are pervasive in western

Height Chart

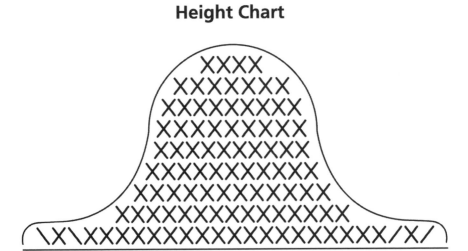

The "\" represents the height range for women and the "/" represents the height range for men. The "X" are areas where they overlap.

society, it is impossible to tell what significance biological difference might have. In addition, because gender roles and expectations change across time and cultures, we should be cautious about concluding some essential maleness or femaleness underlies them. For example:

- earlier in this century men did most of the teaching and office work;
- physicians in Russia are predominantly women;
- men play the major role in childraising and child care in many societies;
- women were active participants in craftwork and manufacturing in colonial America;
- men are affectionate and emotionally expressive in many cultures in Asia, Eastern Europe, and other parts of the world.

GENDER AS A SOCIAL CONSTRUCTION

Masculine and feminine roles are socially constructed, i.e. invented by people and then taken to be fixed in nature. When people use the word "masculine" to describe behaviors, archetypes, myths, rituals, or anything else, they are putting these things in a socially constructed container and leaving out the things they think don't fit, even if these qualities are present. I believe that there is no single behavior, expression, activity, symbol, stance, or psychological quality that is inherently or exclusively male. Throughout history, male and female roles have been created to reflect the ways any particular society divided up tasks and behaviors.

Many of what are currently touted as traditional male roles are throwbacks to patriarchal, feudal societies in Europe or to patriarchal, hierarchical civilizations such as that in ancient Egypt. The roles of warrior, priest, king, and magician were roles that elite men in these societies were allowed to play. The societies and the roles maintaining them were anti-democratic and patriarchal. Many times they promoted ideas of male separation, isolation, and independence that I hope will become obsolete in today's interdependent and more democratic society. If we accept these male roles, we are fostering a notion of responsible but nonresponsive leadership that perpetuates hierarchical thinking and structures. Teaching a boy to be a warrior or a king teaches him that he is above changing the diapers and that there are others — commoners, usually women — who should do that kind of work.

"We need men like they used to be." "Why aren't men responsible any more?" "If only men were more..." "Men used to be so..." "We need to restore men to their place at the head of the family." The feelings expressed in all of these statements draw on a Western nostalgia for a mythical past when men supposedly led their families with responsibility and caring. This nostalgia ignores the history of male abuse in many families, a history that includes desertion, controlling behavior, drug abuse, financial irresponsibility, incest, battery, and physical abuse of children and women. Such nostalgia ignores the tremendous burdens of responsibility on men to meet a continuously expanding set of expectations to provide the good life for their partners and children. It also ignores the role that men have played in upholding very exploitative and hierarchical social structures.

The families of our past were not uniformly happy families, although they may have looked less conflicted from the outside than today's families do.[4] Nor was the community the same. Extended family networks were often intact, there were greater levels of community and governmental support from the mid 1940s through the 1970s, and children had a broader social safety net than they do now. Restoring a falsely remembered masculine role in today's fragmented and devastated communities would not get us very far towards solving our most pressing social and economic problems.

Those of us who are tempted to cling to traditions that promise security, order, control, and discipline must guard against such answers to the confusion we face. In communities of color, in poor and working-class communities, and in immigrant communities — all of which are under great attack — this is a particularly strong temptation. Some people may want to romanticize their cultural heritages and pretend that everything bad has been adapted from white mainstream culture, or may want to return to a non-Western tradition without questioning the fundamental values of that tradition.

I urge caution here because I think we can neither reject traditional approaches to raising boys nor accept those traditions indiscriminately, especially when they leave out women. For example, I think that initiation rituals and rites of passage are important for boys. And there are culturally specific traditions and models worth adapting, particularly those that build young men's self-confidence, education, spiritual understanding, empathy for all life, and connection to a social community which gives meaning, direction and responsibility to their life. Unfortunately, male initiations have often been used by men to welcome boys into exclusive spheres of adult male power and to separate them from women. Instead, we can take the useful and positive practices, modify them to meet changing circumstances, and mix them with contemporary ideas and understandings to create rituals that emphasize interdependence and affirm young men's respect for and interdependence with women.

The challenge for parents and teachers in raising boys is to acknowledge the tremendous influence of socially created gender divisions and traditional male roles without accepting them as natural. We can try to overcome these divisions and to change these roles as we face a constant social backlash that tries to reestablish gender role differences based on genetics, body chemistry, historical patterns, or cultural traditions.

It may be difficult for you to accept the fact that forms of male behavior are not biologically determined or unalterable. You don't need to accept my emphasis on the social construction of gender differences to find this book useful. At the same time, you might want to try the following exercise. Make a list of what you consider to be male and female qualities. Look at the qualities carefully and see if there are any that the other group does not exhibit.

EXERCISE

(Enter Qualities here)

Women are:	Men are:

Generally I find that what people list as male or female qualities are actually human qualities that they have been taught to attribute to either men or women. Masculine and feminine are the two mutually exclusive containers into which most of us have learned to put all human behavior. Our training to think that gender differences are important or biologically fixed is deep and not easily dislodged.

Recently several parents have said to me, "I hate to admit it, but when I watch children play (or my child play) I've come to conclude that boys really are different than girls." They say this as if they are resigned to the fact that there are major biological differences between girls and boys.

For those of us who raised children in the 1970s, 1980s, and early 1990s and consciously tried to apply nonsexist childraising techniques within our families, it may be difficult to acknowledge that we didn't raise nonsexist children, or at least children who did not reflect gender-based differences. Perhaps if we feel that we failed or at least underestimated the task, some of us fall back on biological explanations for why it didn't work. For me it is more realistic and more accurate to admit that we ourselves were not suddenly free of gender bias, that the social training for boys and girls to act differently is massive and starts from before birth, and that there were far too few of us attempting this undertaking to transform society's norms (so far). As a result, our children demonstrate some traditional gender-based differences. Maybe the boys are more active and aggressive than the girls, for example. But there is still no convincing evidence that this difference is biological — despite constant, serious, and well-funded attempts to demonstrate that it is. There is strong and completely convincing evidence that girls and boys are not very different emotionally, physically, or psychologically when they are born, but that we systematically train girls and boys to be different.[5]

Throughout this book there are Questions to Ask Yourself. Please take a few moments to reflect on your responses to these questions before continuing.

A question to ask yourself

What would you lose if you assumed that although there are biological differences between men and women, there are no psychological qualities that either men or women have a monopoly on?

THE "ACT LIKE A MAN" BOX[6]

How is gender constructed in Western society? From a very early age, most boys are told to "act like a man." Even though they have all the normal human feelings of love, excitement, sadness, confusion, anger, curiosity, pain, frustration, humiliation, shame, grief, resentment, loneliness, low self-worth, and self-doubt, most are taught to hide the feelings (except anger) and appear to be tough and in control. They are told to be aggressive, not to back down, not to make mistakes, and to take charge, have lots of sex, make lots of money, and be responsible. Most of all, they are told not to cry.

At the Oakland Men's Project, which I helped to start over 20 years ago, we've called this rigid set of expectations the "Act Like a Man" Box because it feels like a box — a 24-hour-a-day, seven-day-a-week box that society tells boys they must fit themselves into. One reason we know it's a box is because every time a boy tries to step out he's pushed back in with names like wimp, sissy, mama's boy, girl, fag, nerd, punk, mark, bitch, and others even more graphic. Behind those names is the threat of violence. Most boys end up in a fight sometime in their youth to prove they are in the Box. If another boy comes up to you in the hall at junior high school and calls you a wimp, a girl, or a fag, you have to fight him to prove you are in the Box.

The columns on either side of the Box show widespread expectations our society holds for men. The abuse, pressure, and training boys receive to meet these expectations and stay in the Box produce a lot of feelings, some of which are listed in the middle of the Box above. Yet they have to cover over those feelings and try to act like a man because one of the strictures of being a man is not to show your feelings. Some of the names that boys get called are listed on the left of the Box. On the right are listed some of the other kinds of abuse that come with the training to be in the Box.

"Act Like a Man" Box

wimp ▲

girl ▲

sissy ▲

mama's boy ▲

nerd ▲

fag ▲

punk ▲

mark ▲

bitch ▲

tough

aggressive

competitive

in control

no feelings

don't cry

take charge

don't make mistakes

succeed

anger
sadness
love
connection
confusion
low self-worth
resentment
curiosity
excitement
isolation

have money

never ask for help

angry

yell

intimidate

responsible

take it

don't back down

have sex with women

▲ hit/beat up

▲ teased

▲ isolated

▲ rejected

▲ forced to play sports

▲ sexual assault

There are cultural variations of this theme, but its prevalence in Western cultures is striking. Boys develop different strategies for trying to survive in the Box, some might even sneak out of it at times, but, for many, the scars from living within the walls of the Box are long-lasting and painful.

If we pay attention we can easily see the Box's effects on boys. Just watch a group of them together. They are constantly challenging each other, putting each other down, hitting each other, testing to see who is in the Box. They are never at ease, always on guard. At an early age, most start to hide their feelings, toughen up, and will make a huge emotional effort not to cry. Many boys stop wearing colorful clothing or participating in activities that they think might make them vulnerable to being labeled gay. They walk more stiffly, talk more guardedly, move more aggressively. Behind this bravura they are often confused, scared, angry, and wanting closeness with others. But being in the Box precludes closeness and makes intimacy less and less likely.

Our desire for closeness with them is often at odds with our desire to toughen them up so they will not be vulnerable. We may fervently want them to get out of the Box, but there can be subtle and not-so-subtle ways we reinforce their training. For example, most of us stop holding boys when they are four, five, or six years old. We might say to ourselves that we don't want our sons to remain babies, that they need to grow up, that it's a tough world out there. But boys, young men — every single one — need respectful, physical affection from the adults around them. They do pull away from us as they get older and face peer pressure to be unemotional, particularly in public situations. But primarily it is our discomfort rather than theirs that deprives them of the hugs, kisses, and physical affection they need into their teen years.

We may become fearful for their safety and offer only lukewarm support if they show interest in activities that are not traditionally male. We may encourage them to participate in athletic or other competitive programs because we think it is good for them, without questioning the values they learn from their activities.

There are probably times that we give up, say "boys will be boys," and don't challenge the messages and training they receive from TV, movies, books, sports, and their peers. We can remind ourselves that "boys will be men" and they need our support in figuring out how to be men who are not trapped in the Box.

Questions to ask yourself

Is there an age beyond which you find it hard to hold or hug boys? Why?

What damage did you think it would do if you continued?

Are there any ways you have withheld affection or nurturing from an older boy because you were worried about the effect it might have on him?

Are there any names that you use to refer to boys who are not in the Box?

Has there ever been a time when you worried that your son or another boy wasn't tough enough?

Are there any ways that you encourage boys to toughen up, get over their pain, or take it like a man?
Are there activities that you are uncomfortable having boys participate in — for example, playing with dolls, dancing, wearing bright colors, jumping rope?

The key to staying in the Box is control. Boys are taught to control their bodies, control their feelings, control their relationships — to protect themselves from being vulnerable. Although the Box is a metaphor for the social pressures all boys must learn to respond to, the possibility that a boy will have control over the conditions of his life varies depending on his race, class, and culture.

Being in control is not the same as being violent. In Western societies hitting people is frowned upon except in particular sports or military settings. It is deemed much more refined to retain control by using verbal, emotional, or psychological means rather than physical force. Financial manipulation, coercion and intimidation, and sexual pressure are also condoned as long as no one is physically injured.

Clearly, the more money, education, and connections a man has, the easier it is for him to buy or manipulate others to get what he wants. Wealthy and upper- or middle-class white men are generally promoted and celebrated for being in control and getting what they want. Poor or working-class men and men of color are usually punished for these same behaviors, especially, but not only, if they use physical force.

Why are boys trained to be in control? Most boys will end up with one of three roles in society — to be workers, consumers, or enforcers. A small percentage of boys are trained to give orders — to be bosses, managers, or officers. The Box trains boys for the roles they will play, whether they will make decisions governing the lives of others or carry out the decisions made by those at the top. I will have more to say about this training in Chapter 2, but I think it is clear that the Box prepares boys to be police officers, security guards, deans, administrators, soldiers, heads of families, probation officers, prison guards — the roles that many men, primarily white men, are being trained to fill. Men of color, along with women and young people, are the people more often being controlled.

Many men are under the illusion that being in the Box is like being in an exclusive club. No girls allowed. All men are equal. For working- and middle-class white men and for those men of color who aspire to be accepted by them, the Box creates a false feeling of solidarity with men in power and misleads many men into thinking they have more in common with corporate executives, political and religious leaders, generals, and bosses than they have with women.

In this book, I examine closely the training that boys receive to "act like a man" and offer suggestions for countering it because this training sustains and perpetuates an undemocratic and unjust social structure. Although many of us are not happy with how it works, few of us talk to our sons about the gender-role training they are receiving. We may not point it out to them or notice with them the consequences for themselves, other men, and women. We may not challenge them to think critically about that training and to

© Kathy Sloane

develop the communication and problem-solving skills that would get them out of the Box.

It is essential for young men to discuss and reject the behavior outlined in the "Act Like a Man" Box. It is liberating for them to understand the reasons why they feel so pressured, the consequences of this male training for them and for those around them, and the roles they are being prepared to play in the larger society. These roles are discussed more fully in the next chapter.

WHAT KIND OF MEN DO WE NEED?

This book is not about raising boys to "act like men." Every boy who survives childhood becomes a man, a physically mature adult human male. So what are we raising boys for? This is not an easy question to answer. To some extent I don't think we can know yet. New roles and new responsibilities have to emerge out of the lived needs of new times. However, there are some common values I think we need as a foundation for any progressive future we can imagine.

One of those values is the elimination of rigidly defined, mutually exclusive gender roles that lock men and women into expectations and behaviors that are limiting and distorted. We will have achieved little if we do not seriously undermine male and female gender roles and must be constantly vigilant to ensure we do not recreate them in new guises.

I want to raise children who are responsible, cooperative, caring, and competent, regardless of their biology. I think we need young people who understand and are willing to challenge all forms of social injustice based on economics, race, gender, sexual identity, and ability.

Finally, I want to raise boys differently because they demand it from us. They are constantly challenging our ideas and childrearing practices — constantly asking if what we are doing is relevant, current, appropriate. We can gain a great deal if we heed their challenges and question our practices.

PART 1

Becoming Allies
to Our Sons

2 The Big Picture

WHO ARE OUR SONS?

Some of you reading this book have biological, adopted, foster, or stepsons. Many of you have nephews and male cousins as well. Others of you may be teachers, counselors, coaches, or Boy Scout leaders. All of you have boys in your life in some way. I am using the word son to encompass a number of relationships that we, as caring adults, can have with boys and young men.

Questions to ask yourself

Which boys, if any, look to you as a parent?
Which boys, if any, might look to you for advice, guidance, or role modeling?
Which boys, if any, are you responsible for in your job or profession?
Which boys in your extended family, neighborhood, or circle of friends
might you reach out to?
For men, which boys or young men might you be a role model for
(think of nephews, cousins, younger brothers, neighborhood guys,
boys you coach, teach, lead, or minister to)?

Most of us have one, two, or a few boys in mind when we think about raising sons. This is important because we need to be very specific when talking about sons. You need to test what I suggest against the reality of the lives of boys you know.

But the lives our sons will lead will be heavily determined by the lives of many other boys in the world. If we think of some boys as our sons, and disregard the lives of the rest, we perpetuate a world of inequality, exploitation, and violence in which the lives and dreams of many boys are discarded.

Our culture pushes us to separate "us" from "them," our team from theirs, our kids from theirs. Since we already have class and racial divisions in our lives, we may easily see most boys as problems and our sons as our responsibility. If we are white, it is easy to see boys of color on the street or at school as not our sons. If we are well-off, it is easy to see boys from poor and working-class families as not our sons. It is easy to see boys from other cultural and racial groups as not our sons. It is even easier to see boys in gangs, boys dealing drugs, or boys who have dropped out of school as not our sons because the media usually portrays them as dangerous and alien.

One of our challenges is to see every boy as one of our sons. The more we can do that, the less we will be willing to accept policies that throw away any young man. In a society where some children are uncared for or neglected and in which competition and violence reign, none of our sons or daughters are safe, no matter how strong or independent or caring or nonsexist we raise our sons to be.

We are responsible for each other's children. It makes a profound difference in our actions and in the world when we say of every boy we encounter, "Here is one of my sons." If people did this, boys themselves would be different. They would feel wanted, loved, and supported. We would be building more schools than prisons. Boys would see their value, and our future, in their eyes.

Although this book focuses on raising the sons in your immediate life, you can only do that effectively by valuing the boys around you regardless of your relationship to them.

Questions to ask yourself

Which boys are hardest to see as your sons? Those who are:

Suburban?

Urban?

Rural?

Poor?

Well-off?

Disabled?

Gay and bisexual?

African American?

Asian American?

Latino?

Jewish?

Native American?

White?

Immigrant?

Gang members?

When you see boys or young men that you don't consider to be your sons, try to look past their dress, their attitude, their bravado. Look into their eyes. See the full, loving, competent, creative, and caring human being who is there, although perhaps well-camouflaged. Know that he is probably scared, just as you may be; he is struggling to figure out the world, just as you may be; he is wanting love and connection, just as you are.

I think we each want the world to see the goodness, the talents, the efforts of the boys we know, and we can practice seeing those qualities in the boys we don't know.

AND OUR DAUGHTERS

Our sons are growing up in a world with our daughters. Just as it is dangerous to throw away boys we don't consider ours, it is equally counter-productive to ignore the lives of girls. Some of you have daughters, some of you are women, so you have an immediate touchstone for guiding you. Those of you who are men can keep the lives, safety, healing, growth, and opportunity of girls in the forefront of your thinking as you raise boys. We can affirm that everything we want for our sons we want for our daughters; nothing that boys gain can be at the expense of girls.

Keeping this in mind may be a challenge. You may want your sons to have the opportunities other boys have. You may look at rich, white, powerful males and want your sons to have access to money and power as well. But it is not equal opportunity if it is at the expense of girls.

This book is not about equal opportunity or success as they are traditionally defined. My vision is of a society in which all our children share a world of opportunity, participation, safety, and caring. To acheive that vision can leave no child behind; we can throw no child away.

CO-PARENTING WITH SOCIETY

I am raising two sons and a daughter with my partner, Micki. You've probably noticed, as I have, that we aren't raising our sons alone. Co-parenting with us are movies, TV, contemporary music, organized sports, advertising, our sons' peers, adult male friends, and an array of professionals including teachers, principals, coaches, counselors, and doctors.

We should be modest when we evaluate what effect we have on our boys' lives. We can be an important influence. But many times we are not the primary influence. I think that the period when our moral and political influence is greatest is when our sons are between the ages of four and twelve. That influence may well ground them through the rest of their lives. But as they enter adolescence, other influences become much more important. Our presence is still crucial, but our influence is not nearly as powerful.

Many of us have a tug-of-war theory of parenting in which we imagine our sons tied to the middle of the rope. We see ourselves as pulling against the media, peer pressure, and the temptations of modern society for our sons' attention and allegiance. This inaccurate perception puts us in a position where we feel constantly embattled, always fighting to save our sons from the evil influences "out there." This represents a religious framework for seeing the world in which we are good and righteous. Arrayed against us, tempting our sons to sin, are drugs, sex, music lyrics, gangs, and the more traditional vices of laziness, sloth, aimlessness, and frivolity.

There is one important element left out of this view of parenting. Our sons are not simply unthinking and gullible people tempted by horrible but tantalizing fates that we must help them resist. Boys have feelings, thoughts, ambitions, dreams, and the capacity to make their own decisions. We need to realign ourselves so that we are on their side. This involves working to help strengthen their ability to make good choices about their lives. We can trust that they will pick their own directions, activities, friends, and future if, during their childhood, we have given them the information, skills, and support they need to make good choices. They will make mistakes. They will make choices we may not like or approve of. But we can remember that they are leading their lives, not ours.

Given the intense battery of negative messages we receive from the media about boys and young men, it is sometimes difficult to remember the positive qualities of our sons. They may have difficulty themselves staying centered in their own strength. We can keep reminding ourselves to affirm their beauty, strength, intelligence, creativity, and uniqueness.

A question to ask yourself

Think about some of the boys and young men you know. What shifts inside of you when you assume that your son, your nephew, your neighbor's boy, a young man on the news, a young soldier, your student, or any other young man is beautiful, strong, intelligent, creative, and unique?

Until the children of black mothers,
black mother's sons
are treated like the children of white mothers,
white mother's sons
We who believe in freedom cannot rest
We who believe in freedom
cannot rest until we're done.[1]

As the lyrics from this song by Sweet Honey in the Rock indicate, our challenge is to be allies to our sons and to provide opportunities for those qualities to shine in every young man in our society. Assuming these qualities are inherent in every boy and young man we encounter leads us to the deep inner knowing that every mother's son is one of our sons. This practice leads us to trust our sons, to reconnect with them, and to be proud to stand by their side.

Given the divisions in our society, it is not surprising that we may find it difficult to identify all boys as our sons. I want to look at the issues of power and violence and becoming allies more closely in the rest of this chapter to see what keeps us separated from so many of the young men in our society.

POWER

Before I talk about how to support our sons, how to be their allies, how to raise them to be allies to others, I want to talk about power. If we did not live in a society in which some groups of people had more socioeconomic and political power than others, it would not be so important to be allies.

For example, men as a group have more socioeconomic and political power than women as a group. If we look at any major institution we will see men at the top, making the important decisions, being paid more, and having greater status and respect than women. If we look at our national governments, the courts, the directors of large corporations, heads of hospitals, superintendents of schools, or the people in any number of other positions of power we would find the same fact: men are overwhelmingly in control.

We know it is true that women can perform any of these jobs with competence because we have examples of women who have done so. But overall, women do not have the same access to these opportunities as men do. At every level we find that women are paid less, receive less respect, and are subject to more harassment and abuse than men. These institutions implement policy and procedures that favor men as a group. The men in charge make corporate policies, legal decisions, educational programs, and health-care decisions that disadvantage women. Some people call this system sexism, patriarchy, or male supremacy. Whatever we call it, and however much we want to believe that women now have equal opportunity, it seems clear that there are still serious barriers to women achieving the same economic, educational, and political opportunities that men have.

This inequality of power has specific consequences for women and others for men that I want to look at briefly. Since women as a group have less power, they have less power to protect themselves. This makes them vulnerable to violence from men and from male-run institutions. Women are vulnerable to emotional abuse, financial exploitation, harassment, battery, and sexual assault.[2] In addition they face job and housing discrimination, poorer health care, less protection through the criminal justice system, and much more limited educational opportunities than men. These are all forms of violence. As Martin Luther King, Jr. stated so eloquently, "Violence is anything that denies human integrity, and leads to hopelessness and helplessness."

On the other side, what benefits do men, in general, receive for being men that women don't have equal opportunity to receive?

- Boys are called on more in class and encouraged to go farther in our education system.
- Boys have role models of men in positions of authority.
- Men are given affirmative action in the form of veterans' benefits, old boy networks, housing loans, farm subsidies, retirement benefits, and so on.
- Men are paid more than women for comparable work, receive better benefits, and are promoted faster and into higher positions.
- Men are given preference in housing rentals and in job applications for male (i.e., higher-paying) occupations.
- Men see themselves represented in the media in a variety of powerful roles.
- Men are safer at home and on the streets and are generally better protected and responded to by the criminal justice system, especially by the police.(This is much less true for men of color.)
- Men's needs for sex and for sexual fulfillment are socially recognized.
- Men have access to pornography, sex shows, sex for hire, and other forms of exploitation of women's bodies.
- Men can usually find a woman or hire a woman to cook for them, clean for them, take care of their children, take care of elders, respond to them emotionally, and take care of them when they are sick.
- Men can generally count on women's labor to do all of these tasks in the society at large as teachers, nurses, home help, cleaners, counselors, cooks and waitresses, and other caregivers.

If you are a man you might be wondering why you aren't on top of the world if you indeed enjoy all these benefits. If you are a woman you might be wondering how it is that men can't see the advantages that they enjoy. Two factors make it hard for men to see how they benefit from being part of a more powerful group.

1) Those benefits are normal — taken for granted, seldom questioned or even pointed out. If the benefits are pointed out, it is usually by women, who are easily discounted precisely because they are women.

2) Those benefits are attenuated by the other complex power relationships in our society based on class, race, physical ability, education, religion, sexual identity, and other factors. It is, therefore, easy to point to some men who are part of other less-powerful groups and claim that men have it hard too, maybe even worse than women. For example, if you are a man of color you might say that white women enjoy many more benefits than you do. If you are poor or work-

ing class you might point out that the middle and upper classes are where most of these benefits have accumulated in society.

In a society that is stratified by many different factors, it is important to look at how they are all intertwined. Gender can not be isolated from the others. Only if we understand how this system of benefits and costs operates can we resist it effectively. Below is a chart that shows some of the ways that power is divided up in this society.

The Power Chart

MORE POWERFUL GROUPS	LESS POWERFUL GROUPS
adult	young people and seniors
men	women
the rich	the poor
white people	people of color
bosses	workers
heterosexuals	lesbians, gays, bisexuals
Christians	Jews, Moslems, Buddhists
able-bodied people	people with disabilities
formally educated	not formally educated
born here	recent immigrants

If you look up and down the Power Chart you will see that you are in, or have been in, groups on both sides — more powerful and less powerful. As children, most of us know what it is like to be vulnerable to violence from adults. This gives us some idea of what it is like for people in other groups on the right side of the chart. We all grow to be adults and so become more powerful. We each come to know what it is like to be in a powerful group and to have some power over others. Some of us are in more groups on the right column and are multiply vulnerable to violence — we have less ability to protect ourselves than those who are predominantly on the left.

These are socially constructed categories. Those with the most power want us to believe that we have different interests and needs if we are on the left or the right in any particular category. In particular, they want people on the left side to think that they are separate and better than those on the right and should not care about those "inferior" people who just get what they deserve. We are told that it is natural for men to have power and high-paying jobs and natural for women to be thin, take care of the children, and earn less. We are told it is natural for white people to have more political control, more access to higher education, and better-paying jobs. We are led to believe that these categories are natural and the benefits or costs attached to them are inevitable because we hear over and over again that people on the right side of the chart are to blame for their problems. We are told that —

- They don't work hard.
- They aren't smart enough.
- They don't have what it takes.
- They are dishonest.
- They are not ambitious.
- They are not as smart.
- They are not as experienced.
- They are too emotional.
- They haven't lived here long enough.
- They are immoral.
- They are sinful.
- They are undeserving.
- They need us to take care of them.

If we believe these lies about other groups, we have to believe them, to some extent, about ourselves — because we all find ourselves on the right side of the chart at some point. Any category we belong to on the right side of the chart makes us vulnerable to economic exploitation, discrimination, stereotypes, violence, and the daily indignities of living in a society that devalues and belittles us and our cultures. Because it can seem daunting to challenge this system, we may find ourselves passing on our pain, frustration, and anger to someone with even less power than we have. We may yell at our kids, abuse our partners, gossip about our co-workers, and blame recent immigrants, welfare mothers, teenagers, gays and lesbians, or some other group for our problems. When we do so we perpetuate a cycle of violence that keeps power and control concentrated in the hands of some — and keeps all of us apart, misinformed, mistrustful, and fearful of each other.

Who benefits from this cycle of violence? To some extent nobody does because we are all caught up in hurting others and being hurt ourselves. To some extent we all benefit a little because most of us can find someone with less power than we have to whom we pass on our pain and anger. One group benefits enormously from this system of power and violence: the wealthiest people in our society.

THE ECONOMIC PYRAMID

On the following page is a pyramid representing the population and wealth of the United States.[3] A corresponding pyramid for other Western countries would look similar with slightly more or less concentration at the top. As you can see, one percent of the population controls nearly half of the wealth of the country. The top 20 percent controls so much wealth that the rest of us are literally fighting over the scraps. The remaining six percent doesn't go very far divided by 80 percent of the population. Wealth has always been concentrated in Western countries, but the amount concentrated at the top of the pyramid has increased dramatically during the last twenty years.

Since about 1980, due to the political and economic policy decisions of govern-

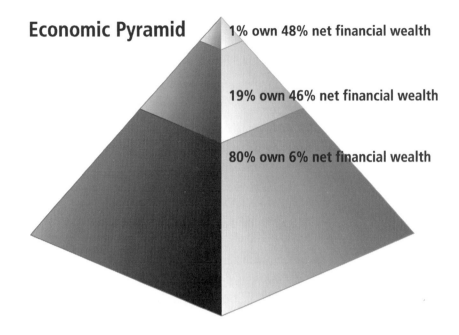

Economic Pyramid

1% own 48% net financial wealth

19% own 46% net financial wealth

80% own 6% net financial wealth

ments, multinational corporations became larger and more dominant in the global economy, and wealth became increasingly concentrated in the hands of fewer people. The result has been the rapid movement of capital and jobs from country to country, as national governments competed to offer corporations the lowest-waged workers, the most lax environmental standards, and the least government interference. Many of these countries were left with debt, social instability, unemployment, and environmental devastation when capital moved elsewhere.

Most young people clearly have no position in the present global economy except as consumers. Unemployment rates are astoundingly high for young men, and many of them have no prospect of stable work lives earning livable wages in safe working conditions. In other words, a large number of young men are economically expendable — and they know it. They are aware of the lack of jobs for adult men they know, the lack of training they are receiving in their schools, the lack of social investment in their futures. They can also see the increased preparation for social control in the form of police, prisons, immigration restrictions, drug programs, and courts. They understand that they are not considered to have an active role in the dynamic future of this country.

The people at the top of the pyramid don't want us to notice that they have cornered such a large share of our wealth. They have developed various ways to keep us distracted from talking about, much less doing anything about, the unequal distribution of power and wealth in our society. For many of us, just surviving — trying to get our share of the crumbs — keeps us distracted. It is not easy putting food on the table, shelter over our heads, and clothes on our children's backs. Others of us turn to sports, movies, video games, computers, romance novels, pornography, or public scandals and trials to distract ourselves. Some of us use alcohol and other drugs to numb our pain. The media — largely owned by large corporations such as General Electric, Westinghouse, and Disney — provide us with distractions in the form of courtroom and political dramas, and scapegoats in the form of welfare mothers, recent immigrants, and young men — particularly young men of color.

At no time in recent history have young men themselves been so attacked and blamed for being the cause of our current social and economic problems. Every day we are assailed with headlines about the danger that young men pose to our lives and property and to young women.[4] Many of us have come to fear for the lives of our sons and fear the damage they may do to our communities. As long as we fear relatively powerless young men and do not turn our attention to the powerful multinational corporations that make most of the decisions that affect our lives, we will not be able to get together to solve our most pressing social and economic problems.

People have always resisted injustice and the concentration of wealth and power among the few. These struggles continue today. In your community, efforts to organize are probably being made by workers, women, students, neighborhoods, communities of color, environmentalists, and peace activists. We don't hear about them regularly on the news because the corporations that own the media don't want us to know about and be inspired by these efforts. They are not described at length in our textbooks because the same corporations want to protect their interests. [5]

Questions to ask yourself

Using the three-part economic structure described above, where are
you and your family situated on the economic pyramid?
What category does your son or the boys you live/work
with fall into, if different?
What kinds of educational opportunities are available for
most of the boys in each category?
What kinds of work opportunities (including illegal or semilegal ones)
are available for most of the boys in each category?
How is masculinity typically defined for each category? What resources do men
in each category have for defining their masculinity?
How is respect typically gained by men in each category?
How do these dynamics vary by racial group?

Some of our sons are growing up in families in the top two categories — the segment of the population that runs the country and controls 85 to 95 percent of the wealth. These boys are being prepared, through education and other investment in their lives, to be the political and corporate leaders, professionals, and managers who will lead economically comfortable lives in exchange for their collaboration with the economic, racial, and gender hierarchy.

The remainder of our sons are being raised to stay in the bottom category. Those in the upper half of this category will be raised to hold professional and lower management jobs, often employing, supervising, or relying on services from those in the bottom half who hold low- and minimum-wage jobs. Many in this latter group will end up unemployed, on welfare, or homeless.

Although it makes a crucial difference where a boy is on the economic pyramid, all young men today receive at least some training to define themselves as men who control women and men with less power than they have. Most are encouraged to define their self-respect and their place in society in terms of a masculine identity and to use these masculine qualities to support and maintain their economic advantages.

GETTING BY, GETTING AHEAD, GETTING TOGETHER

Since all young men find themselves on the economic pyramid in a situation not of their own choosing, they must figure out what strategies they are going to use to make their way in the world. Boys from families at the top of the pyramid have lots of choices and are encouraged from an early age to think strategically. They are told that they have bright futures and they see many examples of men who resemble them who are bosses, intellectuals, artists, scientists, athletes, or politicians. They can be reasonably assured that the system will support whatever choices they make.

Boys in the middle of the pyramid are told that they have a future, but it depends entirely upon what they do, how much they accomplish, and how hard they work. They are given lots of examples of men who have made it. They are also given examples of men who haven't made it and are told it was because these men made mistakes, had bad judgment, did not work hard enough, or didn't seize the initiative. Many come to believe that they are the arbiters of their future.

Many boys at the bottom of the pyramid are told that they have no future. Their parents may say, "You'll never amount to anything." Their teachers may say, "Why don't you try this mechanical arts course?" The police may say, "Just another punk on the street." These young men don't have models of men like them who are successful, and they don't expect support for their success. Some live with the most graphic violence, and they despair even of staying alive.

Whatever our position on the economic pyramid, there are three kinds of strategies we can develop for living our lives:
• Getting by
• Getting ahead
• Getting together

Most boys are only told about the first two — getting by and getting ahead. They are told that our efforts will determine where in the pyramid they will end up and therefore they should try to get ahead. However, many of them know that they don't have equal opportunity and that only some can get ahead, so they resign themselves to getting by. Getting by is survival mode.

We all need strategies for getting by. When faced with a bully, a dangerous neighborhood, exploitative work, disrespectful teachers, or abuse in our family, we have to get by. We have to live day by day, hoping we make it through. For some young men, getting by is a major accomplishment. For others, getting by is a realistic strategy for not attracting too much attention from those who might hurt them. For still others, getting by is a way to avoid the competition and aggression needed to get ahead. Young men can develop some very sophisticated and effective survival strategies for getting by in difficult circumstances. We need to respect strategies for getting by.

However, getting by does not lead us to a future that we help create. There is little hope, no planning, and little change in a life guided by a getting-by strategy. It is also quite isolating because we cannot trust anyone. We need to be constantly cautious of others and protective of our bodies and our feelings. We can only react to the threats that we perceive around us. We often make short-term choices to stay safe that actually lead us into greater danger. Getting stoned is a getting-by strategy. Joining a gang is a getting-by strategy. Doing the minimum schoolwork is a getting-by strategy. Avoiding conflict and risk are also about getting by. But boys don't start out trying to get by; they start out trying to get ahead.

Getting ahead is a more proactive strategy because we are trying to get somewhere. Our goals may be focused on education, work, success, or the development of personal skills and expression in the arts, on the playing field, or in the community. Getting-ahead strategies combine personal abilities with social circumstances to focus on some external goal beyond mere survival. Society supports — in fact, acclaims — getting-ahead strategies. We are all pushed to achieve, compete, succeed, get ahead by any means necessary. Most of the advice adults give young people encourages them to get ahead — study hard, say no to drugs and sex, get an education, get a job, get some training, don't get pregnant. Many after-school academies, job-training programs, continuing education classes, sex education programs, and rite of passage programs are set up to help as many young men and women as can be reached to get ahead. These programs often measure their success by how many young people they graduate; how many get into college or get a job; how many don't get AIDS; how many stay on the path to success as it has been defined in this society — a good education, a good job, some health benefits, an apartment or house, a car.

Everyone needs to get ahead. In a society where even survival is not guaranteed for many of us, getting ahead is no small achievement. We need an education and a job. We need economic security, health care, and a stable family network. But getting ahead can also be costly. What do we have to give up to get ahead? Do we have to fit in; lose our accents; cover up our sexual identity; disavow our less successful or immigrant family members; hide our cultural heritage, values, and traditions; exploit others? Getting ahead often means disconnecting ourselves from the family, friends, and neighborhoods we grew up in. It may mean working long hours and dangerous shifts and putting the other parts of our lives on hold.

We and our communities can end up paying tremendous costs for our getting ahead. Our capitalist economy is structured so that people can get ahead only at the expense of others. If I win, you lose. If my business succeeds, then ten others must fail. If

I get into this college, then twenty-five other qualified applicants will not. If I get this job, then someone else will be unemployed. Because of the artificial scarcity of resources, because of the concentration of wealth among the top 20 percent, climbing the ladder of success invariably means stepping on the shoulders of others. Getting ahead strategies are necessary but they are not enough.

Young children have a natural inclination to do things with others, to be team players, to be sociable. However, boys in particular are quickly taught that getting ahead is an individual process and that they are in competition with others for any goals worth attaining. They learn, through the training to "act like a man," to become competitive, aggressive, independent, and insensitive to others. Many give up on cooperation because it is not encouraged. They are fed superhero fantasies and develop great ambitions. They expect to go far and may have parents and others encouraging them to do so. They can see that Superman is a man. Michael Jordan is a man. So is Bill Gates. So are presidents, judges, and astronauts.

Most boys begin life with the sense that there is nothing they can't do. For some of them, that vision is quickly dispelled as the social realities hit them. Every put-down and discouraging comment deflates them; every assault distracts them; every test, grade, paper, evaluation, award, and sports competition defeats a few more of them. The better they are, the better the competition gets. At each level there are few winners and large numbers of losers. As they grow older they can see the racial, economic, and cultural barriers more clearly. They begin to understand the compromises the men around them have made.

All boys must face the reality of the limits on their lives. If a boy is from a poor or working-class family and/or is African American, Latino, or Native American, he quickly learns of his limited possibilities and adjusts his expectations accordingly. He sees the kind of jobs the men in his community have, the kind of educational opportunities he has available, and the kind of money he can expect to make. He may feel the lack of positive expectations from his teachers, counselors, and parents. He may receive negative expectations, punishment, and discouragement from those same adults. Many boys begin to see those limits at age eight, nine, ten. Some see them much earlier.

Although our society can tolerate, and even encourages, spectacular success for a few (very few) athletes and entertainers, economic and social mobility in the United States and other Western countries is actually quite limited. At some point in adolescence if not earlier, most boys come to grips with what they can actually achieve in their lives. The more resources they command because of race, family, money, and education, the higher their ambitions can lie and the longer they can hold on to their aspirations. Hope fades early for many, replaced by lowered goals, lowered self-worth, broken hearts, and anger.

A similar process occurs when a boy realizes he is gay or bisexual. The limits to what he can achieve become clear as he comes out and faces rejection from family or friends, discrimination, or verbal or physical attacks. He, too, may begin to lose hope of getting ahead.

Adults who work with young people participate in this process in two ways. Some teachers, principals, counselors, parents, social welfare workers, police, and probation officers are fed predictions about where boys will end up and they act accordingly, channeling them into their expected roles. Essentially they accept the stereotypes and believe that what individual boys can achieve is limited by their economic status, family background, race, gender, or other salient factors.

Adults with more optimism, determination, or caring will reach out to boys reject-ed by others and try to buck the predictions or temper the pain and frustration. Sometimes they will succeed. There are successful programs around the country that help young men in trouble turn their lives around and go to college, find a job, get off drugs, or become bet-ter fathers. Our society can tolerate some flexibility in where particular boys end up. However, if the odds are that 97 out of 100 boys in the neighborhood will not get to col-lege, then pointing to the three who do go does not change young men's perception of the odds, although it may motivate a dozen to try for those three positions.

At whatever age a boy understands the odds and decides that he can no longer get ahead, he begins to try to just get by. This is the stage when boys often get into trouble. Many of us who are adults feel responsible for encouraging boys not to give up. But if we can only see two strategies — getting ahead or getting by — we will not able to help young men get together.

Getting together means working with others so that we all get ahead. There are lots of examples of strategies for getting together to change things — unions, liberation move-ments, the civil rights movement, demonstrations, organizing, boycotts, support groups. This strategy involves groups of people with less power, opportunity, and resources who get together to broaden participation in society. Getting together is a process of getting beyond ourselves and realizing that our gain cannot be at someone else's expense. Realizing that, in the long term, we are all in the same boat and we are too interconnected to survive if some people are excluded from sharing in our social wealth.

No one gets by without help. No one gets ahead without an extensive network of support from family, friends, neighbors, teammates, and co-workers. Understanding how interconnected we are can help our sons begin to see who they might get together with.

If young people think about it at all, they usually start out thinking about getting together as an expanded form of self-interest within a limited group. The "us" may be a family, school, neighborhood, gang, or racial/ethnic or religious group. Even most adults have difficulty imagining broad categories of people as part of the "us." The decline in union membership, the lack of support for boycotts and other consumer actions, the scapegoating of welfare recipients, recent immigrants, and young people, all point to the fact that many of us fail to include significant groups of our country's population as part of "us." Young people are strongly influenced by their parents' sense of who the "us" is. If we walk across picket lines and don't identify with other workers, our sons will not under-stand the potential for solidarity with other working people. If we blame less powerful groups for social problems, our sons receive the message that those groups are not part of "us." All of us would benefit from broadening and making more diverse the people we con-sider "us" — the people we are in solidarity with. We can't get together, we can't bring our sons together with us, if we are in this for ourselves, if we see most people as them and not as us.

© Kathy Sloane

Questions to ask yourself

Which groups of people in this country (if any) is it hard for
you toconsider part of the "us"?
Are there any groups of people in this country that you wish would
leave, be less demanding, or change their attitude?

Getting together means building on common ground, reaching for common goals, meeting common needs. This kind of coming together is not easy. We are constantly pressured to pull in the gates and raise the drawbridge — a pressure fueled by the lies, stereotypes, and distortions we receive about others. But this narrow-minded approach to the world just makes it easier for those with more power to manipulate our fear of others.

In the sociopolitical environment we live in, boys can use our guidance in getting together. Our guidance must be based on our understanding of our sons' positions in economic, racial, and other hierarchies. Most importantly, we need to understand that changing which boys are in which roles does not make the system more equitable. I don't believe that increased participation in the present system can be a substitute for substantial change in how the system operates. We have to challenge all levels of inequality and violence.

For example, helping more men of color reach the top of the pyramid makes for a more colorful patriarchy but doesn't challenge the values on which it rests. Similarly, getting more women of whatever color into the powerful and controlling positions in society doesn't necessarily change the dynamics and exploitation of the economic system.

Similarly, the affluence of Western countries is based largely on the appropriation and accumulation of wealth from poorer countries by military and economic exploitation. Democratizing our society, even including women in the political and economic structure, would not necessarily lead to less exploitation and violence in the larger world.

A third strategy for parents and teachers is to reach out to all boys and help them develop their full potential while helping them understand and deal with the ways that they are being marginalized by the larger society. Providing this level of support and understanding allows them to succeed individually *and* to get together with others to challenge the unequal opportunities they face.

Partly that means helping them connect up with other young people who are similarly motivated to create change. Throughout the world, young people are coming together to battle for their rights and for social justice. In the U.S., for example, young people have been in the forefront recently in fights to maintain affirmative action, to protect immigrant rights, to preserve the environment, to change the educational system, to defend young people, and to extend workers' rights. There are many youth groups with a focus on community service, and some focused on social justice. There are some grassroots community groups that include young people as vital members of their constituency. (Some of these groups are described in Chapter 18.)

MAKING CHOICES

Individual young men have decisions to make about how they are going to respond to the choices and pressures they face. These choices can be to get ahead and support our present hierarchical structures or to get together with others to subvert them. Usually their choices will combine elements of both.

Each young man's choices are limited by his economic status, by his racial/cultural position, by his sexual identity, and by other personal and social factors. Even young men who make the same choice will have different chances of successfully achieving their aspirations because of how the social structure responds to young men's choices. For example, a white, middle-class young man and a Latino, middle-class young man may both choose to study hard, stay in school, and go to college. The white young man will likely be encouraged by family, school, and community, and doors will open for him. The Latino young man may have support from his family and some teachers, but lack of role models, discouragement from taking academic courses, discriminatory discipline, peer pressure, racism in the curriculum, racial prejudice from counselors and teachers, and police harassment may close doors and make it more difficult for him to succeed.

We cannot say that society systematically determines these young men's choices. Young men respond to the options they perceive for themselves. However, it is also not enough to say that these two youth are making the same choices. Choices are made in a social and economic context that supports the choices of some young men and works against the choices of others.

Our role as parents in this process is manifold. We can give our young men an understanding of the choices they face and the consequences of making those choices. We can also give them some sense of the context that creates these choices so they understand the forces working for and against their success.

As they decide to pursue certain paths, we can support them as they work to achieve their aspirations. Along with this, we can help them understand the different choices that people of different classes, races, and sexual identities have, and the ways they are being pressured to define themselves as masculine in juxtaposition to women, regardless of the choices they are making. Provided with this understanding, they can choose to work with us in our efforts to transform the hierarchical systems of class, race, and gender that limit every young person's choices.

A key skill that boys need, therefore, is the ability to analyze critically the larger social, political, and economic reality so they can see where their choices lead and what effects those choices have on others.

Questions for us and our sons to reflect on

What are the social implications of a man becoming an accountant in a large corporation, or a street corner drug dealer, or a teacher, or a truck driver? How have people in those positions gotten together with others to build up the community? Are there some positions from which this is easier or more difficult? Are there some positions from which it is impossible to build the community? How do these concerns relate to making a living, contributing to the support of a family, maintaining personal health, creating economic security, raising children, or living in community?

We don't know what the world will look like next year, much less in a decade from now. I think that part of our task in raising sons is to give them the tools for developing their values so that, as times change, they will have the tools for making informed, responsible choices throughout their life. In developing their ability to make good choices we are acting as their allies, and preparing them to be allies to others.

WHAT DOES AN ALLY DO?

Now we come to the crucial meaning of being an ally when we live in a social system where a small number of people control vast amounts of wealth, Being an ally means we are on the side of those with less power, working for safety, equality, and justice for the bottom 80 percent and an end to the whole class system.

To consider what an ally does, I want to look at three different levels where we interact with each other.

1) Prejudice. If you look at the power chart and the economic pyramid and see where the people who control television, movies, textbooks, newspapers, and radio stations are situated, you will understand why we all have so much misinformation about each other. Lies, stereotypes, caricatures, and misinformation are continuously put forward to confuse us. This misinformation creates scapegoats to keep us distracted from noticing who has power. We all have prejudices about each other. It is not possible for any of us to be raised in this society and not absorb some of the lies we have been fed. As an ally, we each have personal work to do to learn about the groups we have prejudices and stereotypes about so we can develop honest and respectful relationships with members of those groups.

2) Interpersonal relationships. We are all in relationships in which we are in a more powerful group vis-a-vis the person we are relating to. Our power may come as a parent, a teacher, a co-worker, a doctor, a supervisor, a store owner in relationship to a employee, or an employee in relationship to a customer. There are literally thousands of ways that we have some power over someone else because of our age, skin color, gender, sexual identity, physical ability, formal education, job, or wealth. We may have just a little more power, or we may have a lot more power, but we have some ability to influence that person's life. We can either turn our pain, anger, and frustration into abuse of them, or we can break the cycle of violence and be an ally to them by providing them with support, information, resources, connections, or appropriate interventions. Our challenge as an ally is to use our power to support that other person rather than using it to hurt them.

3) Institutions. I have described how we confront systemic patterns of power and violence involving whole groups of people. We have also noticed that people are constantly organizing to end the violence and distribute wealth and power more equitably. An ally joins those struggles by participating in community efforts to end the cycle of violence and the unjust distribution of power and wealth in our society.

As an example of how the three different levels operate, I will cite my own position as a man. My first task as an ally to women is to eliminate my own prejudices against women and learn what women's experiences are really like. Then I can support women in my interpersonal relationships with them, both eliminating any controlling or abusive patterns I have and learning how to support women's leadership. Finally, I need to join community struggles for equal rights for women, for an end to male violence against them, and for full inclusion and equal opportunity for every woman. As a male worker, I would naturally be building alliances with other workers, male and female, focused on workplace issues. As a white person, I would try to be an effective ally to men and women of color, and as a father, an ally to my children.

Being an ally is a complex series of commitments to and for oneself, to other individuals who have less power, and to others in groups that have less power. Out of our commitment come our actions.

Throughout the rest of this book, I will use the word "we" to refer to those of us who value equality, democracy, and justice and want to be allies to our sons so that they can be strong and loving participants in the struggle to create a just society.

Questions to ask yourself

What do you want from people who are your allies?
If you are a young person, what do you want from adults?
If you are a woman, what do you want from men?
If you are a person of color, what do you need from white people?
If you are a person with a disability, what do you expect from
people without disabilities?

There are some general qualities I want in my allies. I want them to be respectful, honest, committed, caring, and supportive. I want them to listen to me; to inform themselves about who I am; to recognize discrimination or harassment when it occurs; to empathize with what I experience; to share power, information, money, and other resources; and to be passionate for justice. Most of all I want my allies to stand by me when I need them. When I am being put down, abused, denied access, discriminated against, or attacked I want my allies to intervene, interrupt, organize, take action, and challenge injustice, even when I am not present. To do this effectively my ally needs to be courageous, a risk taker, creative, strong, imaginative, and humble.

I also know what qualities I don't need in an ally. I don't need an ally who takes charge, takes over, one who is arrogant, dominating, controlling, who doesn't listen, or who can't work cooperatively. Nor is an ally effective if she or he is always cautious, afraid of making mistakes, anxious to be polite, safe, and politically correct at all times.

Being an ally answers the two essential questions: "What do I stand for?" and "Who do I stand with?" If we ask those questions for ourselves we help every young man decide how he is going to answer them. In my daily life I am constantly called on to make decisions about when and how to be an ally. Each time I act as an ally I decrease my own isolation, strengthen my integrity, and participate in building a better world. Clearly, as a society we can only develop the collective power and resources needed to end the cycle of violence and injustice if we, as adults, are strong and effective allies for young men so that they, in turn, can learn how to be allies to others.

To be effective allies to our sons we need to look at what we bring to the complex challenges of being a parent, teacher or youth worker. The next chapter provides some tools and suggestions so that our prior experiences do not hinder our role as their allies.

3 Mothering, Fathering and Co-Parenting: What Gets in our Way?

WHAT WE BRING TO PARENTING

Each of us brings a variety of personal experiences to parenting. These can be experiences from the parenting we received ourselves as children and from what we saw and see as models of parenting around us in real life or on TV and in movies and books. For any adult to create new models for how boys can become men, it is important that they be clear about what we bring to our parenting so we can put aside our own negative experiences and draw on positive ones. I want to look at our gender-role training and some of the experiences that might interfere with your being a good ally to our sons.

IF YOU'RE A WOMAN

Women come to the parenting of boys with feelings and expectations from their life experiences. I think it is important to examine these and draw on the insight and experience they provide. If these experiences are left unexamined, they can intrude in unexpected ways on the pleasures and challenges of raising boys.

First, there are all the things you have learned about men and boys — all the messages you have received and internalized about who males are, what they do, and how they act.

Second, you bring your personal experience with men and boys in your life — your brothers, fathers, male cousins, uncles, male teachers and bosses, boyfriends and partners (if you are heterosexual), and complete strangers who interacted with you in memorable ways. Some of that experience will undoubtedly be negative. A woman in this society cannot fail to have been, or to have seen other women being, assaulted, harassed, discriminated against, or treated as inferior by men.

Third, women bring their internalization of the female role — all the ways they have been trained to be a woman, to act like a lady, to be a good girl, including the ways that training contained messages about how women were supposed to relate to men.

Finally, women bring their experiences of how they have seen other women in their lives relating to men. These experiences start with their mothers and other female relatives and run through girl friends, female colleagues, and media images of women relating to men. Obviously these areas overlap. But I think it is important to separate them out and look at how each might have affected what women bring to relationships with boys.

While as a mother you probably love your son with great depth of feeling, any of the kinds of experiences listed above may cause you to have deep ambivalence about raising a boy. You may fear raising a son who will treat women disrespectfully; you may be angry at your son for being like men who have mistreated you or other women. These are understandable and realistic fears. At the same time, your son may be like or remind you of his father, your father, or other men in your life, and that may trigger a variety of responses, both positive and negative.

Insofar as your son is receiving messages from society about how to act like a man, he will indeed, at times, resemble men and act out male training in ways that are upsetting. You may have decided to raise him to be the opposite of men in your life who were dangerous, abusive, or unresponsive. In any of these cases it will be hard to stay focused on who your son is if you see him partly through afterimages of males you have known.

You may have no ambivalence about raising a son, but you are still likely to be affected by some of these issues. The following questions should help you reflect on just what you do bring as a woman to the experience of being a mother to a son. I know that such questions can encourage stereotypes. But used in this context, I think they can help us see what general feelings we still carry with us from prior experience and training.

Questions to ask yourself

What have you learned about men?

How would you complete the following sentences?

Men are...

Men usually...

Men never...

Boys are different from girls because they...

Boys lack...

Boys should be able to...

Boys won't have to...

Compared to girls, boys are more...

Compared to boys, girls are more...

Most of the men in my life have been...

It is not just that you have been constantly barraged with messages about what boys and men are like from early childhood. You have also had lots of experiences with boys and men directly. Some of those experiences may have been painful or abusive. If you recognize the feelings of pain and anger these experiences produced, you can deal with them or compensate for them. If they are unrecognized, they can sabotage your efforts to raise boys who will not be abusive. The exercise Experiences of Abusive Behavior from Men will help you identify these experiences.

EXERCISE
EXPERIENCES OF ABUSIVE BEHAVIOR FROM MEN[1]

The following exercise will help you identify and think about the effects of any negative experiences you have had with boys or men. It may bring up painful memories and feelings. If so, please stop and talk with someone about these feelings, seek support, and work through them.

Put a check mark by any of the following statements that apply to you.

1. I have been interrupted by a man talking loudly.
2. I have noticed a man thinking that what I had to say was not as important as what a man had to say.
3. I have noticed a man judging my body as I walked down the street.
4. I have noticed a man looking at my breasts while talking with me.
5. I have been told that my future wasn't as important as a man's.
6. I have been treated as less important than a boy by a teacher.
7. I have been given less training or education than a man for a job.
8. I have been paid less than a man for doing comparable work.
9. I have been harassed while walking down the street.
10. I have been called a bitch, slut, or a whore by a man.
11. I have been harassed on a job site.
12. I have been with a man who only wanted sex from me.
13. I have been lied to, manipulated, or deceived by a man.
14. I have had a man try to control where I could go, who I could see, or what I could do.
15. I have had a man yell at me, threaten me, or otherwise try to intimidate me.
16. I was molested by my father, another male relative, or another adult male when I was a girl.
17. I have been hit by a man.
18. I have been sexually assaulted by a man.

Even if you checked few or none of the statements in the Experiences of Abusive Behavior from Men exercise, you have probably encountered men and seen media portrayals of men who have done those things. My goal is not to have you forget prior negative experiences or to forgive men, but simply to be able to come to the boys in your life with as much openness, love, and hopefulness as you can and with as few echoes from these experiences as possible.

I think it is important that you receive validation and support for your feelings from other adults so that you can be present with your son without being unduly influenced by experiences with other men. He is a person struggling to be caring and responsible, trying to find his place in the world, and he needs your guidance, not your projections. He can neither replace the other men in your life nor heal the hurts from them.

You may have had positive experiences with men that you want to pass on or that inspire you.

Questions to ask yourself

Think of a time in your life when a man came through for you — a time when you needed support and a brother, father, son, lover, co-worker, or other male was there when you needed him.

Who was that person?

What did he provide?

What do you carry with you from that experience?

What did that experience teach you about how men can be?

I believe that when we are raising boys we are most effective when we reach out to the caring, loving, strong, capable, and responsive human qualities they all start with. Then we can nurture those qualities and guide boys towards full participation in the community.

As well as your experiences with men, you bring your experiences with women and as a woman to parenting. We could construct a long list of expectations you may have that say what girls are supposed to be like and how they are supposed to act. What is important here is to look at thesocial expectations girls are taught about how they should relate to men and children. Some of these expectations are that women will:

- put their needs aside in favor of men's.
- act less smart than men or hide their intelligence.
- look to men to take care of financial or physical tasks.
- be dependent on men.
- acquiesce to men's demands.
- take care of the children.

- cook.
- clean house.
- defer to male authority.
- manage the feelings in a family or relationship.

Questions to ask yourself

Which (if any) of these expectations were present in your family?
Which (if any) were you taught?
Which (if any) occur in your present family?
Which (if any) of these expectations do you see your son or
his friends adopting?
Which (if any) do you find it hard to let go of as expectations for yourself?

These are social patterns which exert tremendous pressure on most women to fall into at least some of these ways of behaving around men, not least because some men get angry and even violent when women don't. These expectations are so strong that it is easy for women to continue these patterns with their sons as they grow up.

It may not be easy to alter these patterns, but the first step is to notice them. Talking about them with friends, getting support from other adults, discussing them within your family — these can be steps to building more gender-equal relationships within the family and helping everyone to get out of the boxes of gender socialization.

MOTHERS ARE NOT THE PROBLEM

Despite a constant barrage of blame and disparagement from the media, women are still the primary caretakers of boys as well as of girls. Although there are men who continue to claim that there is something problematic about women raising sons, most single mothers, lesbian mothers, grandmothers, stepmothers, paid caretakers, and women in heterosexual relationships are doing wonderful jobs of raising boys, biologically related or not, often in spite of great adversity. When I talk with successful adult men they commonly attribute their success, their values, their self-discipline, and often their inspiration to their mothers. Some go on to mention how their mothers raised them in an environment of male violence, poverty, lack of external support such as childcare, or public disapproval of single-parent families.

This personal testimony is in sharp contrast to a public discourse in which mothers are routinely blamed for the failings of men. The scapegoating of mothers continues even when it is commonly the rejection of female values and the overidentification with patriarchal male values that lead young men to be uncaring, exploitative, and violent.

Some of the men I talk with also mention their fathers and the wonderful support and nurturing their fathers provided them. However, the greater number mention what they did not receive from their fathers, referring to the lack of nurturing, praise, support, and often the lack of physical or emotional presence that make father/son relationships so troubling to many men. The absence of an adult male, psychologically or physically, in the lives of many young men sometimes leads us to the false conclusion that we need to bring men back into the lives of boys at all costs.

© Kathy Sloane

DO BOYS NEED MEN?

I think boys do need — we all need — men to be fully involved in childraising. With so many young people stranded without adequate community support, we need men as well as women to see themselves as primary childrearers of their own children and of all the young people around them. We cannot raise another generation of children with most men uninvolved in parenting without disastrous consequences.

But that is not the whole story. There is an often stated message in our society that at some point in a boy's life he needs a man to show him how to become a man. Many single mothers worry that they need to find a man — a lover, coach, teacher, minister, mentor, therapist, or uncle — to be a male model. Many fathers or father substitutes are ready to step in when they judge that women are creating soft boys, that boys need toughening up or setting straight. If boys are getting into trouble, mothers are the ones who are blamed because it is assumed they are not authoritative enough to set limits.

It seems to me that most advice to women about raising boys has come from men who want to disempower subtly or not-so-subtly mothers and create a mystique around maleness. There have been many warnings about not coddling boys, with the implication that coddling damages them somehow. And there are lots of suggestions that women should reduce their presence in their sons' lives and turn them over to men who know better how to initiate sons into the sacred rites of manhood. Besides being self-serving, this kind of advice is damaging to boys. Boys need strong and caring women, mothers, and other-mothers throughout their childhood and adolescence.

Mothers are not the problem; men are not the solution. There is no evidence that women-raised sons are inadequate or incompetent or lacking in any way at all, even though there are lots of assertions and attempts to demonstrate so.

Boys and young men need female parents fully in their lives. It is important that a woman not give up her claim to full parental respect and involvement just because a boy reaches a certain age or his father says, "I know how it is for boys." He may or may not know. He may be projecting his own emotions onto his son, he may be out of touch with current youth culture, or he may be reluctant to relinquish his male authority or traditional values. We do not need men to step in and "correct" a pattern of "over-mothering""by separating sons from women and initiating them into men's mysteries. I hope that men will resist any temptation to take their sons off and make men of them in all-male environments. It is not true that men and boys have to go off alone when things get serious, or intimate, or important. And I hope that women can resist the social messages that say they are inadequate to the task of raising a son and therefore should find a suitable male to whom they can hand their son.

Questions to ask yourself

Women are fully capable of raising successful sons alone or with a male or female partner. Can you repeat this statement without qualifications?
Are there any ways that you have doubted your own ability to raise a son?
To counter the negative social messages about women raising sons, where can you get support for sustaining your confidence in your parenting?

IF YOU'RE A MAN

Most boys in western societies were raised to be men in fairly traditional ways. Even if you had progressive parents who challenged these norms, you could not completely escape the pressures to act like a man. Precisely because of that training you have much to offer your sons because you know the destructiveness of that training and the controlling behavior and abuse it produces. You know the pressures your sons face and can help them discover alternatives. But you will be much more effective if you are clear about what you carry from your own experiences.

One influence on your understanding of male parenting is what you learned from your father, stepfather, or other father figure who provided you with a visible model of what men are like. Few men were not influenced by their father's presence (or absence) in their lives. You may have consciously tried to emulate him or to be as different as possible. It is important to acknowledge the influence of your father and father figures, building on the positive aspects and leaving behind what isn't useful.

Questions to ask yourself

Describe your father or other father figure, relating as much as you know or remember about him.
What kind of person is/was he?
What did he talk about with you?
What didn't he talk about with you?
How did he express his feelings?
How did he relate to women, to children, to other men?
How might your mother or sisters or his peers have described him?
Complete this sentence: What I learned from my father is...
If he were standing in front of you today, how would you complete this sentence, "Dad, I need(ed) you to..."?
Who were father figures in your life besides (or instead of) your biological father?
What did you learn from them?
List any qualities you think are important in a parent that you learned from your father or other father figure.

Many boys experience a lack of physical affection past the age of three or four, and a lack of emotional support for dealing with the everyday pressures to measure up. Many boys are physically abused, and one out of every five or six is sexually molested as a child.[2] Boys are trained, through the use of violence and the lack of alternatives, to fulfill people's expectations of what it means to be a man.

Your sons face constantly shifting but similar pressures to what you have faced. You will be able to be more fully present for them as you recover from your own history of growing up male. What have you done with the pain and anger of being hit, yelled at, called names, or simply pressured to act like a man? Have you hidden the pain or used alcohol and other drugs to cover it up? Have you ever stopped yourself from showing affection, hugging, or touching another man because of how it might look? Have you become more cautious in the way you dress, talk, and behave? Have you ever limited your activities to those accepted as manly? And what about when you became older? Have you ever been so mad that, while driving, you drove too fast or lost control of the car? Have you ever felt like committing suicide or taken out your anger and pain on family and friends?

The pressures, and the dangers, that boys face today are not so different from those you may have faced when young. Nor are the typical responses. Boys still turn to self-destructive violence, high-risk activities, abuse of others, and silence to control or cover the pain and anger they feel about how they've been treated.

Questions to ask yourself

How did you cope with the pressure to act like a man?
When you were young, did you worry that you were not tough enough;
did you exercise to make yourself tougher?
Were you disrespected by adults or told to act like a man, take it
like a man, be a man, or simply grow up?
Were you called wimp, queer, fag, or other names by adults or other boys?
Were you in a fight at some time in your childhood; were
you hit by your parents?
What do you carry with you from these experiences?
How can you use your experience growing up as a boy in positive
ways to guide your parenting?

One of the strongest messages boys learn from male training is to hold themselves in, not to show any feelings, except anger. It is often not safe to speak back or fight back against the people who are inflicting violence on them. The only way that many men think they can deal with the pain is to perpetuate a cycle of violence in which they pass on their pain, anger, hurt, and frustration to someone who is weaker than they are. Therefore, one effect of male training is to encourage men to take out their anger on other people, and on women in particular.

The Power Chart discussed earlier illustrates why women become targets for men's violence. Most boys learn that women are inferior, less important, and, in fact, provoke or are responsible for violence that happens to them. In addition, they learn to expect women to take care of them physically, sexually, and emotionally. They are presented with many models of women who seem to be doing just that in the thousands of advertisements they are exposed to. It is often difficult for men to imagine the profound effect that these images have in building their expectations that women will take care of their needs. Of course, the images themselves are just a reflection of the greater patriarchal social structure that keeps power, status, money, land, and control in the hands of some men and relegates women to the margins of society, along with other disenfranchised groups.

The exercise Passing on Abuse to Women will give you a better sense of how the patriarchal social structure affects men's personal relationships with women, which in turn has an impact on the way they parent their daughters and sons.

EXERCISE

PASSING ON ABUSE TO WOMEN[3]

*Put a check mark by any of the following questions to which
you answer yes.*

Have you ever:

1. interrupted a woman by talking louder than her?

2. not valued a woman's thought or opinion because she was a woman?

3. found yourself looking at a woman's breasts while talking with her?

4. found yourself unintentionally distracted from conversation, thought, driving, or another activity because you were sizing up the bodies of women going past you?

5. been dissatisfied with the body or sex appeal of a woman you were with because she wasn't as pretty as the woman you had thought you would end up with?

6. made a comment in public about a woman's body?

7. discussed a woman's body with another man?

8. been told by a woman that you are sexist?

9. been told by a woman that she wanted more affection and less sex from you?

10. lied to a woman with whom you were intimate about a sexual relationship with another woman?

11. left care for birth control up to the woman with whom you had a sexual relationship?

12. downplayed or minimized a woman's fear of male violence?

13. used your voice or body to scare or intimidate a woman?

14. tried to control when and where a woman could go or what she could do?

15. threatened to harm a woman, her children, her possessions, or yourself if she didn't do what you wanted her to do?

16. hit, slapped, shoved, or pushed a woman?

17. had sex with a woman when you knew she didn't want to?

Unless you question and interrupt any behavior you have learned to belittle women and to be complicit with sexism, you will pass that training on to your sons. They look to you as a role model who will show them how to treat women and how to relate to "women's" issues. As well, because society tells boys that women are not as valuable as men, many boys tend not to listen to women as much as they listen to men. Therefore, you have authority in the eyes of boys simply because you are a man. I hope you will use this authority carefully, not to enhance your status or dominance, but to amplify the concerns that women have about male violence and injustice. There are so many ways to contribute to the dangerous mystique of maleness that you need to be vigilant, constantly talking and working with women so that you support women's equality and leadership and don't perpetuate male dominance.

Boys need you as a caring adult ally who supports women, who contradicts the negative messages boys receive about women, and who participates as a responsive and responsible member of the community.

Our actions at home and in public are the most powerful modeling we can provide our sons if we want them to become activists for social justice and gender equity. I know that I am not and will never be perfect. What my sons need to see is that I am trying to make changes as I grapple with these issues in open and honest ways. Then they understand that these are serious matters and deserve their attention as well as ours.

Questions to ask yourself

If we are heterosexual, this modeling is most powerful in our homes.
How are decisions made in your family?
How are chores divided up?
Do you listen to women and respect their intelligence and leadership?
Do you tease your daughters about their sexuality or belittle their
intelligence or athletic abilities?
Do you put down your partner, tell sexual jokes, or comment
on women's bodies?
Do you use pornography?

After assessing your behavior at home, you can look at your public actions.
Do you interrupt jokes, put-downs, and sexual harassment of women, intervene
in situations where women are being abused or discriminated against, and fight
alongside women for gender justice in all parts of our society?

There are a few things to remember as you think about how to nurture your sons.
1) It is never too late to begin. No matter how old your son or how distant your relationship, you can change how you relate to your son.
2) It makes a difference. Even if you are physically removed or only see your son occasionally, you count in your son's life. He may look to you for guidance, for support, for answers to questions he may not be able to ask anyone else. He does listen to your stories, mistakes, triumphs, ideas, even when he doesn't

show it. He also watches what you do.

3) It heals us when we reach out to our sons. When we parent our sons well, we heal from and move beyond the pain, abuse, absence, disappointment, and frustrations we may have carried over from our own childhood.

DO WE NEED TO BE TOUGH TO BE STRONG?

Men need to be aware of the drive to be tough. It is easy to assume that your son needs to be tough in order to succeed in the world. That is probably what you were taught. You probably want him to be gentle and caring — but you may become concerned when you see signs of what you think is weak behavior.

Many men carry two ideas from their male training that intersect here. One is a sense that the world is dangerous for men: if you're not tough, people will walk right over you. The other is that the worst thing in the world is to have a son who is gay. If your son cannot defend himself or if he is gay, you may feel that you have failed as a man or as a father.

I have faced the fear that my son might not be able to defend himself. When Ariel was eight he came to me after having been threatened by a bully.

"Robert said he's going to kill me tomorrow at school."

"He said what?"

"He's going to get some kids and kill me."

"Why would he say that? What happened today?"

"He's always bossing everyone around, so today I hit him. He chased me after that, but the bell rang so he said he would get me. I can't go to school tomorrow."

At this point I had conflicting responses. On the one hand I wanted to cruise by the school and show this bully who he was messing with. I wanted to protect my son. On the other hand I was afraid that if my son were pushed around this time he might become a permanent wimp and always be picked on. Maybe it was time to stop coddling him so that he could learn how to take care of himself. Maybe I should teach him how to fight, then send him back out there to fend for himself. (And, of course, I was conveniently over-looking the fact that Ariel had landed the first hit.)

This monologue going through my head had nothing to do with my son. These two loud, conflicting voices come directly out of my training to be a man, reinforced by experiences growing up with other guys in the neighborhood.

To help my son get out of the Box and resolve this situation, I had to stop this inner chatter and listen to him so that I could figure out how best to support him. That meant putting him in control, letting him make the best decisions he could given the choices he felt he had. I had to quiet my voices and help him discover his. Our conversation continued something like this:

"Sounds like you're scared."

"Yeah, he's eleven and I'm only eight. He'll clobber me, and he has big friends."

"Well, you have to go to school, but maybe we can figure something out. What do you think you could do?"

"I dunno."

"Could you get some help at school?"

"I don't know. The playground teacher never notices what happens and my regular teacher won't deal with stuff on the playground. She just says to take it to the playground teacher."

"What about the principal?"

"What can she do? Why don't you come to school with me?"

"I can't stay with you all day. Could you talk to Robert?"

"What good would that do, he'd just hit me."

"What if you talked with him with an adult there?"

"That might work, but what about when they left?"

"What if it was the principal who was there?"

"That might work. But I can't just go into the principal's office and do that. Can you come with me?"

"I suppose I could come in the morning to be with you when you talk with the principal."

We were able to work this conflict out and avoid further violence.[4] Not all situations are so easily resolvable, but my questions and suggestions helped Ariel see that he had more choices than fight or flight. He could be strong without being tough. Two things were clear to me. It was important for my son to decide how he wanted to deal with the conflict, knowing he had my support. And more violence wasn't the answer.

Most boys are taught that you are a winner or loser, champ or chump, bully or wimp, in the Box or out of the Box. They learn that there is no in-between, no complex alternative. What we must do is help boys see that they can think through a situation and come up with new ideas that go beyond traditional either/or thinking.

Being tough does not protect boys from violence. In fact, it can bring on more of it. *A boy's best protection is to be able to think for himself, solve problems, communicate, and connect with people.* These are true survival skills. They are also the beginning of leadership abilities.

I know that when your son comes home scared or in tears, it isn't helpful to say (even though you may think it), "Get back out there and whip his ass or you'll have to deal with me." But any pressure on your son to take care of himself, not to cry, not to retreat, not to make mistakes, and not to ask for help conveys a similar message.

The two most common responses from men when their sons face conflict and are scared are to withdraw or, alternatively, to become aggressive. They withdraw because they are uncomfortable around their feelings and don't know how to reach out to their sons. Or they become angry and try to bully boys into acting like real men and toughing it out. Neither response is useful.

Instead, you can be with them without answers. It is okay to be uncomfortable. It is okay to wait for them to talk with you. It is okay not to take action immediately. You need to learn, and model for them, what it is like to simply be there in quiet strength for someone who needs you.

Questions to ask yourself

Are you (or would you be) uncomfortable when your son comes
home defeated, scared, or having run from a fight?
How do you feel when he needs to cry on your shoulder?
Can you be fully present for him or do you panic and withdraw
or become more aggressive in your discomfort?

MORE THAN COMPANIONSHIP

Father-son time together is important because young men need the benefit of all the female and male attention they can get in today's difficult environment. There can be something deeply nurturing and supportive in a father's presence or companionship with his son. Just hanging out together, playing sports, going fishing, watching a game can make a connection. I encourage you to enjoy those times and take pleasure in the company of your son. For many boys, these times of male companionship are all too rare.

However, challenge yourself to give more to your son than just your silent presence. He needs you to talk with him, and he needs you to hold him.

Talking about personal affairs is not something many men are comfortable with. At most they may confide in their partner or a special male friend. They are often uncomfortable around their children when it comes to expressing how they feel. If this describes you — just give it a try. Talk about your life, your joys, your sadness, your family, your challenges. I don't mean in a one-time, no-holds-barred, "here's my life" unloading. Steadily but in brief segments, as part of your everyday interaction with your son, talk about yourself. He may not appear to be listening, but he is. He may not appear affected, but he is. He may not even be respectful. But it shifts deep waters when adult men open up and talk with their sons. It is a sign of respect, sharing, and trust, and a demonstration of emotional literacy that no young man is unaffected by.

Besides talking with your son you need to remember to hold him. When he is young, physically cuddle him in your lap, hug him, kiss him, and shower him with loving affection. Even when he is older, hold him in your arms to greet him, acknowledge him, or give him a shoulder to cry on. Learn to hold his feelings. To sit with him with he is upset, scared, or sad. To jump with him when he is excited or celebratory. Your presence can become a safe space where he can be fully and completely who he is, in touch with his deepest feelings because you hold him with secure, loving arms.

Although you face unique challenges as men raising boys, you also can expect special joy in your connections. Because your son looks to you for understanding of the range of how he can be in the world, when you model life-affirming, anti-sexist nurturing you pass on to him a history of concern, caring, and commitment that will benefit us all.

A LISTENING PARTNERSHIP

In the previous two sections we have looked at some of the particular issues that women and men bring to parenting boys. As adults who care about our sons, we don't want the unresolved pain, confusion, and fear we bring from our backgrounds to interfere with our ability to be there for them. Although as men and women we may have somewhat different issues (and there is a lot of overlap!), we all bring emotional issues to our parenting. It is our work to sort them out. If we don't, those issues will surface in our relationships with our sons and communication may well break down as our son realizes that instead of understanding his situation, we are projecting from ours.

The Parents Leadership Institute, a San Francisco Bay area group that offers classes, workshops, and resources for parents, describes how a listening partnership can help us clear out some of these issues so we can refocus on our children. Simply put, a listening partner is another adult who will give us a block of time and listen intently as we talk about our concerns as a parent. The listening partner provides support and care, suggestions if we ask for them, but not criticism. It is immensely useful to have a partner, friend, support group, or colleague who will provide this kind of attention to us so that we don't pass on our concerns to our sons or daughters. It also allows us to sort out our thinking and often to come up with new ideas for resolving particular challenges with our sons.

An essential part of being an ally to another person or group is to get support for ourselves, not from that group, but from a peer, family member, or friend. Establishing a listening partnership is a valuable support to our ability to parent effectively. It can also help us if we are co-parenting with another adult who disagrees with us on basic approaches to raising our son. We don't have to raise our sons by ourselves without support.

IF YOU ARE CO-PARENTING

Many of us are not parenting by ourselves. You may be reading this book and thinking, "I agree with all this, but my male or female partner really needs to hear it." Although there are lots of advantages to co-parenting — i.e., shared resources, more time, energy, relief, and support — there are inevitably differences in values and differing approaches to childraising.

The differences in perspective between you and your partner can sometimes seem like huge chasms. If you are in a heterosexual relationship, some of the issues that arise may be based on your and your partner's different gender training. I have found that men, in general, are more concerned than women about their sons being, or appearing to be, gay, about their engaging in activities that are not traditionally male, and about their level of achievement. Men have higher self-investment in their son's success, and they are more punitive when their sons break the rules.

Many men, although they might profess otherwise, fall back into the traditional male role when it comes to raising sons. For example, if his son would rather try out for a theater or dance audition than the football team, a father may become angry. Consciously or not, he may fear his son is gay and that this choice of activities will reflect badly on him as a father. In such a situation, the mother may find it harder to create space for her son to develop his full humanity when his father doesn't support her efforts.

Talking about nonsexist childraising with your partner doesn't always help because such discussions are abstract. You can agree on principles but may meet conflict when you come to resolving particular issues. It is often more useful to take a specific situation and talk out how the two of you want to handle it. On the other hand, if that approach is too charged, you might want to start by coming to agreement about some general values you both want to pass on to your son and then applying these to concrete situations.

For example, rather than arguing about whether guns or violent games make boys aggressive, you can talk about what values you want to develop in your son. If you can agree that you want your son to care about others and to be able to work cooperatively, then you can look at his toys, games, or other activities to see if they foster these values. You have a common basis for evaluating specific items.

If you and your partner disagree on an issue, you don't need to present a united front to your son. In fact, it is important to let him know that you disagree with your partner, and it is often appropriate to invite his involvement in the discussion. Covering over differences is not necessary. As young men determine their own values, they need to see how different adults live their lives. It is always an advantage when more than one adult is parenting a boy because each adult brings different experiences and perspectives. Most boys are able to sort out these differences and decide for themselves how they want to do things.

There are no values or stands that are fixed in stone or that can be labeled the right way to do things. As a co-parent you can model not the correct answer, but a healthy process that nurtures your relationship with your partner as well as the growth of your son. A healthy process is one in which difference is valued and cooperative results support all involved. (If the differences are extreme or lead to conflict, outside mediation or counseling can be useful.)

In particular, if you are a woman, I think you should expect respect for your own well-being. This teaches boys that women are to be respected and it teaches girls to expect respect. Boys rarely learn to respect women if they see women they know being disrespected.

You also need physical and emotional safety. If you or another female are being verbally, emotionally, or physically abused in your family, that abuse will contradict the positive values you try to teach your son. It may be possible for you to relate to your son differently when you are alone, but anything you might teach your son would be undermined by the violence he sees. Your seeking help is not simply for his sake, but to ensure your own safety.

Co-parenting develops over time. The first major change occurs when the first child is born and adults who might have been living relatively independent lives have to coordinate their schedules and childraising practices much more tightly. All of a sudden they need to agree on decisions about meals and shopping and childcare that work for both partners. This is particularly hard for some men to accept because they are often much less used to giving up control of their time and activities and may expect a female partner to do more of the childcare and housework. When our first child was born it was hard for me to acknowledge the importance of regular meal times. I was also used to watching Sunday football games and resented the fact that I couldn't just relax in front of the TV for three hours without interruption. I didn't anticipate the constant demands of a newborn and was used to having a lot of discretion in how I spent my time. Working out an equitable distribution of responsibilities with Micki, my partner, required that I let go of some of my expectations and take her needs into account. These discussions should begin even before a baby is born, because patterns set in those early years are hard to change later.

Arrangements will naturally change over time as external circumstances and your children change. Micki and I often have to shift primary responsibility for shopping and cooking dinner and after school carpooling as our work demands change. Our goal is to balance household responsibilities between us equally and we have to review and discuss how things are working on a regular basis to ensure that everyone's needs are being met.

Although the issues have to be worked out when a child is born, many men are, unfortunately, not as concerned with childraising issues at such an early age. A father may be very involved with his son in a nongendered way, but he often doesn't feel the gender stakes are very high so he "allows" the mother more control over his son's life. Then when his son gets older — sometimes at kindergarten age, sometimes much later — such a father will become worried about his partner's feminization of their son and about the son's ability to make it as a guy. This is the point at which the stakes rise and the father tries to regain control of how his son acts, what activities he participates in, and how he looks. Most men who are not involved with their sons in their younger years have a point at which they will claim their "father rights" as their own fears kick in.

If a mother has similar fears that her son is not masculine enough she will, perhaps, compromise her own best thinking and let the man make decisions that are not in the son's best interest. She may be so relieved that he is finally paying more attention to his son that she is afraid to challenge how he is doing it. This is when boys get pushed to participate in sports they don't want to do, to talk or walk in ways that make them uncomfortable, to let go of dolls or stuffed animals they are attached to, to spend less time with their mother, and to learn to stuff their feelings, not to cry, and to take it like a man. Of course, mothers can initiate these changes, pushing boys into the "Act Like a Man" Box, though they usually provide more affection and are less punitive then men at this stage.

It is crucial that both parents talk out their fears about their son's masculinity. Otherwise men step in, women retreat or are pushed out, and the son is pushed into the Box. Many boys are experiencing the same fears that the adults have. Discussing these fears with them — what they are based on, how we learn them, how they are reinforced — helps boys feel less need to prove themselves masculine enough to pass the inspection of their peers and adults. Having two or more adults describe their experiences and feelings about these issues helps boys see that there are multiple ways to respond.

There is no guarantee that we will have a stronger influence over our son than a co-parent does, and there may be times when we despair that we are "losing him" altogether. However, there usually comes a time, possibly not until he is an adult, when our son will respond to how we raised him. It is not easy to stay true to our values while being flexible and working out ways to co-parent. It is a long-term balancing act that requires communication, perseverance, strategic thinking, and the ability to keep our son's needs at the center of our attention. Although it is not easy, co-parenting offers many rewards. When it works well we have someone to share the joys and delight of watching our children grow and thrive, to comfort us when they don't, and to puzzle through unfamiliar and unexpected occurrences with us. A challenging and supportive partner can enhance our own best attempts at parenting.

Whether we are single parents, co-parents, or have a more complex parenting arrangement, there are two more very significant issuesI want to look at so we can be more powerful allies to our sons. The next chapter looks at homophobia and how we can support our sons whether they are gay or straight. The subsequent chapter examines the complicated dynamics of race and racism so that we can support and guide our sons through the difficult challenges of living in a multiracial society.

4 Challenging Homophobia

A major factor that keeps many of us from supporting our sons when they try to step out of the Box is homophobia.[1] We fear that our sons might be gay or might appear to others to be gay if they don't look, talk, and act "straight" — which usually means tough and in control. A common fear of heterosexual men and women is that if their sons are weak, scared, confused, or just not physically strong they are gay. This fear arises because many people have a deep misunderstanding of what it means to be gay.

For men, especially, the concept of homosexuality can trigger confusion and fear about their own sexual identity. Some men see their son's sexual identity as a reflection on their own masculinity. In addition, in some cultures the strength and success of a son, which often includes being heterosexual and fathering children, is seen as proof of his father's success.

Some of our sons are homosexual or bisexual, others are heterosexual. Many more are confused about their sexuality and may not become clear about their sexual identity until later in life. For still others, sexual identity may change over time. In any case, we generally don't know and can't predict which boys are, or will become gay, bisexual, or straight. Most of us assume that any boy is heterosexual unless we have some visible evidence that he is not. This presumption of heterosexuality leaves very little room for boys to operate in whether they are gay, straight, or bisexual.

Questions to ask yourself

In what ways (if any) have you assumed your son or other boys you interact with are heterosexual?

What would change in your behavior if you assumed that any boy you interact with might be gay or bisexual, including your son?

Young men constantly have to alter their behavior, dress, way of talking, or physical posture to prove to others that they are not gay. One of the quickest way to make a boy jump back into the "Act Like A Man" Box is to call him a fag, wimp, or sissy, or to indicate that you think he might be homosexual. Any leadership, any creativity, any imaginative acts can be immediately challenged and defeated by homophobic comments. When we accept the "Act Like a Man" Box in any form, and accept the homophobia that keeps it in place, we make all boys unsafe and we promote violence. For example, as adults, whenever we describe things using words like wimp, soft, or weak in a derogatory way, or use strong as a synonym for aggressive or violent, we are fueling homophobia.

Another confusion is often present in our homophobia. A boy's sexual identity has nothing to do with his toughness, his physical strength, his gentleness, his desire to dance, or his lack of interest in football. He can be violent and aggressive — and be gay. He can be people-oriented or physically frail — and be heterosexual.

You may sigh with relief to realize that your son isn't necessarily gay even if he is not athletic, likes dance, or shows some other "nonmasculine" symptom — but that sigh confirms your homophobia.

It is important to ask yourself why you are scared your son may be gay. Do you need more information about what it means to be gay or bisexual? Do you need to talk with parents of gay children?[2] Are you worried that a gay son is a reflection on you or on your parenting? Are you worried that even talking about sexual identity will affect your image in the eyes of your son, or of other boys or men?

All children experience tremendous pressure to become heterosexual and to present themselves as heterosexual for their own protection.[3] This is extremely destructive because most young people have strong, natural desires to be close to members of their own gender, to experiment sexually, and to express the love and tenderness they feel for other young people. To have all this off-limits because one might be, or might be mistaken for being, gay or lesbian takes a heavy toll on young people's relationships. This pressure to pass as straight is even more destructive for gay, lesbian, and bisexual youth because it denies them the opportunity to be affirmed in who they are. Consequently many resort to alcohol and other drug use, other self-destructive activities, or suicide.

For all boys, the consequences of homophobia are particularly great. Being violent towards others is often a direct result of homophobia. Any man who is called a wimp, sissy, or fag can prove he's not by fighting the guy who challenged him or, if that is too dangerous, by attacking someone who is less powerful. Similarly, our political leaders often try to demonstrate their toughness by going to war, advocating mean-spirited and aggressive social or international policies, and generally parading as not weak, soft, and stereotypically gay.

Homophobia has made it difficult for boys to get together because they are afraid getting together will make it appear to others that they are gay. Their only model for success is to go it alone, leaving them unable to participate effectively in cooperative or group efforts for community development.

There are many men, straight and gay, who have stepped out of the Box — who are strong and powerful without resorting to violence to get what they want. This concept can be very confusing to young men, so it helps to use examples such as Gandhi and Cesar Chavez- two men who were strong and powerful but did not use physical force or violence to get what they wanted. What did they use? In a classroom I might hear the following responses:

- They used their minds.
- They used their hearts.
- They cared for people.
- They spoke up.
- They organized with lots of people.
- They used their faith.
- They were smart.
- They moved people.
- They used their compassion.

Cesar Chavez and Gandhi didn't go it alone. They organized with people. They got ahead by getting together. Just like them, all men have sources of strength besides their fists. Using these sources of strength helps us get out of the Box. When these men stepped out of the Box, did they get called names? Of course. Did people attack them and try to get them to be violent? Of course. The other ingredient it takes to get out of the Box is courage.

Every boy needs to learn about the men in his particular culture who challenged not just the gender roles, but all forms of injustice and violence. We have the opportunity to provide them with models of men who are strong and powerful fighters for justice but who do not use threat, intimidation, and violence to get their way.

We can encourage boys to try out atypical or nonviolent male behavior and show them models of adult men who do. Often boys will say they simply can't do something — wear pink, take dance classes, express their feelings in public — and will not be able to explain why they feel it is impossible. They are usually responding to peer pressure and its homophobic underpinnings. It doesn't work to simply ask them, "But why not?" Until they have a concept of homophobia and have practice in recognizing it in themselves and others, they won't have a vocabulary to describe what is going on.

Part of our challenge is to help young men to develop the other kinds of strength they have, to break down their isolation, and to stand up for what they believe in. Then they can act from their strength and not respond out of fear of other people's homophobia.

Boys cannot get out of the Box unless they see others doing so. They need role models. It supports them when see us, the caring adult women and men in their families, challenging the gender-role stereotypes and restrictions and challenging our own homophobia.

If you have any hesitation or questions about these issues, talk with other adults to clarify where it becomes difficult for you to talk with your son about homophobia. Make a commitment that you will not let your own misinformation or prejudices overlay your discussion of these issues with him. You may need to do some reading for yourself or talk with lesbians and gay men to prepare you for these family conversations. You can start by answering the questions below.

© Cathy Cade

Questions to ask yourself

While growing up, where did you learn homophobic messages?

How old were you?

What was told to you to justify these messages?

If you are straight, do you have any doubts that lesbians,
gay men, and bisexuals deserve the safety, respect, and equal
opportunity that other citizens have?

What would you have to change in your own comments or behavior
to eliminate homophobia from them?

What are ways that your homophobia may lead you to want to toughen up
your son, or to discourage him from participating in activities which
have been traditionally less masculine in reputation?

Who could you talk with to explore these issues further?

ADDRESSING HOMOPHOBIA AT HOME

Boys bring home homophobic remarks in two or sometimes three phases while growing up. The first phase is between the ages of six and nine when they come home saying words like "fag" and "queer." They often don't know what the words mean but they know they hurt.

Talking about the meaning of such words, defining lesbian, gay, and bisexual people, and discussing why these words are hurtful usually ends the behavior, especially if there is a general practice of respect towards others within your family. At this age we can name homophobia, describe how it operates, give examples from our own lives, and discuss the costs of it with them. This gives them an opportunity to ask questions, to think further about it, to question the wisdom of acting out of this fear. We don't need to talk about sexuality at this age if we feel it is inappropriate. The subject is not sexual activity — what people do in bed — but sexual identity — what kind of public behaviors and activities are delineated for males and females.

If you are not lesbian, gay, or bisexual yourself and don't have close family members or friends who are (why not?), you can use books to introduce boys of this age to the issue — for example, *Heather has Two Mommies* by Leslea Newman, *Jenny Lives with Eric and Martin* by Susanne Bosche, *Tommy Stands Alone* by Gloria Velasquez, *A Day with Alexis* by Sarita Johnson-Hunt, and *Elliott and Win* by Carolyn Meyer — and talk more about sexual identity.

Another phase comes when boys are older, know more about homosexuality, and have picked up negative value judgments from their peers and the media — perhaps even from you. They may also be confronting their own sexual confusion at this stage, wanting to make sure they pass as straight. The pressure on teenage boys to be heterosexual, tough, in control, and unfeeling is so great that many wear their homophobia as a protective coat to cover their insecurities and fears. You can continue to discuss sexual identity and provide your son with information, including videos and books, to help defuse some of the homophobia at this age. However, discussion is no substitute for actual contact with a diversity of lesbians, gays, and bisexuals.

Boys at this age, although facing pressure to appear heterosexual and to join in gay-baiting, also have a wonderful sense of justice and compassion. They are capable of understanding the damage that homophobia does to the lives of gay and bisexual youth, as well as the dilemmas it presents for straight youth. When given a chance to think about the issues and to talk about their own feelings and ideas they are often fair-minded and open. They may not be capable of challenging the homophobia of others because of the personal danger of being attacked themselves, but they can decide not to participate in put-downs or attacks on others.

Our sons are looking to us to model how to respond to homophobic comments, put-downs, jokes, and other forms of abusive behavior. We are better allies to them when we increase our own commitment and ability to notice homophobia and to intervene appropriately.

Questions to ask yourself
Where do you notice homophobia in the boys around you?
How might you interrupt it and raise the issues discussed in this section?
What makes it hard for you to challenge homophobia when you see it?

The third phase occurs for some young men when they become so heavily involved in anti-gay subcultures in sports, religious groups, or in gangs that all you can do is come to an uneasy truce about what is acceptable language and behavior in your house. This phase is not necessarily permanent but it can be very painful to watch your son receiving his identity and his external adult support from a source that is based in part on a deeply rooted and constantly reinforced homophobia. Be clear about your values and your expectations for his behavior in your presence, but don't expect to have a major impact on your son's attitudes during this phase. Remember that even at this stage you cannot make any assumptions about what his sexual identity is.

Although you may not be able to influence the behavior of a particular young man who is caught up in homophobic and other anti-social behavior, you can work to make anti-bias curriculums that address issues of gender, sexual identity, and homophobia available for adolescents in schools and youth programs. You can also put pressure on schools and youth programs to design interventions that produce a safe environment for gay, lesbian, and bisexual youth and to respond to situations where homophobia is present. These actions help minimize the prevalence of homophobic attacks and are an important way to support gay youth.

SUPPORTING GAY YOUTH

If your household acknowledges gender diversity and celebrates diversity in sexual identity you have created a sound foundation for supporting your gay son. If you have been able to work with your son's school, religious organization, youth programs, and other institutions on these issues, you will also have begun to build a base of support for him.

If your son tells you that he is gay, he needs you to be unqualifiedly proud and supportive. Of course you may have fears for his safety as a homosexual in a society in which there is still so much homophobia. Put that fear aside for the moment and perhaps talk about it with other adults. The response your son needs from you is support and pride based on your love for him.

A gay son needs both support and advocacy. One part of that support is expressing your love for him. You can let him know that when things get hard you will be there for him. If he faces discrimination, abuse, or danger you will be an ally to him and help him respond.

You can support him by providing connections to gay youth organizations; by providing magazines, books, and films about gay life; by participating in organizations like

PFLAG that support gay youth; and by welcoming his gay friends and whatever representations of gay culture he brings into your lives. Your own life will become much richer from all of these activities.

The anti-gay climate in so many communities makes it imperative that each of us reach out with support to all gay youth. Because so many are rejected at home, turned out or forced out on their own, or face isolation and danger at school, a great number of gay youth become depressed, engage in dangerous activities, use alcohol or other drugs, or commit suicide. Having an adult who accepts them, talks with them, and provides them with support and resources can make all the difference in their lives.

In addition to our support, our advocacy for gay youth is also crucial. Our neighborhood or school may well be unsafe for them. We may need to challenge organizations to insure their safety and to eliminate homophobia from policies, curriculums, programs, and informal practices. We may need to organize with other adults and with young people to address a wide variety of issues and to make sure that the needs of gay youth are addressed in every program or issue that affects the community.

Gay youth do not know that we are their allies unless we give them visible evidence. Because so many adults are homophobic they cannot assume that we are any different. If we avoid assuming that young people are heterosexual; include references to gay, lesbian, and bisexual people in our speech; and wear buttons and T-shirts, or display other gay-positive materials, we let them know that they can come to us for support. You can find many additional suggestions for being allies to gay youth in the book *Free your mind: The Book for Gay, Lesbian, and Bisexual Youth-and Their Allies* by Ellen Bass and Kate Kaufman.

5 Dealing with Racism

Some of the expectations for and pressures on boys are universal, but the pressure to be a man has a great deal of cultural specificity. In addition, there are striking differences, based particularly on race and class, in the ways that boys are treated. It is important we understand them.

As an example, when a white boy in elementary school is in a fight, adults may praise him for taking care of himself, assume he is passing through a phase, or ignore his behavior because "boys will be boys." He will often be disciplined lightly or given another chance because in spite of "bad boy" behavior he is assumed to be basically good inside.

Adults, especially white adults, often assume that African American and Latino youth are violent and uncivilized. When such a young man gets into a fight, his behavior may be seen as typical of his culture, dangerous, or a mark of long-term pathology or dysfunction. He will probably be disciplined more quickly and more harshly than his white counterparts. Concerned adults may note to each other that he has a tendency to be aggressive and should be watched closely.

Adults, especially those without extensive exposure to Asian American culture, often believe that Asian American boys are not tough or physically aggressive; they do not know how to respond to an Asian American boy who gets into a fight. Because his behavior is seen as atypical, he may not be judged a serious threat to other boys and may not be disciplined seriously, though his aggression won't be considered a positive sign and might be held against him in the future.

Of course these descriptions are generalizations, and adults respond differently depending upon their own sensitivity to racial stereotypes. But in many circumstances boys receive differential treatment from the adults around them based on their race. It is quite possible that none of the boys mentioned above would receive sensitive and caring intervention from adults. As allies to young men we have to take racism into account all of the time when thinking about their needs.

IF YOU AND YOUR SON ARE WHITE

When babies are born they are unaware of racial difference and attach no intrinsic value to skin color. They begin to notice racial differences and their effects between the ages of two and five. Throughout their childhood they are bombarded with stereotypes, misinformation, and lies about race. If they are white they are pressured to become racist in their attitudes and behavior. Without our intervention they will become the racist shock troops of the next generation. This is why we must begin teaching our sons at an early age to embrace differences and to become anti-racist activists. We can start this process by assessing our home and family environment for evidence of racism.[1]

It is challenging to raise white boys in the highly racist society we live in. Although racism is highly visible, it is strongly denied. Racism is often talked about either as an issue of the past, as if we had solved it, or as an issue of interpersonal relationships — "I treat everyone the same, I'm color blind." This dynamic allows white people to feel comfortable with racial disparities in income and education while giving them scapegoats for current economic and social problems.

As even a cursory look at our communities will show, racism is still omnipresent and pervasive. It not only devastates the lives of people of color but it is also harmful to white people because they absorb lies and stereotypes about people of color, are taught to fear them, and have their attention diverted from the white corporate and political elites who make the decisions that affect their lives.

It takes practice to see the everyday effects of racism. People of color know that everything that happens to them during the day is influenced by racism. (Not *determined* by, but influenced by racism. There are obviously many other factors at play, including one's own efforts, personality, abilities, class, and gender.) The question that should always be in front of us is "How is racism operating here?" Not "Is racism a factor?" but "How is it a factor?" Once we can identify how it is a factor, we can begin to figure out strategies for addressing it. As white people, we need to learn to see through what I call a racial lens, in order to see the difference that race makes. The best way to teach our sons to view the world this way is to show them how we use our own racial lens.

Many times differential treatment is quite obvious. We can see that young men of color are treated differently than young white men in school or on the streets. We can see them channeled into non-college tracks and can see them disciplined more often, more harshly, and with less tolerance than white youth. We can see white people stiffen up and lock their doors when young men of color are present, and we notice how the police treat young men differently based on race.

It is not as easy to see how a person of color has been treated with less warmth by a shopkeeper, followed around the store or charged more by a salesperson than a white person was. It may be harder to notice that people of color are systematically turned away from apartment buildings, jobs, houses, and apprenticeship programs that white people walk right into. To improve our ability to see through this racial lens we need to listen to people of color talk about their experiences, to read what they write, to look at the studies of discrimination in housing, jobs, and education.

For example, I did not realize that people of color were followed in some of the stores where I shopped until I listened to them describe their experiences and read about how prevalent such behavior was among shopkeepers. This new information allowed me to see that the smile I received at the door was not what my friends of color received. It also allowed me to speak to the manager about changing store policies and to avoid shopping at stores which were unresponsive.

We can also teach our sons that racism keeps people of color the center of attention and white people the center of power. We always need to ask: When people of color are the focus, who really has power here? Is our attention being distracted from the source of our problems? Are people of color, such as recent immigrants, being scapegoated for economic problems?

In order to raise white sons as allies to people of color, we probably need to do some work on racism ourselves. We all can benefit from increased practice identifying racism and developing strategies for combating it. In addition, many of us may not know the histories of communities of color in this country; we may not have read much literature of other cultures; we may not have many close contacts with people of color.

During early childhood years we can point out and comment on the racism in the books, videos, computer games, TV shows, and advertising that our children are exposed to. Just as many of us point out gender inequities, introduce female heroines, and comment on sexism when we see it, we can do the same for racist situations and materials. We can simply state our own feelings: "I don't like it when all the action heroes are white and all the enemies are people of color." "How come we never see people of color who are scientists in this science series? I know there are many."

Our sons need to listen to the experiences of people of color. Placing our children in multicultural childcare settings, encouraging multiracial friendships, reaching out to co-workers and colleagues who are of diverse backgrounds, and choosing professionals like doctors and dentists who are people of color are all ways to broaden our children's experience. Our society is so highly segregated that any of these efforts may turn out to be more complex than we imagined. But that complexity also can become material for understanding how racism operates and for introducing our children to the issues. (It can also bring us up against our own prejudices, fears, and resistance.)

If our neighborhood or school is segregated, we can still introduce our children to a multicultural world experience that breaks down stereotypes. The best and often most accurate way is to read what people of color write about their lives. There is a multitude of new children's books that realistically portray the lives of adults and children who are African American. There are a substantial number of books about the lives of Latino/as. Books by Native American, Arab American, and Asian American writers for young people are few and hard to find, but there are some good ones available.[2] Many of us, especially if we are in large cities, have access to photo exhibits, live musical performances, museums, and cultural centers where we can take our children. Hearing and seeing examples of other people's diverse experiences is extremely valuable for our sons.

If we understand that we live in a multicultural society, we will begin to question any situation where people of color are not present. For example, if our sons are in a Boy Scout troop, a little league team, a Math Olympics team, or a religious school class that is all white, we will ask ourselves, "Why is this group all white? Are there any barriers that keep people of color out?" Then we might question the curriculum or program. Is it multicultural? Does it reflect the diversity of the larger community? What values are being taught? Are issues of racism being addressed? Are other groups excluded, such as girls or gay youth?

There is nothing wrong with all-white groups if they aren't intentionally exclusive. But because such groups have often been breeding grounds for various forms of chauvinism and racism, we should monitor them carefully and push them to be as inclusive and multicultural as possible. Very often what appears to be a natural racial division is based on larger patterns of discrimination. For example, if all students in a school are white, the clubs in that school will also be all white. You may think it's only natural that there are no children of color in the area. But they may be absent because of discriminatory housing, job location, or zoning patterns. Such segregation is by no means natural. It is the result of institutional racism, and we need to scrutinize the often invisible factors that produce segregation.

When we notice and remark on the ways that people are separated and treated differently, it validates our children's own perceptions and lets them build a sharper awareness of how racism works. When my son was caught shoplifting a couple of years ago, the store manager called me and released him to my care without calling the police and having him arrested. Of course, my son was scared when he was caught and was relieved that he was not taken to jail. He was fined and banned from the store but did not get an arrest on his record. Afterwards, when we talked about this incident I asked him how Charles, an African American friend of his, might have been treated if he had been the one caught shoplifting. I didn't tell him he would have been treated differently. I asked him what difference he thought it might make. We had a thoughtful discussion of what might have happened if the store had called the police, how his friend might have been treated, what it would have meant if he had an arrest record. I brought this up not to make him feel guilty or lucky, but to give him practice in noticing that race makes a constant difference in how people are treated.

It is hard to know at what age we should begin talking about institutionalized racism and the history of racial injustice, because we don't want to overwhelm our children. I think that by age eight to ten, young people are capable of understanding patterns of discrimination such as slavery or the Holocaust or the genocide of Native Americans. They can begin to see the difference between individual white responses to people of color, and government or corporate policies.

I think it is crucial that we be honest with our children about racial inequality in the larger society. When we are answering their questions about poverty, homelessness, or AIDS, we can discuss the ways that racism makes people of color more vulnerable to these problems. We can point out how people of color are blamed for having these problems while the large number of white people in the same situation are not blamed as much or are not even discussed. For instance, there are more white people than African Americans on welfare in the United States, but the media often present images of welfare mothers who are black, not white.

Because people of color are disproportionately presented as problems in our society, with their positive contributions correspondingly minimized, our children need to understand these messages for what they are — part of the reinforcement of white dominance —

and need to realize that people of color's anger about racism is legitimate and arises from the discrimination and abuse they experience.

Another effect of these biased representations of people of color is to reinforce the unstated belief that white people are superior. In almost every interpersonal and institutional setting the assumption is that white is better because white people are in charge, white images are taken for granted, white history is taught in our schools, and white people receive more respect. This instills in white boys a sense that they are entitled to respect, power, and inclusion, and justifies disrespect for, violence towards, and exclusion of people of color. Our sons need to hear from us that white is not superior and that white people are not smarter, nor do they work harder than people of color. They will only understand this if they have a grasp of how racism works as a system, a set of interlocking institutions that denies equal opportunity to people of color in education, housing, and jobs.

When we talk about poverty, for example, we can discuss job discrimination and unequal funding for education. This will help our children understand the social roots of individual problems. Whether the issue is race, gender, economics, or disability, nothing is more important than to give our children insight into the systematic nature of power, violence, and blame at a level at which they can absorb it. We do this not to excuse abusive or destructive behavior, but to put it into a context and to help our sons move beyond blaming individuals for social problems.

On the other hand, if our child gets into a conflict with a boy of color, we don't need to go into an explanation of slavery or racism to help him sort out how to respond to an interpersonal conflict. Racism is part of understanding how situations develop, not an excuse to avoid holding either our son or the other youth responsible for what they do. When a conflict arises it is time to help young men sort out their feelings and decide how best to resolve the situation.

What if your son is white and you hear him making racially disparaging comments about people of color? Demonstrating racial solidarity with other young males is often one condition of being accepted as a man by others. For white boys this sometimes means signing on to white racism and proving that you have the "courage" to put down and abuse people of color. The most extreme examples are white hate groups, but many young white men affirm their manhood by participating in less dramatic examples of white racist solidarity.

If your son is making racially disparaging comments, ask him to talk about what he means, why he is making generalizations, where he heard this "information." Tell him how you feel about his remarks and discuss with him how his remarks might make it unsafe for or contribute to violence towards people of color. You may discover gaps in his understanding that you could remedy with books, videos, or further discussion.

Your son may contend that language is not important, that he has heard members of other cultural groups call themselves those words, or that his comments were not really serious. This may bring up more discussion about the importance of respect, the impact of words, the different ways one speaks about one's own cultural group as opposed to others, and the issue of safety and violence.

I want our young men to be active participants in the struggle to end racism, not just to use correct or polite language when referring to people of color. However, language (and the climate it creates) either promote respect or encourage objectification, stereotypes, and abuse. Derogatory comments, posters, or graffiti should not remain unchallenged by us.

Teaching tolerance is important but not enough. Teaching tolerance produces adults who say, "I treat everyone equally. Why can't they treat me that way?" or "I am colorblind so racism isn't a problem for me," or "There's no racism here because there are no people of color here," or "My family didn't own slaves." Of course, in a multicultural society, we need to raise sons who are not prejudiced and who treat everyone with respect. But racism affects everything we do, every day of our lives. Just as with gender, we can help our sons notice the difference that race makes and understand the institutional nature of racism.

Young white men will have many conflicting feelings as they become exposed to the realities of racism. Anger, sadness, fear (of retaliation), shame, guilt, outrage, powerlessness, hopelessness, defiance — these are all typical white responses to knowledge of racism. We need to honor those feelings and allow them to be expressed without trying to soothe them away.

Honoring their feelings is important because white males do get put into categories and do get stereotyped. They may hear people of color say, "All white men are responsible for or benefit from racism," or "All white people are racist." When this happens and our sons protest, it is useful to point out to them that this is the same boxed-in, fearful, and dehumanized feeling that people of color experience all the time because of racism. We can teach our sons to listen carefully to what people of color say and not to take it personally. Even if we try to treat everyone equally, it does not mean that everyone is treated equally. People of color are understandably mistrustful of white people who say they are against discrimination or mistreatment but do not recognize racism when it occurs and are not doing anything to stop it.

It empowers white boys when they see that they have a role to play in ending racism and all forms of social injustice. Historically there have always been white men who have been strong allies to people of color in the fight against racism. White men took stands against slavery, lynching, and other forms of racism. Many white men supported the civil rights movement, and some lost their lives doing so. White men continue to fight against hate crimes, police brutality, housing and job discrimination, biased news coverage, the unequal incarceration of youth of color, and other forms of racism. There are probably local people, possibly members of your extended family or community, who are also models of white men who have been allies to people of color in the fight for racial justice.

At the same time, we can help our white sons recognize that white people in general have been resistant to acknowledging and ending racism. We need to be honest about our own role and the roles of our foreparents. Many of us have relatives who did not support the civil rights movement or the struggles for racial justice by Latino/a and Native Americans. Adult white men, either actively or passively, are the biggest supporters of racism in this country. Some of us have family members who are today speaking out against or acting against equal opportunity, school and residential integration, immigrant rights, and affirmative action.

Young people need to see that they can choose to support racist policies or they can choose to become anti-racist activists. We can present all sides — the complex dimensions of white responses to racism — so that our sons will see that they have moral choices to make. When they understand how racism is institutionalized, they will know that they are not responsible for it, but they are responsible for how they respond to it. Will they stand for racial justice and equal opportunity? Will they stand with people of color?

Questions to ask our white sons

Why do you think our neighborhood, school, summer camp,
college prep class, or social group is all white?
Why are so many young men of color tracked into non-academic courses?
Why are there so few positive images of people of
color on TV and in the movies?
Why are African American men funneled into violent sports but not into less
dangerous ones, or into manual labor but not management?
Why is so much of the music you listen to produced by African Americans?
Who makes money off it? How does racism work in the music industry?
(Our sons will only be asking these questions if we are.)

IF YOU AND YOUR SON ARE AFRICAN AMERICAN, LATINO/A, NATIVE AMERICAN, ASIAN AMERICAN, OR ARAB AMERICAN

I am white, raising white sons. The best source of advice about raising young men of color is the mothers and fathers of color who have been doing it so well for so long. However, there are not many written resources for parents of young men of color, and the ones that do exist do not share the concerns raised in this book, so I offer the following suggestions with caution in the hope that they are useful to spark further discussion and strategizing.

It is a very dangerous world for young men of color, particularly if they are African American, Latino, or Native American. They are many times more likely to experience violence; to be discriminated against, harassed, or attacked by teachers, storekeepers, and police; or to be killed than white youths are. The survival of our sons is crucial and we need to be concerned about the bottom line: getting them into adulthood alive and healthy. It may be difficult for us as parents to overcome the overwhelming expectation that our sons are endangered. We may fear the violence that they are being set up to confront and become victims to. We may be scared for their lives. Their very survival can come to seem our best hope.

Most young men of color do survive. But what if they survive and:
• it's at the cost of other people of color?
• they beat up their partners?

- they make corporate decisions to destroy the environment?
- they help end affirmative action or support attacks on immigrants?

If we are only concerned about the survival of our sons, we can only help them develop strategies for survival — how to get by or, at best, to get ahead. If we believe that our sons are an endangered species[3], we lock ourselves into this kind of thinking.

African American, Latino, and Native American men have been described as endangered species, and this phrase certainly speaks to part of the problem. Black men, in particular, are too often seen as less than human, as another species, as objects to be studied. It may have been the intent of the person who coined the phrase to point out that we pay more attention to the status and lives of animals than to African Americans, but the repeated use of this phrase only reconfirms unstated beliefs that black men are indeed another species — if not endangered, than dangerous.

Are African American or Latino or Native American men endangered? Not in a biological sense, certainly. Though they experience higher mortality rates, shorter life spans, poorer health, fewer jobs, higher imprisonment, most will survive.

Are they under attack? Most assuredly. Our African American sons — boys and men — in particular are systematically targeted for violence, punishment, segregation, imprisonment, and discrimination in work, housing, and education. The negative misinformation and stereotypes about young black men have created a climate in which they have become the embodiment of danger in the imagination of mainstream America. This demonization is used to justify the outrageous levels of incarceration of African American boys and men.

The process begins quite early. Young boys of color are often seen as cute, energetic, or perhaps even creative preschoolers. But at some point between the ages of four and seven many are perceived as rambunctious, disruptive, and threatening by teachers (who are often white) and become feared and unwanted at school. The boys begin to receive messages that they are out of place in the educational environment. Not all teachers alter their perceptions and expectations of young boys of color as these children proceed through elementary school, but many do. Many teachers and administrators expect boys of color to be disruptive and start disciplining them more than their behavior requires, often more punitively than they discipline white boys engaged in similar activities.

Not all boys of color get pushed out of school, but few are encouraged or expected to succeed. African American, Latino, and Native American boys are at highest risk for negative treatment, as are boys from families that have recently immigrated. Boys of color from middle-class backgrounds and those from more established Asian American communities feel these effects less strongly. Even if they are successful at school — by the standards that white boys are judged by — they are more likely to have their intelligence doubted or discounted. For many of these boys, unfair discipline and adult expectations of failure increase dramatically throughout the elementary school years. By junior high school, many are seriously discouraged in school and more and more marginalized in school culture.

This reality has a profound effect on the hearts and minds of young men of color. There are a wide variety of responses. They can succumb, resist, rebel, overcome, manipu-

late, or reject these expectations, but they cannot ignore them.

Because of the huge pressure within our society to abandon young men of color or to lock them up and throw away the key, our sons of color can feel that survival at all costs is their only choice. We can apply a contrary pressure to pull them back into the community and get them involved in activities that help them feel their power to take leadership and to make change. We are also in a position where we must value the choices they make while at times challenging those choices.

Young men of color face many difficult situations with few completely positive choices. It may not be easy for us to accept the choices they make and stay present with them to help them figure out what's best for them. Some of our young men decide to join gangs for personal safety or to be part of a group. Others may use alcohol or other drugs to cover their pain or to socialize with the guys. Rather than condemning those choices, we can try to understand why our sons made them and what options they thought they had. Whether as parents or as community members we must be careful not to rush to judgment. It is only by listening to young men of color that we can understand what those choices mean to them. Then, by asking the right questions, we can help them think about what they want to do, what they think they can accomplish, what are the costs of their choices, and what other options they might have available to them.

Many of their decisions are based on fear and anger. Fear for their lives, fear for their future, fear for their families, fear for their friends. Anger about racism, anger about poverty, anger about injustice, anger about lack of opportunity, anger about being systematically discounted as young people.

As caring adults we can acknowledge their fear because it is real. This may be difficult. Adults of all racial backgrounds have trouble seeing the fear that many young men of color experience because we ourselves have been taught to fear them. Since we are afraid of them, we can't see that they are afraid as well. We might fear that their anger will be directed at us. We might fear it will set them up for violent confrontations with peers, or with the police and other authorities. We might fear it will lead to them being murdered because they are too outspoken or visible, as some civil rights leaders have been.

We need to honor their anger because it is righteous. They need to hear from us that their anger is appropriate to the magnitude of the injustice in this society and that anger tempered with reason and community solidarity is a natural and powerful guide to action. Without anger there would have been no civil rights movement, Chicano liberation movement, American Indian Movement, or the thousands of everyday acts of resistance to racism by people of color.

Because our society offers young men of color so few ways to participate meaningfully in the community, they are constantly provoked to turn their anger into violent and destructive acts. These acts are the only ones that receive adult attention, produce a response from the system, and show up on the radar of the community. We can be allies to our sons of color by helping them articulate their fears, by supporting them, and by validating their feeling that they are in danger. Then they can develop realistic strategies for dealing with it.

We can teach our sons to express their anger in effective ways. They should try not only to relieve it but to guide it into activity that makes a difference. We can also remind them of men from their cultural backgrounds who used their anger to fight for change, to better the community. We can teach them to draw, write, compose, act, dance their anger.

If we have provided them with some understanding of how the entire system of power and violence works in our society, many will come to see how their personal decisions and strategies either support the status quo or help make change possible. They need a detailed knowledge of racism to help them survive. This knowledge needn't become an excuse for destructiveness, blaming, self-blame, hopelessness, passivity, or irresponsibility. When these responses do come up, we can challenge young men of color to take responsibility for their own lives, with our support.

We face some particular challenges when raising sons of color because the media and our textbooks distort our cultures in specific ways. On the one hand, there is a preponderance of images of African American and Latino youth and men as criminals. On the other, there is a severe lack of images of them as intellectuals, political leaders, scientists, and artists. Our sons need to know that this distortion sets them up to be feared and scapegoated for social problems. These messages also perpetuate violence against their communities.

Native American, Arab American, and Asian American youth are so rarely portrayed in the media that it creates a problem of invisibility. There are few ways for boys from these cultures to see themselves in positive adult roles.

Asian American boys also face slightly different challenges because the stereotypes, pressures, and expectations they encounter may seem more positive. They are expected to behave, to be cooperative, and to perform well in math and science. Their cultural background, their life experience, and their unique personalities are no less devalued than other boys of color by these "positive" stereotypes. Nor is there any less pressure on them to be tough, together, and in control. As their parents, we can help Asian American boys see the variety of responses men of their community have had to these pressures. They also need to know that being accepted at times as an honorary white person will not necessarily exempt them from having to deal with prejudice, stereotypes, abuse, hate crimes, and institutional discrimination. They have an important stake, and an important role, in the struggle against racism regardless of their personal ability to succeed.

Adults often assume that Asian American boys are not and should not be in the "Act Like a Man" Box. Yet the message Asian American boys receive from the media is that being tough and aggressive is the only way to succeed. If they are from families that have recently immigrated to this country, they may lack the personal skills or material resources that boys from more established Asian American communities have access to and will have even fewer options to succeed by mainstream male standards, as problematic as those are. The challenge of proving how tough they are in the face of adult skepticism may encourage them to be competitive and aggressive towards other boys, abusive towards young women, or self-destructive. Without an understanding of how American male socialization works, and without help to understand the unique pressures that they face as Asian Americans, they cannot develop strategies that help them get ahead *and* get together.

The few leaders from communities of color who are portrayed as successful are made into exceptional heroes, ideals beyond our reach. As part of this phenomenon, men of color are shown as lone heroes, divorced from community and unconnected to the women who were often the backbone of political struggle. We can present young men with a range of counterimages of men and women who have achieved in a wide variety of fields of human endeavor. However, this approach has its limits because it focuses on individual achievement and does not refer to the background of political organizing and community pressures that opened up doors for those heroes. Individual achievement stories can seriously distort history and our understanding of how change happens. They can leave young people feeling discouraged and guilty that they are not able to achieve at the same levels as the people they're told about.

For example, Martin Luther King, Jr. is held up as a great leader, which he certainly was. But he was also part of a widespread struggle for racial justice involving tens of thousands of poor and working-class people, young and old, who came together during the civil rights movement. He was surrounded by powerful women leaders such as Septima Clark, Rosa Parks, Ella Baker, and Fannie Lou Hamer, who barely get mentioned on the same page. Just as important, the civil rights movement was preceded by thirty years of struggle for access to jobs, housing, the military, and decent education by people whose names we may never know.

We need to be mindful of the way that political organizing is taken out of our histories as well. Rosa Parks is commonly described as a simple woman who got on the bus one day, was tired, and refused to move to the back of the bus. In reality, she was part of a well-organized community that had been fighting against the bus company for many years.[4] They had attempted other strikes and boycotts, each one stronger and more nearly successful than the one before. The bus boycott initiated by Rosa Parks' action was not spontaneous but was carefully planned and executed by an organized community.[5] We diminish the participants' thoughtfulness, intelligence, persistence, commitment, and passion for justice if we focus solely on Rosa Parks or claim that it was a spontaneous event without forethought and planning. This kind of distortion makes getting-ahead strategies seem more successful at producing change than getting-together strategies.

Rosa Parks, Martin Luther King, Jr., Cesar Chavez, and Nelson Mandela were all successful because they got together with other members of their communities. Some young men will become great leaders, but *all* have roles as participants in the social struggles of our time. When they identify with ordinary people working for safety, dignity, and equality, they are much less vulnerable to self-destructive behavior and interpersonal violence, because they can see how those actions undercut their community and its efforts to achieve equality and justice.

Without role models and accurate historical information, our sons of color will not understand why they should join current struggles for social justice. Instead, we will more likely find them making racially disparaging comments about other people of their own racial group and sabotaging their own efforts to get ahead. One of the most devastating impacts of racism on young men of color is the internalization of racism. This leads to self-destructive violence such as suicide, drug use, and high-risk activity. It leads to competition with other young men and violence towards young men and women of color. To counter this pattern, you can help your son identify the strengths of his cultural tradition and the insights of its leaders. Use books, videos, and other resources. Draw on family members, friends, and members of religious and other community organizations for examples of how men in your community have participated in community struggles for justice. Let him develop pride in his cultural and racial identity, and help him understand the powerful forces of white supremacy so he does not blame himself or others in his racial group for perceived failure.

You can point out to him the parallels between how white society treats people of color and how he treats other people of color. If he feels himself part of a larger struggle to combat racism, he will see other youth of color as allies in that struggle rather than as competitors for scarce resources. It may be hard for him to stay focused on this when other young men of color, possibly from his own culture, are the ones confronting him. You cannot protect your son from these attacks. You can prepare him to make the best choices he can. He needs tools for self-defense so he feels good about his body. He needs conflict resolution and communication skills so he can solve problems effectively. He needs to know he has your support for the choices he makes. He won't always be able to avoid a fight, but you can encourage him to do so whenever possible. You can encourage him to run away, to get help, to help others in trouble, to cry, and not to have all the answers — in other words, you can encourage him to be fully human. Don't let your own fear, powerlessness, gender training, or personal pain get in the way of your being there for him.

We can always keep the needs of the community in mind. If we support young men of color and they become successful but forget their connections to their family, friends, or neighborhoods, what does it do to them and what is it worth to us? We can define success not at the expense of, but as the support of, the community. We can talk about capitalism and the way it can absorb members of minority groups, making them tokens of change who are then used to justify attacks against the rest of us for not making it. We can talk about tokenism and co-optation and what it means to sell out one's values and one's community. We can ask our sons, "What do you stand for? Who do you stand with?"

IF YOU ARE A PARENT OF A SON OF MIXED HERITAGE

There are increasing numbers of children of mixed heritage in the United States, although their existence is only slowly being recognized by mainstream society. There are few books, studies, or accounts of growing up of mixed heritage, and even fewer organizational resources for parents. We know little about the growth and development of these children and almost nothing about the gender issues they face.

I do know, from those who I have talked with, that boys of mixed heritage encounter many of the same pressures other boys do to stay in the "Act Like a Man" Box. However, they face confusing contradictions about how to respond because they are responding to more than one set of expectations from peers, teachers, and others.

Boys of mixed heritage who are secure in their identity can become valued participants in our struggles to end racism and create a multicultural society, but first we must value them as whole and complex and not pressure them to choose a particular heritage to identify with. They have access to two or more cultures and potentially have deep insight into how our entire cultural-racial system works. We will learn much from their experience if we can help them process it thoughtfully.

You can begin by helping your son celebrate all of his cultural heritage, not just the part that is yours or that you are most comfortable with. Help him sort out his feelings about the confusing expectations he receives from others by asking him lots of questions about what he feels and experiences. Talk with other parents of mixed heritage boys and look for resources. Remember that he is Vietnamese and African American, not half of each; he is Puerto Rican and Jewish, not one or the other; he is white and Latino and Native American and brings all of himself into every experience and every encounter.

IF YOU ARE A WHITE PARENT OF A SON OF COLOR

If you are a white parent, stepparent, or foster parent of a son of color, you have a particularly challenging job because you cannot use your own experience to guide you. In fact, your own experience may get in your way. Things that worked for you as a white child may not work for a child of color. It might be hard to acknowledge that your experience will not always serve you well in guiding a son of color into adulthood. Your greatest resources at those times are your son and other parents who are of the same racial/ethnic group as your son (or, if your son is of mixed heritage, people who are of similar combinations as your son). They will have had to deal with white people's attitudes towards them and with the complex cultural codes of their own cultural group.

Your son knows much more than you do about what he is experiencing and what it means to be him. Especially if he lives in a predominantly white environment, he will be the best judge about how he is treated and whether it is racist or not. You can encourage him to tell you what he experiences at school, in the neighborhood, and at friends' houses. You may need to learn to hold back your tendency to defend other white people, to minimize the prevalence of racism, or to underestimate its effects (see the next section). Even if you care, and sometimes *because* you care, your son may not tell you everything that happens to him because he wants to protect you from being hurt. At times he may be confused about whether what he experiences really is racism and whether it is important enough to talk about. Always be sensitive to the presence of racism. You don't have to assume it is present, but you can ask him if he thinks he is being responded to differently than others because of his skin color. Your son will pay fewer costs later and your family will remain stronger if you acknowledge the realities of racism and the effects it has on your son.

Your son needs to have a deep understanding of his own cultural heritage. Become knowledgeable about his heritage so that you can help him learn about it. You may fear that valuing and celebrating your son's cultural history and traditions will take away from your ability to create a united, loving family or to celebrate your own traditions. On the contrary, our families can support much diversity, and all family members will benefit from a richer, more inclusive family heritage.

Your son may go through several phases of responding to being different, especially if he is in a predominantly white community. He may try to pass at times. He may try to assert his individuality and uniqueness without attaching significance to his racial difference. He may strongly identify with his racial/cultural heritage in defiance of his white peers, sometimes in defiance of you. He faces a daunting task as he is trying to deal with his own identity without a lot of structural support. He needs encouragement to talk about what he is going through and he needs loving support and acknowledgment of the difficulties he has to contend with. You can expect that he will eventually find his own way, especially if he has strong familial love and support.

IF YOUR SON COMPLAINS ABOUT AN
INCIDENT OF RACISM

Intentionally or unintentionally, subtly or obviously, boys of color will inevitably experience racism in this society. If you live in a predominantly white community there is great likelihood that it will be ignored or minimized. Your son needs you to be his ally — to listen to him, validate his experiences, and advocate for him within his school, youth group, religious congregation, or neighborhood.

You can begin by having him describe what happened, assuming that racism is probably occurring. He has most likely developed good antennae for picking up racist attitudes and policies.

If the incident happened at school, your son may be responding to overt acts of discrimination, or he may be picking up on teachers' and counselors' unstated assumptions about what he can accomplish. You will not be supporting him if you tell him "The teacher probably didn't mean it like that," or "It's always like that," or "Maybe you were mistaken," or "It shouldn't matter," or "You shouldn't take it so seriously." Whether it was intentional or not, racism probably occurred and it does matter.

Once you've validated your son's perceptions (or gently challenged him if you are absolutely convinced that something else was going on), you can ask him what he wants to do about it. How is he going to respond? What choices does he have? What support might he want from you or others?

Similarly, if he has been followed around in a store, you can acknowledge that this happens a lot to young men of color. Help him decide what his best response is, both personally and politically. How can he respond when he notices it happening? How have other people dealt with that situation? Is it worth confrontation, picketing, a boycott, a letter to the local newspaper, a community meeting, or another form of protest?

Our sons may be harassed by men and women of color — a police officer, a store worker, a teacher — who has some authority within the system to carry out a racist agenda. Sometimes they have to do so to maintain their jobs, position, or authority. Other times they have simply internalized mainstream values. In either case, painful as they are, these occurrences are also opportunities to discuss how this happens, how prejudice and internalized racism can be passed on within the community.

Often our sons of color are already marginalized and discounted both because they are young and because they are not white. Therefore, advocating for them in the community is particularly important. They need us to notice when they are being treated unequally and to be outspoken on their behalf. Your efforts may make you disliked or unwelcome by teachers, counselors, school board members, police, or other groups you need to confront. Unfortunately, your efforts to obtain fair treatment will give you great insight into how racism operates in your community as you meet denial, minimization, and other forms of resistance. While your actions may strengthen the bonds within your family, you will need support from others, possibly from parents of color who are fighting the same battles on behalf of their children.

Reach out for support. Talk with other parents. Read whatever you can. Listen to your son. Keep on struggling on his behalf because you are potentially struggling on behalf of all our sons of color when you, with the credibility of a white person, speak to other white people about the realities of racism that your son faces.

In this new century, racism will certainly continue to be a dominant issue for us and for our children. Our sons benefit from having us as anti-racist activists so that they have the opportunity to join us in the struggle to end racism. Whenever we are thinking about how to raise our sons as allies, we can take into account their racial/cultural heritage, as well as our own, so that our childraising strategies are caring and effective.

PART 2

Everyday
Challenges

6 Getting Started

We now come to the more practical part: how to apply the ideas outlined in Part 1 to our everyday interactions with boys. Talking about power and violence, male roles, sexism, racism, and economics doesn't prepare us for the everyday challenges of parenting. How do we teach our sons to care for themselves, their community, and the natural world, develop their leadership abilities, and think about the moral implications of their actions. More practically, what do we do when they want to play with guns, bring home pornography, go out for little league, get into a fight, or lose themselves in computer games?

Our sons need us to be their allies every day, each step of the way, working these issues out together. Whether it is youth culture or family culture, toy guns or real guns, discipline or self-discipline, the challenge is still how to teach them to stand for compassion and justice and to stand with those who are organizing for change.

APPRECIATING BOYS

Before the daunting circumstances and responsibility of parenting discourage us, we can reaffirm that boys are wonderful. If we cannot find joy in their company and teach them to enjoy their lives we will have offered ourselves and them little beyond fear and worry. The

© Kathy Sloane

best motivation for raising sons is our love and caring, our joy, and our vision of the tremendous potential each human being brings into the world. The resiliency, creativity, caring, and courage we see in boys remind us how much boys add to the world and how much leadership they can provide.

Before reading further, think about a boy in your life.

Questions to ask yourself

What do you love about him?
What is special or unique about him?
What positive qualities does he bring out in you?
How does he challenge you to grow?
How will you take the time to appreciate his presence in your life?

Because there are a lot of suggestions in this book, it can seem like every minute should be thought out and taken advantage of. We can easily become too serious in our attempt to support our sons. Most of what I suggest should not add extra time to your day or extra expense to your budget. I am talking not about more, but about better: better communication, deeper connection, increased respect, more effective problem solving, greater growth and responsibility.

BECOMING AN ALLY TO OUR SONS

The rest of the book deals with specific issues, from personal growth and relationships in the family, at school, with other boys, and with girls and women, to the political involvement that is at the core of raising boys to become allies. But first I want to mention some key concepts for being allies to boys.

The core of being an ally to your son is being a loving and challenging presence in his life — someone who will listen and will give support when required. Our courage and caring become a model for him as we invite him to join those of us working to develop our community.

Stop

Stop the other things you are doing or thinking and pay full, loving attention to your son. One of the simplest and most profound gifts we each have to give is our loving presence. Many boys suffer from its absence. Although we may spend a good deal of time with our sons and even more time taking care of their needs, there may be very little time that we are simply and fully present with them. I find that I'm often thinking of other things, planning other events, preparing for the next activity, paying half-hearted attention to my children. I have to remind myself that my time with my sons is incredibly valuable, even if I am not doing anything, accomplishing anything, or going anywhere.

Look

See the beauty, intelligence, and grace of your son. Some of us gaze with wonder at our boys when they are young, but become too busy or distracted to do so later. Some of us never had the time or energy to see our sons for the wondrous gifts to the world that they are. Many of us have high-stress jobs with too much to do. Take a moment, stop what you are doing, and look at the boys around you. It only takes a few minutes to stop and really look at our sons and see them for the beautiful and unique people they are.

Listen

When we have stopped and looked at our sons, we are then able to listen to what they are saying and to discover who they are. We may need to be prepared to listen at unexpected times and at odd moments. Sometimes we can arrange a time and quiet place to talk. Other times we need to be ready to drop what we are doing and listen even if we are tired or cooking dinner or finishing up some work. Boys, like the rest of us, don't know when they will need us to be there for them. When they are ready to talk we can either listen at the moment or try to arrange a not-too-distant time when we can give them our full attention.

We can also be listening at other times. We can take in what our sons are communicating not only through their words but also through what they do, how they act, what they draw and write, what music they play or listen to, and how they relate to their friends.

Ask (thought-provoking) Questions

Our sons will become critical thinkers by using their minds and developing their capacity to ask the right questions. Every time we ask them a question that begins "Why do you think...?" or "What do you think about...?" or "How do you feel about...?" we sharpen their ability to reflect thoughtfully on the world around them. We are asking them to use their imagination — to question the way things are, opening up the possibility that they can be different.

I was asked many questions as a child, but they were factual questions: At what temperature does water freeze? Why? What is the capital of Alabama? Name the oceans of the world. How many miles from the sun to the earth? There is nothing wrong with these questions. They are actually a way that some parents prepare their children for the many tests they will have to take in their lives. But an unrelenting diet of factual questions leads us to ask what, not why, and to focus on the facts, not the feelings. These questions encourage us to memorize and regurgitate information, not to deepen our ability to think reflectively.

Open Doors

- Provide alternative information and other views.

  In a society in which the media is controlled by large corporations and our textbooks are provided by the same sources, we are not able to think critically unless we have alternative information that allows us to see the lies, gaps, and misinformation we are being presented with. Finding magazines, books, music,

art, photos, cartoons, comic books, and graffiti with different perspectives can open up doors for our sons.

• Provide alternative experiences.

Our sons need different kinds of experiences to expand their thinking. They need exposure to a variety of environments, people, jobs, and activities so their own vision of what is possible can grow.

• Provide connections to other resources.

Through our network of friends, through our work, and through our religious and community organizations and activities we have access to jobs, educational opportunities, recreational activities, travel, internships, opportunities for community service, and political involvement that most young people are denied. We need to connect them to these resources.

Advocate for Young People

• Work for full inclusion and participation of youth.

Adults continue to make almost all public policy, funding, and programming decisions affecting young people, giving youth no voice in the decision-making process. Wherever we go we can be advocates for young people's full, not just token, participation on committees, boards, staffs, government agencies, and school boards.

• Advocate when youth are not present.

We are often in a position to advocate for young people when public policy, youth programming, funding, and educational policy decisions are being made with no youth present. We need to speak on their behalf while pushing for youth representation. We may also be in situations with other adults where young people are being talked about disparagingly. It is important that we not collude with other adults in being disrespectful towards young people just because they are not there to defend themselves. It is always appropriate for us to gently challenge generalizations made by other adults about teenagers and younger boys and girls. We can similarly challenge unfair or unrepresentative portrayals of youth on TV, in the movies, in ads, or in newspapers by writing letters, making phone calls, and organizing with others to change the way young people are portrayed.

Get Involved with Public Policy Issues

Most public policy affects young people, although their voices are not represented in public discussion. Welfare reform, education funding, drug policies, funding for needle exchanges, accessible health care, rent control, living wage laws, adequate childcare, and parental leave are all issues that affect youth. We need to use our political leverage as adults to put the interests of young people in front of the public so that public policy is not created at their expense.

Get Support

I think it is difficult to be good allies to our sons if we do not have support. We will simply become burned out and ineffective. We need to get together with other adults and share our feelings, thoughts, ideas, hopes, and disappointments. Building an adult network of support for ourselves is a crucial step in maintaining our own physical and mental health so that we can remain effective allies to our sons.

These are general guidelines for paying attention to our sons and their needs. I also want them to be able to pay attention to themselves and attend to their own needs. Helping them connect to nature and to their inner selves sets the stage for their being able to care for themselves physically and emotionally. All of these aspects of care will prepare them to take care of others and to take care of the natural environment.

7 Finding a Place in the Natural World

If our sons find a strong, secure place in the world, they can reach out to others and help build community. Their place is really a series of places reflecting our sons' connection to the natural world, to their family culture, to their spiritual practice, and to youth culture. Each of these "places" can provide part of the foundation for the compassion and commitment to others that we want our sons to develop.

THE NATURAL WORLD

Young people are fascinated by nature. Whether it's an insect or a bird, a pretty flower or an interesting leaf that catches their eye, they will stop and look and ask questions about the environment in which they live. My own children have always brought home bugs and worms and seeds and put them in jars to see how they'll grow or change. If we stop to look and value the natural world around us, they will too. If we notice the phase of the moon, the color of the twilight sky, the patterns of the clouds, they will too.

In your busy life you

© Kathy Sloane

may not always feel able to stop and notice the world around you, but it only takes moments to appreciate a flower, an animal, or another natural part of our environment, and you and your children gain tremendously when you do.

Connecting to the natural environment is particularly important for boys because they are often encouraged to deny or downplay any empathetic response they may have. Their games are more likely to destroy objects rather than appreciate them, kill rather than heal, manipulate rather than nurture. Children's natural curiosity about how things work can be encouraged alongside a respect for the role of those beings in the total scheme of things.

It is a delicate balance and you need to find your own comfort zone in guiding boys to respect and learn from nature. It is possible to teach boys to hunt, if that is part of your cultural heritage or is important to you, and still respect the lives of animals. It is possible to teach boys to cut down trees and plants and still have reverence for the life of plants.

What is important is the ability to see the connections and the interdependency between people and all other life. In urban environments it is more difficult to see those connections because our food comes from a store, our water comes from a tap, and there may be few plants and animals visible (although you may be surprised to find how many animals and plants live in the city). Through discussion; through books, TV shows, and videos; and through noticing with your son what is going on around you, you can help him make these connections.

Boys can also learn to care about the natural environment by growing plants or caring for a pet themselves. It takes little work to stick an avocado seed into a jar with some water or to have a caterpillar or mealy worm in a container and watch a wondrous transformation. Taking care of plants or animals and watching their life cycles is a revelatory experience that gives boys practice in nurturing. Caring for animals and plants brings up feelings of love, joy, fear, inadequacy, curiosity, pride, and sadness as the things a boy cares for live and die, thrive or fail despite his hopes and efforts. Talking about these feelings is good practice for a boy who will one day need to talk about the same kinds of feelings when they are produced by the relationships he has with other humans.

Acknowledging and celebrating the natural cycle of the year is also something that takes little time but is tremendously rewarding. If you point out the solstices and equinoxes as they come around each year, your son will start to see and understand the cyclical and connected aspects of all life. Talking about the changes that are visible in the neighborhood as each season progresses helps boys sharpen their attention to the cycles of life. Observing the cycle of the moon shows them one more cyclical pattern in our lives.

These connections are more visible and accessible in rural settings, but even here they must be noticed and valued or boys end up feeling disconnected from the natural environment. This can lead to their becoming manipulators of nature and destructive of the life around them.

Most young people readily feel connected to the environment and are motivated to work on its behalf. Such activity can be one of the easiest ways to involve young people in social action. Many of us live in neighborhoods where the community is challenging toxic waste dumping and other forms of pollution. Some of us live in areas where logging, mining, or drilling endanger the environment. Even if we live in neighborhoods facing no immediate environmental threats, there are still national or global conservation efforts to join. My own children supported "Save the Whales" campaigns and were "Friends of the Sea Otter" long before they were involved in other social action.

You can let your son know about what is going on in your community and what activities people are engaged in to protect the environment. These could be environmental protests, recycling programs, nature centers, and other resources. Encourage your son to figure out what steps he can take to do his part. In their enthusiasm, younger children may sometimes be ready to make more drastic personal efforts than their parents are. My own children want our family to change its lifestyle — to consume less, recycle more, use different packaging, and become vegetarian — at a faster pace than I am sometimes ready for. I find my children's passionate concerns a valuable challenge to my own thinking and my resistance to change.

Environmental issues are also people issues because people make economic and political decisions about the environment. An interest in environmental issues can easily provide a lead-in to discussions of advertising, consumerism, working conditions, and the exploitation of workers and nature involved in the manufacture of products you have or your children want. When you have established a foundation of concern for life around us, you can more easily begin discussing the destruction of rain forests to raise meat for Americans; the use of child slave labor to manufacture products for our homes; the exploitation of women in other countries to make shoes, shirts, balls, and other clothing and paraphernalia for our wardrobes.

Although it's important to be aware of threats to the environment and to be willing to challenge them, I think it is equally important to emphasize the beauty, wonder, interdependency, and healing qualities of the natural world. Awareness of these aspects is what will lead our sons to become environmental activists, but a connection to these qualities of the world have a much more basic value for them. If they are able to connect to these qualities in nature, they will have a tremendous resource available to them for remaining centered — aware of who they are and how they are connected to the rest of the world. When they find themselves pushed to lead lives of alienation and isolation, pressured to live quickly and respond intensely, they need to be able to sit and watch, sit and listen, sit and smell the natural world. When in despair, they need to be able to see the hope in new life. When in pain they need to be able to feel the healing effects of water and air. When we sit with them, we become better allies to them and they become better allies to the world we all live in.

CELEBRATING FAMILY CULTURE

Our sons are sustained by having a connection to nature. They are also nourished by their connection to their family culture. Family is often where we turn when we need support, a connection to our past and to our cultural, religious, ethnic, racial, and geographic traditions. In addition, when we are out in the world trying to get ahead or struggling to get by, our connection to our family culture reminds us that we need to get together. If you want to provide a counterforce to the pressure to be mobile, anonymous, and self-centred, you can provide your son with a solid understanding of and experience in the cultures that he comes from.

Holidays, life-change celebrations, food, music, stories — young boys are often fascinated by traditions that you, as an adult, may take for granted or have lost interest in. You can't practice what you don't believe in or create rituals for the sole purpose of involving your children. But you can offer the traditions you do observe to your son as gifts that he can take with him in whatever paths he chooses in his life.

Even if you don't still follow ancestral traditions, you can give your son a sense of his cultural roots. Boys are usually curious about where their foreparents came from, what languages they spoke, what jobs they did, why and how they came to be here. If family members of an older generation are still alive, it is possible to give your son time to listen to their stories and teach him to respect these elders and develop pride in their, and his, traditions.

Your culture's history may be invisible in the media and textbooks available to your son or it may be presented in ways that stereotype and distort it. You may need to make an effort to dig out the history, correct the lies, and give your son a useful and accurate history of his people. As part of this effort I think you should be honest with your son about the violence in your culture's history, whether your forebears were members of groups that perpetrated it or that survived it.

A respect for other peoples' cultures is a vital component of discussions of your own. If your son is to find his place in his own traditions, he also needs to know how those traditions have a place in a larger national mosaic of cultures. I don't want my sons to be rooted so narrowly in their own traditions that they become chauvinistic and disrespectful of the traditions and achievements of others. Therefore they need to know the full stories of cultural and racial groups different than their own. What did it mean to be an indentured servant, a slave, a Jewish immigrant, an indigenous person, a Finnish immigrant? How did people get here and how did that influence who they were able to become? How did their ancestors survive? What did they accomplish? What did they leave undone? Starting at a young age with books and tapes and videos, you can introduce your son to the variety of cultural and religious traditions in the world. Teach him to understand that cultural systems are integral wholes, not just isolated, interesting customs and holidays. I think boys should understand how cultures interact both now and historically. Our countries were created out of the complex interactions of many different peoples and cultures. Each has left its mark, and contributed to the whole.

If your son learns history he will value the survival and resistance and celebrate the accomplishments of people who came before him. There is much strength, wisdom, and experience to draw on and your son will need these qualities as he goes through life. But not everything that is traditional is valuable. Your son should have permission to reject those parts of his own traditions that are oppressive or that limit the rights of members of the community. Every boy needs to know that he cannot use his tradition to justify women being kept subservient, children being abused, or homosexuals being attacked.

Traditions are constantly changing and it will be up to our sons and daughters to modify the traditions they inherit to meet their needs and the needs of a multicultural society. They can only do that if they know their own traditions and respect and value the cultures of other people.

Questions to ask yourself

What cultural, racial or religious traditions do you identify with?
What parts of those traditions have you found valuable in your life?
What parts have lacked meaning for you?
Which (if any) parts have been hurtful?
Which cultural traditions would you like to pass on to your son?
What would you like him to know about his foreparents?
How can you expose him to the multicultural history of his country?

SPIRITUALITY

Even if we are not part of a traditional religion, there is a spiritual side to our life. Spirituality covers a broad range of beliefs and practices, from traditional religions such as Islam, Buddhism, Judaism, and Christianity, to new or ancient practices such as paganism or wicca. We have many names for the greater reality we are each part of. Whether we call it God, spirit, Goddess, All That Is, Allah, Gaia, or Earth, most of us recognize something greater than ourselves that nourishes and sustains us. We feel connected to other people and to the natural world and, perhaps, to some power even greater than that.

We all need the ability to center ourselves — to let go of the stress and distractions of modern life and reconnect with our own feelings, thoughts, and inner strength. Ironically, this happens best for me when I can step away from the worries and dramas of my daily life and see them in perspective. When I have this perspective I am able to appreciate the beauty and complexity of the world. I am able to see what our role might be in contributing to my family, friends, and community. Appreciating the larger patterns and cycles of the world sustains me in dealing with the personal cycles of birth and death, health and illness, coming together and falling apart. For example, when I am going through a period of personal or family change or have experienced the death of a loved one, I find it healing to walk on the beach and experience the beauty of the ocean and shoreline and the diversity of creatures who live there. I will often sit on the beach and just watch the waves. I gain a perspective on my own feelings from experiencing the magnitude and timelessness of the natural world. I always return to my family and friends renewed from these walks. I gain a similar sense of renewal attending services at the Jewish congregation of which I am a member. Here I experience a connection to a community, a tradition, and to some greater principle in the world. Both at the beach and at services I feel more centered within myself, more connected to others, and more at peace with the world.

Many of us have a spiritual practice and may have already introduced our sons to the rituals, celebrations, and oral or written traditions we honor. But for many young people in our current secular environment, who do not have the benefit of such an introduction, a direct connection with nature can be an opening to a spiritual life. Both my sons took walks with Micki and me when they were children. As they grew older they walked by themselves when they were upset or wanted to think about something or just have some quiet time away from people. Now our older son will go up into the hills above Oakland to relax, to think about things, to meditate, and to appreciate the beauty of the Bay area.

Even if he doesn't develop a spiritual practice, it is an important step for your son to learn how to sit quietly in nature, centered and connected. It can help anchor him in his own inner wisdom and allow him to draw on the wisdom of the natural world around him. It can give him a way to center himself in the face of peer and family pressure.

Martial arts can also provide this kind of spiritual discipline, depending on how they are taught. Yoga, tai-chi, chi-gong, aikido, and various meditational practices can also serve this purpose.

If your son develops a centering practice, he will have a powerful resource for his daily struggles to resist the intense pressure to disconnect from the people around him, to show no feelings, and to become isolated. It will start him on the path to a rich spiritual life that will guide his approach to relationships and community service throughout his life.

CONTEMPORARY YOUTH CULTURE

Young men often become involved in a wider community through cultural participation — connecting with people who share their cultural heritage or with people who share their own youth culture. Visual arts, movement, poetry, fiction, dance, quilting, graffiti, and music are all manifestations of the creative human spirit. They inspire us, heal us, refresh us, connect us, and inform us. Our sons might be isolated and unexpressive in all other areas, but give them a pen, paintbrush, spray can, drum, or guitar and they become articulate. They become involved with and responsive to others. They are drawn outside of themselves into a concern for what's happening to their school or neighborhood.

My friend Jim is a music teacher who believes that every boy should be given a musical instrument and some lessons. I agree with him. Our sons need the ability to express themselves. They need a skill they feel competent in. Most will not become performers, but that's not the point. Studying music or other arts requires self-discipline. It encourages us to express our feelings. It connects us to others who are using the same medium. It makes us part of an historical tradition of people using art to enhance our lives. Some of the most effective youth programs in the country are performance groups, music programs, mural projects, and other grassroots cultural arts programs.

Grassroots culture has been a source of resistance to government and corporate control over culture. Music and art have fueled progressive change and have enabled people to come together and address their needs. Today's youth culture is intensely resistant to mainstream culture and to adult and corporate control over the lives of young people. We need to encourage this resistance because it portends a better future for all of us.

The result will not always be what you want or expect. You may feel uncomfortable with your sons' vitality, his message, or his behavior. His music may strike you as too loud or obnoxious. His graffiti may demand your attention and disrupt your ideas about where art should be. The messages may be racist or sexist or "too radical." You may have to look at some of your own reactions to see where it becomes hard for you to support youth culture and the cultural expression of your sons.

Questions to ask yourself

What did you do as a child to express yourself artistically?

What did these activities provide you?

What support did you receive for these activities from adults around you?

What did they fail to provide that you needed?

Does one of your sons have interests or talents you could support?

What will you do to follow through on this?

What elements of youth culture did you relate to best as an adolescent?

What were typical adult responses to youth music or other forms of youth culture when you were growing up?

How would you judge those responses today?

What are elements of today's youth culture that you enjoy?

Which parts of it have you been challenged by?

Which parts upset you?

What are concrete steps you could take to support youth culture?

As an adult ally, there are some healthy ways for you to respond to youth culture. The first is to really listen, to really see, to ask questions, and to learn what it's all about. The second is to enjoy the parts that you can relate to. Appreciate the vitality, the passion, the grace, the eloquence, and the beauty of it. Take it seriously. Young people have important words for us and they seldom get our attention without bold artistic expression.

Once you understand the complexity of youth culture you can engage in spirited dialogue with your son about parts that you are uncomfortable with. You can explore with him how much of his culture is influenced by consumerism and how much by historical traditions. How much flows out of political resistance to the status quo and how much has been co-opted. How much is genuine rebellion and how much is male posturing and anti-woman in spirit. You can only effectively engage in such dialogue if you are truly respectful and appreciative of youth culture in general.

The most active and powerful response you can give as an adult ally is to free up funding and other kinds of support for youth culture. Young people need your support to fund lessons and classes, equipment, studio and performance space, walls for murals, and publishers for stories, poems, and reports.

It would help all of our young people tremendously if adults gave up the notion that culture is for professional performers and the rest of us can only watch and listen. Everyone deserves opportunities to develop their talents to whatever level they can. It's also valuable to develop the ability to express thoughts and feelings through art and culture. A young man who is centered in himself, who feels he has a place in the world, and who is comfortable expressing himself will have relationships with other people that are characterized by respect, self-respect, and caring.

8 Looking After Ourselves

Physical and emotional self-care are prerequisites for intimacy and responsibility. Our sons can't care for others unless they can take care of themselves, and they can't express their feelings, or empathize with others, unless they are able to identify how they feel. Unfortunately, one of the requirements of the "Act Like a Man" Box is that men guard their feelings.

PHYSICAL CARE

When my ten-year-old son comes downstairs in shorts and T-shirt on a day when I am feeling cold, I sometimes send him back upstairs to put on something warmer. At other times, when I am thinking a little more clearly (or feeling a little less cold myself), I ask him to go outside and see if he's feeling warm enough. If we are going out somewhere and I'm really worried that he will be cold later, I'll bring along a sweatshirt for him to take care of my anxiety.

My two reactions teach him different lessons. Telling him it's cold or he's cold when in fact I am the person feeling cold teaches him that I am in authority and he should obey me regardless of how cold or warm he feels. Telling him to check his body and see how it feels teaches him to pay attention to what's going on with him.

It is important to encourage boys to take care of themselves — to notice when they're tired, uncentered, sore, or hurt; to rest when they are tired and eat when they are hungry (and stop when they are full). One way to do that is to ask them lots of questions so that they get used to noticing. Simple questions such as:

- Are you tired?
- Are you warm enough?
- Did you get enough sleep?
- Did you get enough to eat?
- is your finger still sore?
- Where did you get that bruise?
- Where does it hurt?
- Do you want to take a jacket?

My sons have come to me with questions about bumps, scrapes, cuts, rashes, swellings, bruises, warts, styes, soreness, pimples, skin coloring, fingernails, splinters, and, when they were older, wet dreams, sex, AIDS, and drugs. They are both curious and concerned about their bodies. My partner and I have tried to take their concerns seriously and encourage them to pay attention to their bodies. We have tried not to laugh, belittle, or otherwise discourage their questions. We have told them many times that it is okay to cry when they are hurt. They can't always do that in front of their friends, but at least they know that it's an option.

Boys start out talkative and aware of their bodies. They start to shut down if we tell them not to cry, to eat this, to wear that, not to bother us, and that it doesn't (or shouldn't) really hurt. When peer pressure adds to this by telling them to hang tough and not show pain, they close up. They become adult men who can't ask questions or ask for help, who are vulnerable to accidents, who become insensitive to others who are in discomfort or pain, and who are disdainful of those who express their feelings. These men don't recognize physical symptoms of illness in themselves, wait longer to get medical help than women do, don't take medication and follow other medical advice as they should, and, as a result of all this, die at an average younger age than women do (for example, at age 72 compared to 79 in the United States).[1]

I am not suggesting that we coddle them. Protecting them or treating them like fragile beings does not help them at all. This can be a hard line to draw, especially in two-parent families where one parent has been trained to take care of the children by anticipating their needs and the other has been trained to toughen up boys by ignoring their pain. If you are co-parenting, talk with your partner about how your responses differ when your son gets hurt. How do these responses reflect your own gender training? How do you each want to foster your son's ability to take care of himself *and* get help when he needs it? It is always appropriate to ask your son what he needs with questions such as "What would make you feel better?" or "What can I do to help?" or "Can I give you a hug?"

Strengthening our son's ability to take care of himself physically will not only contribute to a healthier life, it will also help him take care of others when they need help and make him more sensitive to those in pain.

HOUSEHOLD CHORES

There is more to our physical needs than just our health. We need to eat, wash, clean our surroundings, and take care of our possessions. Our sons cannot be allies to women if they expect women, including their mothers, to take care of their physical needs. It is not hard to teach them to cook, clean, wash, and sew, especially if you start when they are young and make it clear that one of your expectations is that every family member will do her or his part.

Learning to cook is both a science and an art and brings great satisfaction to children as well as adults. Vacuuming is maybe not as rewarding, but boys need to see it as another way that people contribute to their own and each other's well-being. It may not be a fun job, but boys should understand that it is not fair that only women and girls have to do it.

In our family, the children are responsible for washing and drying their own clothes at age ten. They start washing dishes soon after that, and by thirteen or fourteen are

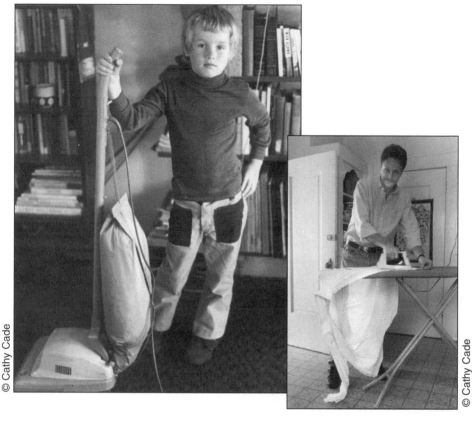

© Cathy Cade

© Cathy Cade

responsible for cooking the family dinner one night a week. They choose the menu and experience great satisfaction and pride in putting a meal on the table. Micki and I have enjoyed the time in the kitchen, teaching them how to measure, chop, bake, fry, and boil.

There is no magic age to begin these tasks. In many families that have little time, energy, or money to spare, children must, of necessity, take on major household tasks when young. However, even if someone is cleaning your house once a week or cooking some of the meals, there are still lots of opportunities for your son to participate in these tasks. He needs to learn the basic skills and, more important, needs to learn that there is dignity, satisfaction, and accomplishment in these tasks no matter who does them.

Girls have always been introduced to these skills early in life and have been taught that it is their responsibility to do them for the collective welfare. We can give boys the same opportunities, both for their own benefit and so that they don't come to expect that women in their family, or women who are paid, will do these tasks for them.

EMOTIONAL CARE

Our sons can also learn to take care of themselves emotionally. One of the most devastating aspects of the traditional male training is the pressure not to show any feelings (except possibly anger) — with the result that boys quickly lose the ability even to describe their feelings. Most are also taught to look to women to take care of their emotional needs. Since girls are trained to notice other people's feelings, they are usually the ones who address emotional issues. The combination of male and female socialization leaves most boys unable to take care of themselves emotionally, relying on women to do it for them.

We know that boys experience the full range of feelings, as girls do. Yet when they are asked to make a list of feelings, boys can often name only three or four rather than the dozens that most of us experience. The only feeling that boys are allowed to express openly — anger — then becomes the funnel for all the other feelings that boys don't think they can safely express.

Feelings Funnel

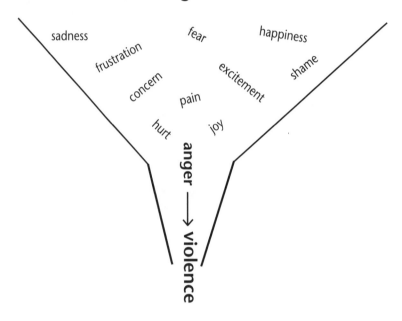

This dynamic gives their anger tremendous power and makes it both frightening and a relief.

- It is frightening because male anger often has led to male violence.
- It is a relief because at least he is expressing something.

Anger is not the problem. Our sons have much to be angry about. Many of them have been verbally, physically, or sexually abused. Others have witnessed acts of violence. Still others have lost family and friends to domestic violence, gang warfare, poverty, and despair. They see the injustice in our society; they feel the pressure to be in the "Act Like a Man" Box. Their anger is righteous and can keep us in touch with how life really is for so many in our society. The problem is not the anger but the misdirected focus of that anger when it turns into violence against family and friends.

Most boys learn early in life that anger goes with violence. They hear admonitions such as "Don't get angry, get even." They hear male excuses for violence such as "I just lost control," or "I was drunk." They hear woman-blaming remarks such as "She deserved it," or "She shouldn't have been in my face like that." These suggest that it's okay for men to be angry and violent — that this is how men take care of business.

At the same time, many young men are afraid of their own anger. They fear they will hurt someone else or themselves. Many feel like time bombs ready to explode. Punitive measures will only incur resentment and more anger.

As adults concerned about boys' anger we fear for them and fear for ourselves. We may get very upset when a boy is angry and it may trigger an angry response in us. Or we may teach him anger management and conflict resolution skills to keep him from getting into trouble or causing trouble.

But what if we assumed that the anger was okay? That it was a legitimate feeling indicating that something was wrong, unjust, painful, or hurtful? What if we assumed the anger was essential for making changes for the better? What if we thanked young men for being sensitive enough to wrongdoing and passionate enough about oppression to let us all know with their anger that we need to do something?

As our sons' allies, we can remind them that their anger is okay but that violence is not. There is no excuse for hurting another person except in unavoidable acts of self-defense. If we can stay with them in their anger, stay present when they explode, we can help them identify what's wrong and develop alternative ways to address the problem. Only when we are not trying to control or eliminate the anger can we appreciate its value and help them to direct it effectively. What our sons need from us is acknowledgment of the legitimacy of their anger and help in expressing and directing it towards effective action for solving the problem, whether this is an interpersonal misunderstanding or social injustice. It is only at this point that they will be able to use anger and communication skills rather than anger and violence.

One side benefit of encouraging artistic expression, as discussed in Chapter 7, is that when a young man has intense feelings, when he needs to process and express what he is experiencing, he can use his instrument, his pen, his movement to take that experience and transform it into something he can communicate to himself and to others. Pouring his heart into a poem or drawing may give his anger a vehicle, his sadness a home, his happiness a medium. Boys are taught that many areas of self-expression will undermine their manliness. Many are afraid of their feelings and isolated from the community. They may already be prone to acting out their feelings by hurting others. These are the ones in particular who need encouragement to pursue their artistic interests regardless of skill level or potential achievement.

There are many people we respect because they stood with others who were angry. The South Africans who rose up against apartheid to fight for independence were angry. The people who were against slavery and willing to fight a war to eliminate it were angry. African Americans were angry about segregation. Women were angry that they couldn't vote. Anger at injustice has motivated many of our greatest freedom fighters. What if we said to our sons, "Be as angry, as focused, and as powerful as Martin Luther King, Jr., as Cesar Chavez, as Sitting Bull, as John Brown, or Nelson Mandela"?

Conversations with our sons about these men would have to include more than just a discussion of their anger. We would have to talk about another emotion that was just as crucial to their success as their anger — one that is even harder for most boys to acknowledge or talk about — love.

All of these men loved people. They had great compassion for others. Their hearts were expansive. One of the most difficult feelings for boys to acknowledge and to express is their love. Just as we must honor their anger, we must encourage the expression of their love.

Children are born in love with the world. They naturally reach out and are concerned about other people, animals, natural objects. Their curiosity, openness, directness, and compassion flow naturally from their love. How sad, and how devastating for all of us, that we train boys to lose or hide their love. They don't want to seem too eager, too passionate, too open, too vulnerable so they hide their love, forget they once felt it. Our best gift to them is to show them our love without qualifications.

We live in a society that rewards people, recognizes their achievements, acknowledges their status. In our families we are probably much better at praising our sons and rewarding their achievements than we are at telling them we love them. Do you show your son that your love remains regardless of what he does? Do you give the false message that love is limited to your family, friends, race, and neighborhood?

We can teach our sons that love involves a daily concern and respect for the well-being of others, the expansive inclusion of their lives with ours. It does not stop when someone fails or makes a wrong decision. It remains even when we are angry with someone. It is not self-denying or self-sacrificing. It fills us up and overflows into the lives of those around us. It guides our action and tempers our anger. It stops our own abusive behavior and redirects our attention towards those who are exploiting others. Everyone touched by our love feels safer, acknowledged, validated, and special. When our sons bask in the glow of our love, they will learn how to become lovers themselves.

A world filled with people who are angry at injustice but overflowing with love for people, animals, and nature — what an amazing place that would be. But to get there we need to help our sons heal from the pain and grief of the losses they have experienced.

GRIEF AND LOSS

Sadness and grief are the feelings that often prevent our sons' being in touch with their anger, their love, and all the other feelings they have locked away. As boys grow up, many suffer verbal, physical, and sexual violence. Some lose friends and family to divorce, abandonment, mobile lives, alcohol and other drugs, imprisonment, drive-by shootings, family violence, homicide, and suicide. Our sons also experience less drastic losses that are still painful and need to be acknowledged. It's a loss when they don't make the team or the cast for a play or other project they try out for, when they don't get the class or teacher or grade they were counting on, when a friend moves away, or when a relationship breaks up.

Some of us come from traditions that have detailed prescriptions for mourning the deaths in our lives. These can help us. But it seems women more than men have permission to mourn losses, to cry, and to set aside time to absorb the shock of losing someone close. Our sons need help in grieving. Many of our sons need help allowing themselves to feel losses and to express their hurt and pain. If they don't get the chance to grieve and heal, their love will become blocked while their anger will be distorted and directed to the wrong channels.

Helping your son grieve can take many forms. You can hold him when he appears sad or when you know he has suffered a loss or defeat. You can ask him how he feels. You may want to share your own experiences of loss with him. If you are a man, you may need to learn to express some of your own grief, both to heal yourself and to provide a model for your son. If your son has experienced the death of someone close to him, you may just ask him to describe or talk about the person he is missing. For any kind of loss you can offer to help him create an appropriate ritual as a remembrance and as a vehicle for his feelings. You can affirm that the loss did occur, that it is okay to feel sad or hurt, that the feelings do matter.

As you encourage your son to express his feelings, you can also help him direct his anger at the source of his problems. If you are a woman, you can avoid beginning a pattern where you take care of your son emotionally, which wrongly teaches him that emotional caretaking is women's work. You can also try to avoid absorbing the feelings that he should direct elsewhere. None of us should have to accept any male's lack of expressiveness or his inappropriate anger.

Most young men want to talk, but they have so much unexpressed feeling inside that those feelings explode out of the funnel as anger. It is not healthy for you or your son if he is allowed to vent his anger on you just because you are there and won't abandon him. He can learn that it is not okay for him to dump his anger and other feelings on his family or on women. If he does do this, rather than shutting him down, you can encourage him to recenter himself, sit down, and tell you what he is feeling. He is capable of learning how to figure out what's really going on. You can keep asking him to talk to you — respectfully. You can help your son learn to recognize his feelings, talk about them, and not feel entitled to dump those feelings on people around him.

A boy whose father is absent or distant, physically or emotionally, may feel a significant amount of anger and sadness about his father. In some families, boys direct those feelings at the mother. Again, if you find yourself in such a situation, you can help him acknowledge the feelings without letting yourself be verbally abused.

If our sons are taking care of themselves emotionally, they are also being responsible for their feelings and how they act them out. When a young man is able to take care of himself emotionally he is not pressuring women to do it, he is not blaming women for his problems, and he is not harassing women (or other males) as a way to bond with men. When he is confronted because his behavior is inappropriate or hurtful, he will be able to listen and take responsibility for his actions. The following questions can guide you in helping your son take care of himself emotionally.

Questions to ask our sons

What are you feeling?

What are other ways you could describe your feelings?

Why are you angry?

How did you realize you were angry?

What is the source of the problem?

What other feelings besides anger do you have?

How can you express your anger constructively?

How can you address the problem you are having?

You should find your own language for these questions rather than using the stilted style above. "What's up?" or "What's going on inside you?" can direct a conversation back to what a boy is feeling. If he has come to you with a conflict or problem, he will probably be focused on what happened, on what somebody else did to him. Eventually he'll have to revisit the situation and decide what he is going to do about it. But he needs to start with his feelings first so he can use his feelings to guide his actions. In the situation described in Chapter 3, when my son confronted a bully in his school, I had to help him acknowledge that he was scared. Once he could do that he could think about what he wanted to do without his fear leading him to do something reckless. In a local high school I recently talked with some students who had experienced the death of a friend. They were very angry over lax security at the school, which had contributed to his death. I was able to help them talk about their grief over their loss. Then, speaking from a place of sadness and anger, they were able to think more clearly about what they wanted to do to improve security and prevent further violence.

You do your son a great service if you gently but persistently challenge him to figure out how he is feeling and to learn how to express himself. This ability will not develop in him overnight. At first you might be met with a lot of "I dunno." Boys do have feelings, and when they are feeling safe enough, they will express them. Even though boys and young men are not aware of their feelings, they are often driven by them. Their anger, pain, sadness, excitement, curiosity, confusion, or frustration get acted out in ways that get them in trouble. Reclaiming an awareness of their feelings puts them in charge so they can use their feelings to guide their behavior into acts of courage, caring, and community

Nurturing Others

Helping our sons learn to express their feelings and guide their anger into constructive action is important, but we must expect our sons to do more than just take care of their own emotional needs. Simply expressing their feelings can leave men as self-centered as they were in the first place. We can provide boys with the skills to listen to, value, and respect the feelings of others. This is obviously important not just in male/female relationships and parenting, but in relationships across any lines of difference.

Men can be as emotionally expressive and nurturing as women, but in general they are not expected to take the emotional initiative in relationships or in childraising. Most of us still expect that boys will turn to their mothers, not their fathers, for those private conversations, intimate questions, and special revelations. We also may expect that women, not men, will bring up relationship problems, pay attention to the emotional temperature in the room, and initiate the processing of difficult issues in the family.

There is plenty of evidence that these are not gender specific skills. Just as they can learn how to cook, change a diaper, and clean the house, boys and men can learn emotional, expressive skills. Women are not born with sensitivity to tension within a relationship or to their children's emotional well-being. Some women never develop such skills, but because they are female, society expects them to pay attention to the emotional state of everyone around them and blame them when they don't take care of these things.

Boys need to have practice at nurturing so that their natural inclination to take care of people and things is encouraged and developed. Give them dolls, give them stuffed animals, give them plants, give them pets, or give them younger children to take care of, keeping the challenge suitable to their age and abilities.

Boys can learn to notice when people around them are depressed, excited, sad, frustrated, scared, or confused. They can learn to pay attention, listen, ask questions, and provide emotional reassurance and guidance. If boys do not learn to notice the feelings and responses of others, they may grow up to treat people as objects, ignoring the damage they inflict on others through emotional, verbal, or physical attacks. Some men do such harm intentionally, knowing the damage it produces. Many men, however, have been allowed to grow up impervious to the effect their actions have on others.

One way to encourage our son's emotional literacy is to ask him what he notices in others around him.

Questions to ask our sons

How do you think _____ felt when that happened?
How would you have felt if that happened to you?
What do you think is going on inside that character?
What might _____ have been thinking when they did that?
What effect did it have on the people around him/her?
What do you think is going on with (your sister/brother, your father, your cousin, your friend)?

Our sons learn a great deal from seeing us pay attention to their feelings. This is especially true if we are men, because there are so few models of emotionally nurturing men. There are many ways to check on how our sons are feeling. Sometimes words are useful. Sometimes just sitting with them, sharing a story or giving a hug, allows them to share their feelings. Sometimes we can ask directly.

Our sons will also benefit from seeing us express our own complicated feelings. This doesn't mean dumping all our problems on them, but there are many times when it is easy to share feelings about something current, or about a past experience, in ways that let our sons see that talking about feelings is natural, important, and healing. This lets them become comfortable with the idea of listening to others, too. If you are a man, this kind of sharing will contradict the many messages boys receive that men can't, shouldn't, and won't express feelings and that they will be instantly attacked and annihilated if they do. You can constantly challenge the assumption that boys will only make it as men if they are insensitive to the feelings of others and cover up their caring.

There is no man more powerful than one who is in touch with his feelings, who can love and laugh, cry and grieve. One whose anger is compassionate. There is much you can do as an ally to nurture your son's ability to recognize his feelings and develop the skills to take care of himself. This will prevent those feelings from turning into violence against himself and those around him and will bring him into the interdependent circle of caring people who nurture the community.

So far in this section I have been discussing how our sons can find a place for themselves in the world and how they can develop the personal skills to take care of themselves and their surroundings. Now I want to turn to the interpersonal and social skills they need because they are not living in a vacuum. Personal awareness is only useful if it can be connected to social practice. To begin, I want to look at that most central concept: democracy. How do we give our sons practice in democracy?

9 Family Life

PRACTICE IN DEMOCRACY

Democracy is one of our most cherished values and most called-upon traditions, yet most of us have little actual practice with it. Most workplaces are hierarchical and our input is not valued. Some of us work in places where the management comes to us for our input. We are surveyed, made part of focus groups, studied, polled, or simply asked for our opinion on policy matters, but even if our responses are taken seriously, we still are not part of the decision-making process and may feel just as subject to the whim of our supervisors as we did before our input was solicited.

Being asked our opinion so that others can decide is not an example of democracy in the workplace, although it may be a big step forward from total lack of input. Nor is voting a sign of democracy in the political process. Voting for choices that we didn't determine, established by processes that we did not choose, is not democratic. We cannot call a process democratic unless there has been widespread participation in every phase, from researching and gathering information, considering alternatives, and deciding what direction to go, to implementing the decision. The process could be consensus decision-making, voting, proportional representation, or something else entirely. Democracy means active participation in all aspects of the process by all those affected by the decision.

Most of our sons are being raised to assume a powerful and authoritarian role within the family and to give up control at work. They learn that democracy means voting once in a while, but they are primarily trained to remain passive citizens. At the same time, some of our sons — those in families in the top 20 percent of the economic pyramid — are being prepared to take charge, to make decisions, and to assume control. It serves neither of these groups nor the rest of us well to have a small group of well-trained male leaders making decisions for the rest of us. This is undemocratic and leads to political and economic abuse and exploitation.

For democracy to be more than a slogan we need to figure out how to incorporate democratic processes into our everyday lives. Only in that way can we pass on democratic values to our sons. Because most boys are conditioned to hold anti-democratic values that place great importance on control, authority, power over others, competition, and

© Kathy Sloane

hierarchy, it is particularly important that we give them an understanding of and practice in democratic decision making. In addition, boys are often violent because, although they have been taught that the role of men is to be on the top, making decisions, being in charge and in control, in reality they feel powerless and ineffective in their lives. We can counter the allure of violence by offering young men democratic participation that will allow them to feel active, empowered, and effective.

DEMOCRACY IN THE FAMILY

When we hear the phrase "democracy in the family," some of us immediately think this means that everyone is equal, that we have no authority, and that our children can do anything they want. Democracy does not mean lack of authority or lack of leadership. However, it does force us to rethink what authority and leadership mean in a democratic context.

Children want to get their way, yet they have a strong sense of justice and don't want anyone to be left out. I want to strengthen these democratic tendencies by giving our children a chance to practice democratic, cooperative values. The more young people participate in decision-making, the better they are at it and the more they expect to be included.

They will learn to notice when things are not democratic. They will challenge not only our own practices, but also those of the school or the recreational, religious, and other organizations they are part of. It may well feel awkward, uncomfortable, and confusing to adults. It often does to me. When my children are challenging me, one side of me wants to clamp down and say, "Because I said so." Another side wants to say, "Let's look at this more closely." If we can't reach agreement easily, I may become frustrated or tired and return to the side that says, "Enough already, it's still because I said so." But Micki and I have gradually increased our children's participation in family decision-making and I have seen the growth in my children's leadership abilities as a result.

Democracy in our families probably seems like an idealistic and faraway goal. It is. There are many times when, as adults, we must use our authority, power, and responsibility to set limits and make decisions for our children. At the same time, we do not have the right to exclude automatically our children from participating in family decision making because of our belief that they are incompetent, ignorant, irresponsible, or inexperienced. If they are truly any of these things it is our responsibility to prepare them for participating more fully. There are some simple steps we can take to make our democratic ideals part of our everyday practice.

Family Meetings

In order for children (and every adult) to have a chance to participate, there must be an open process for making decisions. One form for this process is family meetings. These can be regular or occasional meetings where all family members sit down together and discuss items that anyone can put on the agenda. If small children are involved, these meetings should be brief and focused on situations of interest to the children. As the children mature and their interests and attention spans broaden, more and more complex subjects can be discussed. You will need to agree on guidelines to make sure the meetings run smoothly. These should be worked out by all family members, kept brief and clear, and possibly written up so that they can be referred to if necessary. It may take time for everyone, adults and children, to get used to some of the guidelines, but if they are sincerely adopted by everyone, they will guide not only family meetings but other interactions within the family as well. In my family, we have agreed to the following guidelines:

1. We respect each other.
2. We don't interrupt each other.
3. We use "I" statements whenever possible.
4. No put-downs.
5. No one can storm out.
6. Anyone can leave if they are too uncomfortable or upset to continue, and the discussion will be continued at another time.
7. Younger children can leave when there are no items left that apply to them (or when they are too restless to continue).

Depending on the age of the child, agenda items for family meetings might include trips; allowances; chores; use of extra money (if there is any); relationships within the family; announcements about work or school or personal feelings; discussion of major family events such as illnesses, deaths, births; changing financial circumstances; changes in family routines or practices such as changing schedules, visitors, mealtimes; curfews; schoolwork and grades; disagreements between family members; family meetings themselves; and so on. The list is endless.

Besides giving practice in democratic decision-making, family meetings also help establish a cooperative atmosphere within the family and provide practice in setting agendas; addressing issues; presenting, explaining, and justifying ideas; and talking through issues — all skills that young people need to develop. As children get older they can become agenda setters and learn more complex facilitation skills.

When boys actively participate in democratic and inclusive, cooperative processes like family meetings, they are gaining practice in emotional caring skills such as paying attention to feelings and working out conflict peacefully rather than through strength and anger.

We want them to learn these skills. Equally, we want them to develop an expectation that all members of the family will have full participation in the process of decision-making. We need to teach boys to expect to participate *and* to see it as an injustice when anyone is left out of the process. We may need to examine our own family practices. Do the males lead the discussions or participate more aggressively in the process? Do all of the children, even the quiet ones, have a chance to put in their comments? Are the women the only ones who pay attention to people's feelings?

Micki and I encourage our children to come to family meetings with proposals. They may say they want a bigger allowance or a later bedtime. We'll ask them to explain why. We might ask them what is typical for their friends. We might ask them what responsibility they will take if they have a larger allowance or a later bedtime. For example, our children have had to take more responsibility for getting up and getting their lunches and breakfasts in exchange for later bedtimes. They have had to set aside some of their allowance to give to community agencies or to buy presents for friends' birthdays in exchange for more money. If we need more information before making a decision, we might send them back to do some research and find out how much things cost or what are the choices. They learn to take their own ideas seriously and do the preparation and planning that will lead to successful implementation of changes.

I regret we did not start these practices in our family as early as I now think possible and we did not carry them out as consistently and thoroughly as we could have. But our children have gained some knowledge of democratic practice; some skill in talking through ideas, issues, and personal relations; and an expectation that they should be included. Their skills in these areas would be much more strongly developed if they were reinforced in their schools.

Staying Out Too Late

Negotiating stay-out times can be a complicated, ongoing process. You have to take into consideration who your son is; what his needs are for sleep, study, chores, and family time; where he goes; who he hangs with. It may help to discuss this with other parents and you may want to establish a family process for working out issues like this. When you reach agreement you need to discuss what happens when the agreement is broken.

For many young men, whether they are in school, working, or both, evenings are usually when they have some freedom and a chance to socialize with friends. It is a time when they control their own life to some extent, without parental supervision. But because they may be tempted by negative aspects of peer pressure to take part in high-risk activities, to ignore their studies, and not to take care of themselves physically, it is also a time when they need some limits and guidelines from parents.

This issue can become a battleground where parental limits are tested and challenged. Or it can be an opportunity to turn a confrontation into a decision-making process that takes into account everyone's concerns. Many times we can stretch our comfort zone and compromise on stay-out times in return for agreements on study time, family responsibility, and communication from our son about his whereabouts and activities.

Before you start negotiating, it helps to decide what your bottom line is while trying to remain flexible. Curfews actually involve a whole series of questions including how late on school nights and how late on the weekends? What does your son have to accomplish before he can leave (i.e., homework, chores, practicing)? When does he have to check in? How much sleep does he need? Does he need to check in at a certain time and tell you where he is, or just be in certain areas? What happens when he stays out too late or doesn't call? Of course all these details change as he matures and shows you he can handle later hours and more responsibility.

Studying and Practicing

Issues that can cause conflict and a desire by parents to set limits include schoolwork and grades, and practice sessions for art, music, or sports activities. What are *your* goals? Do you want your son to get high grades or to love learning? Do you want him to play in the NBA or to love basketball, perform at Carnegie Hall or play music with friends? What role do you want to play? Do you want to have to cajole and threaten regularly to get him to practice? Perhaps he doesn't need to practice every day. Maybe four to five times a week would work just as well, with days off when he has practiced a certain number of days in a row.

Developing study and practice schedules that work for your son will take time and his participation. Those plans are most likely to be carried out when your son is motivated by the intrinsic rewards of the task such as knowing that he is getting better at what he is doing, increasing his self-confidence, achieving certain milestones, and having his progress recognized by others. You can support your son by introducing him to people who love what they are doing and whose self-discipline comes out of that love. Helping your son discover this love of an activity is the best way you can help him develop motivation and self-discipline.

There are things your son will have to do that he may not enjoy but that will get him to places he wants to go. Getting his free throw percentage up will help him make the team; practicing trombone will enable him to play in the band; passing algebra will get him into college. Sometimes intrinsic rewards are not too exciting, especially in a school system where there are plenty of boring textbooks and bad teaching. It will help your son a great deal if you acknowledge that some things are boring or seem meaningless but have to be done because of the results they lead to. Young people understand the connections, and when their feelings of frustration and impatience are acknowledged, they are capable of getting on with their lessons without our being the taskmaster.

Our goal should be not discipline, but self-discipline. To help our sons achieve maximum self-discipline we need to lower our levels of discipline as much as possible and place the responsibility and consequences for behavior on our sons. For example, your son's bedtime, curfew, and other limits can be related to how well he communicates with you, how well he plans his activities, what he needs to stay healthy, and how well he accomplishes the studying and other work he needs to do. Helping him to think through these interconnected issues and to develop mutually acceptable guidelines gives him the tools to make decisions for himself.

Is He Hanging with the Wrong Crowd?

You can't choose your son's friends for him. (You might want to say this sentence to yourself a few times.) But you can help him think about his friends in a reflective way.

Questions to ask your son

What does he like about his friends?

What doesn't he like?

What do they bring out in him — what qualities of his do they support?

What parts of him don't they support?

Your son needs help thinking about his values and his friends' values, his goals and theirs, his future and theirs. It can be very hard not to be judgmental, not to give advice, not to make subtle or not-so-subtle comments, asides, and sarcastic remarks. He needs you to listen and ask questions. If you listen and respect his thinking he will probably be able to hear your opinions if you state them respectfully, once, briefly. He still may hang with guys that you don't like or think are a bad influence on him. It may help to remember that parents have rarely been able to determine who their children's friends are. That is okay because choosing friends is a basic right that all young people are entitled to.

PARENTING NON-VIOLENTLY

If we want our children to participate in family meetings, discussions, and problem-solving, we need to have a family environment that lets them feel safe. Only if we are parenting nonviolently can we create such an environment.

In our house we have simple rules aimed at creating a safe home for everyone. These rules were derived by talking in family meetings about how we wanted to live together. We have found that by the time children are eight or nine (and in many cases much earlier) they are capable of participating in serious discussions about how family members should be treated and what rules need to be established to help family members feel safe. By including children in those discussions we prepare them to think about their behavior and to build skills to live and work with others.

Most of the agreements have to do with violence, bullying, and disrespect. We also have specific guidelines dealing with mealtime behavior, TV viewing, and other household arrangements, but these are constantly revised and modified in family meetings. The basic rules in our family are:

- No hitting, kicking, biting, or hurting others, including the animals and plants around us.
- No kissing, hugging, touching, or other contact with a person who does not want it.
- No teasing or name-calling.
- No throwing things in the house or at people.
- No threats or intimidation.
- "No" means no, "stop it" means stop it — the first time.

We explained the reasons for these rules when the children were old enough to talk, but the limits on violence came first. The rules apply to the adults as well as the children in the house. Adults are not allowed to do any of these things, even in retaliation for children breaking the rules.

Question to ask yourself

How might your family be different if you had some simple family rules for how people treated each other?

When our children were younger we talked a lot about why these rules were important and what our family would be like if we didn't have them. Children easily understand what it is like to be vulnerable to teasing and put-downs from others. They know the value of limits on abusive behavior. But what we emphasize is how we want to live together, not what we want to avoid. Our intent is not to enforce the rules for their own sake, but to help our children learn how to participate in a safe and healthy family environment.

Our children want to live in a safe and supportive environment, but they don't always have the control to stop themselves from hurting others, and sometimes they have no other way to express their anger than to be abusive. So they do break the agreements by hitting, teasing, or calling each other names.

We have found that when children (or adults) break the rules it is usually because they are too tired, too angry, too wound up emotionally or overstimulated, and are therefore uncentered. The most common form of recentering we use is a time-out. A time-out allows a person to separate from the situation, rest in a quiet space, and refocus their energy and attention. We follow a time-out with a brief discussion where we talk about why it was called and hear any further feelings or thoughts the person wants to express. This is a good time to help our sons learn how to identify and express the feelings below the anger.

For small children we calculate the length of a time-out as one minute for each year of their age. For older children the length varies but is never more than fifteen to twenty minutes. Sometimes they want to argue against the time-out as a way to continue a confrontation. We have never found these arguments to be useful when emotions are already heated.

When the children were younger and refused to take a time-out my partner or I would pick them up, gently but firmly, and carry them to their room. When they were older I would say something like, "You need to cool down before we can continue this discussion. You have a five minute time-out. If you don't go to your room now it will be ten minutes." It didn't take long for them to get the message that there was no further discussion until after a cooling out period.

Often during the time-out they will become involved in some focused activity such as reading, writing, or coloring. Then they are ready to reenter the discussion and help figure out what needs to happen next. What I think is most important is that the time-out is a way to prepare for further discussion, not an end to the process. The participants still have to talk about what happened and figure out a solution to the problem that initiated the confrontation.

Over the years we have used time-outs less and less as our children became better at problem-solving and talking through situations. We have raised our expectations of them (and improved our parenting skills), and this has reinforced their ability to participate in family discussions to work out disagreements.

In our family it is okay for our children to be angry, to express their anger, and to go to their room angry. We allow them to yell and even slam a door on their way to their room, though abusive language and destructive behavior are not allowed. Anger is not the problem and we don't want to tell our children that there is something wrong with being angry. What they need to learn is that they are responsible for what they do when they are angry and that, as a family, we have determined that certain behavior is not acceptable. For example, they can't take their anger out on other people or destroy property.

Our assumptions are that no one deserves to get hurt and that there are always alternatives to violence. It is our responsibility as adults to learn to model these alternatives for our children. The following are some of these alternatives:

- Encourage everyone to speak out and say what he or she wants and needs, without demanding it.
- Encourage everyone to talk about his or her feelings, to listen to each other, and to work out negotiated solutions.
- Give time-outs (a quiet time away from others to cool out) when they are too wrought up or involved to behave nonviolently or cooperatively (adults can also have time-outs).
- Instill the expectation that they deserve the respect and love of others; that they are important; that they can control when they are to be touched, hugged, and kissed; that they can meet their needs.
- Devise other ways to express conflict and painful emotions through writing, drawing, acting, playing, and physical activity.

We have noticed that it helps tremendously to acknowledge our children's feelings even when we don't like their behavior. They have many reasons to be angry. They experience great powerlessness in their lives. Their anger is often legitimate, though the way they express it may not be. Our responsibility is to help them see the difference.

I think boys should be taught from an early age that being louder, more aggressive, more intimidating, or abusive is not the way to get what they want. They are receiving constant training that these methods work and that men can rely on them to get their way. If you tell them not to use what they see working (at least in the movies if not in your house) without giving them alternative skills, you leave them confused and anxious, with nothing to fall back on but traditional male power.

This dynamic leads us to a two-part strategy. One is that we can teach boys how to be angry without being abusive. The other is that we can teach them to express the feelings of sadness, frustration, excitement, or confusion that anger often covers over or is mixed in with. Hitting, threats, punishment, intimidation, verbal abuse, and other harsh discipline produces just the opposite effect. Instead of teaching them how not to be abusive, it gives them the message that abusive behavior is justified. Instead of teaching them to express their feelings, it shuts them down and teaches them that their feelings are unimportant. We must teach our sons to work out differences and teach them simple conflict resolution skills such as how to share, how to take turns, how to listen, how to compromise.

Every culture has traditional ways to settle conflicts. We can build on the nonviolent ones and refuse to settle for intimidation and abuse. When boys learn to be leaders and to facilitate alternative conflict-resolution methods, they challenge our preconceived notions that boys will be boys and they provide alternative models for other boys. They show others that there are ways to participate in group activities that are respectful and cooperative. They are also less likely to fall into adult roles that are abusive and controlling.

Part of the understanding in our house is that you can ask for help when you need it, either to defend yourself against aggression or to solve a problem or conflict. We help our children develop alternative, assertive responses to situations that are frustrating or difficult for them — when they are provoked, teased, or bullied, for example. They need help when they are embarrassed or ignored, when they make mistakes or are challenged to fight, or when they need to stand up for their rights.

They also need to know how to empathize with others, stand up for a friend, respond to peer pressure, and behave appropriately when winning or losing in sports. Any of these situations can either be excuses for violence or opportunities for understanding and resolving differences.[1]

WHAT TO DO WHEN AGREEMENTS ARE BROKEN

When your son gets older you face different challenges in working out situations with him. If your son agrees to some expectations about homework or grades or chores and then doesn't follow through, you need to come back to him and say, "This system isn't working. Let's figure out how else to set it up." With this approach he learns that sometimes things don't work out and you have to go back and figure out some other system. The focus is not on his failure but on the situation, which needs a better solution. He also learns that he is responsible for helping to come up with a solution that works, which may mean identifying and taking responsibility for what went wrong on the last round.

If your son breaks the agreements or oversteps the limits you have set, it is easy to want to respond personally, out of your own anger and frustration, rather than in response to his need. It helps to talk about why the agreements are important and how trust breaks down when they are not adhered to. I think this is the most important part of the process. You want to help your son see the consequences of his action — how it affected other family members, how it affected his own health, how it interfered with goals he is trying to achieve.

If you believe that "consequences" are important, it helps to have them spelled out in advance and to have them relate to the violation, although it may not always be easy to determine what is a logical consequence. It is best not to decide on or implement a response when you are very angry. You need to think calmly about what is needed in the situation and what will actually help your son get back on track.

The best solution is to try to work with your son to develop a future plan in which he takes responsibility for changing his behavior and repairing the community bonds he has broken. Other members of the family, including younger children, can also be

© Cathy Cade

involved in this process. However, if you can't reach agreement with your son, sometimes you just have to fall back on your parental authority and say, "From my understanding of what you need and my responsibility for your welfare, I have decided to (ground you, demand that your homework is done before you can leave the house, work out an agreement about grades, lower your stay-out time, institute a mandatory check-in call every night you're out at ___ p.m., etc.)."

It is best to fall back on your parental authority sparingly. As adults, we do have leverage, even over our teens. We control the money and access to family resources that young people depend on, and they still want our attention, trust, and approval. We should not manipulate their needs, but we should exert our authority when behavior is inappropriate, agreements have been broken, or family relationships have been violated.

When you do feel you have to set limits that your son disagrees with, you can respond firmly but without a personal need to blame your son for being male or to subdue his rebelliousness and challenge to authority. It is easy to get into a battle of wills. It is even easier to get into arguments that degenerate into name-calling, sarcasm, put-downs, and the temptation to hit. You are much less likely to be abusive if you accept that you are the authority, the one ultimately responsible, and you don't have to prove that to him.

Having support from other adults is essential to maintaining some perspective when you respond to your son's challenges to your authority. This is the time to check in with a co-parent, friend, or parent support group to talk about what feelings your son's defiance brings up in you and to help you think about the various choices of response you have.

One thing that can get in the way of your being firm is that young people can get very angry when limits are set. Young men can be powerful and even threatening. If your son responds this way, remind yourself that it is okay for him to be angry and that you can help him find appropriate expression for that anger. In some circumstances you may need to determine whether there is a potential for a violent response from your son. If you think there is, your son may need help beyond your parenting skills.

Young men can also be very persistent, demanding reasons, explanations, and endless discussion. You can respect their need to be heard (and you should take seriously any counterarguments they raise), but you don't need to subject yourself to emotional or verbal abuse. You can set limits on the tone and length of the discussion, especially if your son is too upset to continue or is not listening as you explain your reasons to him. You can always continue the discussion another time.

You may find it difficult to set limits because you know your son will be disappointed and possibly not like you for it. You will not always be liked if you are a good parent. Sometimes my children will come to me and tell me that my ratings as a parent have gone way down recently because I've been too mean. But the ratings go up and down, and my children always love and respect me, even when they don't like me at the moment. They always know that we have reasons, which we explain to them, for our actions and we are thinking of their best interests. We try to keep the communication flowing so that we can figure out better ways to make decisions together and take everyone's concerns into consideration. True caring relationships are built on love, mutual respect, and constant communication.

There is no single magic method of setting limits that works for every child (or every parent). But there are many ways to set limits with a child that show you respect your child and respond to his needs, yet that allow you to maintain his and your own dignity and integrity.

If we start by setting minimal, reasonable (at least to us) limits and encouraging our children to take responsibility for choices when they are young, we help them to understand that the limits are guidelines for future responsibility. One way that Micki and I did that with our children was by setting limits on TV watching and letting them decide what they watched within these limits. When they were young we explained that we were setting limits because of the effects of commercials, violence, and stereotypes on their minds and because extended TV watching leads to neglect of other activities and responsibilities. We encouraged them to pursue alternative activities. Later we ended up with a similar structure for time spent on computer and video games. In other words, we started out by explaining our reasons for some parentally set limits, then negotiated changes in the limits as the children grew older. We now leave it up to the children themselves to decide how much they watch. When you start out with minimal limits and reasonable explanations you can end up with no imposed limits at all.

DISCIPLINE

Limits and broken agreements bring us to an issue often thought to be at the core of raising boys: discipline. At home or at school the question of when, how, and whether to discipline boys is a central concern of most adults.

You may have noticed that I didn't mention physical punishment when I discussed options for responding to our sons when they break agreements. In our punitive society we need to discuss physical punishment because it is still widely thought to be necessary for successfully raising boys. Boys are still routinely hit. Either people think it will toughen them up or they think boys are already so tough that hitting is the only thing that will get through.

Are there any situations in which a child deserves to be hit? When I ask this question in workshops, the response I often receive is "No, but..."

- "Not hit, but disciplined."
- "Sometimes you have to do it for their own good."
- "Just a little slap on the booty."
- "Yeah, you have to set limits."

Most people will agree that hitting people is bad and you should never do it. We know the costs — it scares children, lowers their self-esteem, makes them defiant and angry, teaches them that force solves problems and that aggression is okay, and destroys trust and intimacy. But many of us hold onto that "but if."

- "If a child doesn't stop when you ask them to stop again and again."
- "If the child won't listen."
- "If the child is disturbing other people [adults]."
- "If the child is calling people [adults] names and using bad language."
- "If a child is doing something dangerous and won't stop."
- "If a child is challenging you."

In each case the use of force is justified because all else failed. If not force, then other forms of punishment like threats or intimidation are used. What is really going on in these situations? And what is our goal when we use physical discipline or other forms of punishment with a child? How does it affect the practice of democracy in the family?

Questions to ask yourself

Are there any situations in which you think it might be okay to hit a child?

Are there any situations in which you think it might be okay to punish a child?

List any situations in which you think it might be okay to threaten
or intimidate a child.

Was there a time recently when you threatened a child in any way, by threatening punishment, withdrawal of goodies, banishment, or even a bad future ("You'll never get ahead, get to college, make the team, if...")?

Why did you resort to a threat?

What did you gain?

What did it cost you?

What did it cost your relationship with the young person?

What might you have done differently?

Few people like yelling at, threatening, intimidating, or hitting children. If you listed any situations at all in response to the questions above, you probably hoped that you could find alternatives and that punishment, threats, and intimidation would not be necessary. But if all else fails...

Hitting people, especially people you love, is completely dehumanizing to both the person doing the hitting and the person being hit. Most of us know what it feels like to be hit by someone bigger, older, or stronger. We know how powerless, outraged, angry, sad, ashamed, and humiliated it makes us feel. Typical responses from the child being hit may range from "I can't trust you" to "Wait till I get older" to "Next time I'll be real careful I don't get caught." Punishment increases fear, not respect, and obedience, not self-discipline. It does not teach how to live peacefully with others. It does not teach alternatives to violence.

Many of us say that we were hit as kids and it didn't hurt us. In fact, we might say that we probably deserved it. What does it mean to "deserve" to be hit? Children often internalize the blaming messages they receive from adults and do end up thinking they deserved the blame and punishment. But who really deserves to be hit?

If we were hit when we were young, it can be scary to acknowledge that those who hit us were wrong, especially if they were our parents or other people we loved or were dependent on and who loved us. We may have to look at anger and pain we haven't wanted to admit or deal with. We may have to look at attitudes about children that we have carried from childhood — attitudes that children are irrational, devious, manipulative, or out of control. But in order to be caring adults to the young people around us, we must be able to say to ourselves that it was wrong that others hit us, teased us, put us down, or abused us in any way. We were not "bad" and we did not deserve it.

One teen father said to me, "My father never hit me after I was five. All he had to do was look at me in a certain way, or raise his finger, and I froze. I knew that look, and I never got hit any more." This young man went on to admit that he doesn't feel particularly safe with or close to his father. Yet he maintains that the hitting had been appropriate because he was a troublemaker. A troublemaker at three or four or five? He offered this story as an example of the effectiveness of spanking. But I would interpret it as an example of fear and intimidation, and of adults' desperation to maintain control.

Most of our need for control arises because we believe it will bring benefits to us — things like greater quiet, more cooperation, fewer mistakes, less conflict. Our underlying assumption is that our children are fundamentally irrational, uncooperative, too emotional, nagging, demanding, unresponsive, incapable of self-control and therefore we can only get what we want by punishing them. We probably believe that they should not question our need for control but must simply accept our decisions or face the consequences. We often justify our tactics as being in the interest of our children but it is hard to demonstrate any benefits at all to our children from abusive behavior.

Control and punishment are also directly counter to democratic participation. If your goal is to practice democracy in your family, the home environment has to be safe enough for children to participate in discussions, voice their opinions, argue back, and be part of group decision-making. Unilateral and controlling behavior will undermine their safety and therefore their ability to participate fully. Your children will learn to be cautious and accommodating rather than outspoken and courageous.

I am not claiming that every child who has been hit has been irrevocably damaged or that if you have spanked your child you don't necessarily love him. However, now is a good time to step back and understand your own motives of control and fear that have led you to hit your child. Talk with other adults, explore your feelings, make a commitment to find alternatives. There is always an alternative to hitting a child. It is especially important for your son to see you use alternatives to violence in solving problems, setting limits, and working things out. He is taking notes for later use in his own life.

We saw some of these alternatives when we discussed the strengths demonstrated by Gandhi and Cesar Chavez. These men used their words, their minds, their faith, their compassion, and their ability to communicate to be strong without resorting to violence. We each possess similar resources.

We do come home tired, frustrated, and upset. If we have decided there are some circumstances under which it is okay to hit, threaten, or intimidate our children, there may come a time when we will do that. Because we cannot make our best decisions when we are stressed, the only protection we have against acting punitively is to be absolutely clear ahead of time that hitting is never okay, that threats and intimidation are never okay. Otherwise, in situations of panic, we will act out of that panic and end up hurting those we love. When we've done it once, it is a lot easier to do it again.

I think that even the knowledge that we can fall back on punishment gives us less incentive to find alternatives, which makes it more likely we'll end up using punishment. When Micki and I made a decision not to use punishment, it sharpened our thinking about alternative ways to structure our children's environments and to foster self-discipline, problem-solving, creativity, and flexibility.

Is noncorporal punishment any better? Generally, any kind of punishment has the same consequences — pain, fear, and anger. It does not deter misconduct, it does not solve problems, it does not lead to learning and self-discipline, and it promotes violence. As Dr. Rudolf Dreikurs wrote nearly thirty years ago. "Punishments such as spanking, slapping, humiliating, depriving, and generally putting children down are outdated and ineffective means of disciplining children."[2]

Are rewards a good alternative to punishment? Rewards are really just the flip side of the same coin, the carrot that goes with the stick. In either case the focus is on what you want your son to do, which gives you the power to judge behavior. His attention invariably shifts from what he wants, what he thinks, what he can do to what you want for him. This process undermines initiative, learning, self-discipline, and inner motivation. Rewards are simply another way to control behavior. Again, the results are short term and often exactly counter to the long-term goals we have for our children. As Alfie Kohn notes, summing up the research on this issue, "Children who are frequently rewarded tend to be somewhat less generous and cooperative than those who aren't rewarded."[3]

Eliminating punishment in our family has been a slow and difficult process. Micki and I were both raised to spank children, to tease and put them down, and to blame them when we lost control. It was a crucial first step for us when we decided not to use force and verbal abuse in raising our children and to involve them in creating a cooperative family environment in which everyone is fully respected.

We still struggle to develop alternatives to what we learned, and to set limits that show respect for and involve our children. Occasionally one of us has lost control and yelled or screamed or picked up one of the children for a time-out with more force than was necessary. We have found that this occurs less often as we learn ways to engage them in working out conflicts with problem-solving skills. We have learned to step in for each other or suggest a time-out for the other when one of us is simply too tired or stressed to make good parenting decisions. (This is a benefit of having two parents.) We have learned to go back to our children later and apologize for our behavior when we have made mistakes or been unduly harsh. One of the practices that has changed our family dynamics a great deal has been our effort to introduce democratic practice. The more we include the children in discussion and decision-making about family affairs, the less we need to fall back on any alternative problem-solving.

Questions to ask yourself

When you were a child, did your family use physical discipline — hitting,
molesting, slapping, spanking, or other physical force?
What was the effect of this on you and other family members?
Were the children in your family mistreated verbally — put down, teased, told
they were worthless, stupid, would never amount to anything,
or other negative comments?

What was the effect of this on you and other family members?

Do you feel you got as much love and encouragement as you
needed as a child?

Are there ways you want your children to grow up with more love and
encouragement than you received?

What can you do to give them that kind of attention?

Say to yourself, "It is never okay to hit a child." Are there any
"but what ifs" that immediately come to mind?

What keeps you from deciding not to hit, tease, call young
people names, or otherwise put them down?

What steps do you need to take to eliminate hitting
and verbal abuse in your family?

When you are tired, frustrated, or angry, what specifically can you do to avoid
taking out your frustrations on your children (e.g., taking a time-out yourself)?

Make a list of alternative, nonviolent ways to set limits with
young people. Which ones are you going to use?

What guidelines for respect and cooperative living do you think
your family needs to establish?

What are alternative ways for members of your family to
express anger, hurt, and frustration nonviolently?

What steps can you take to make your family praise and appreciate
rather than criticize each other?

Young Men Are Not the Problem

What about older children? What about kids in trouble? What about young men in gangs? Don't we have to be tough with boys? What is the role of democracy and discipline in these situations?

The problem with various forms of punitive discipline is that, besides being morally degrading to both parties, they simply don't work. They don't address the underlying cause of the problem and therefore the problem remains after the punishment is long over, now coupled with additional layers of resentment, shame, and anger.

Boys and young men act out primarily because our schools stifle them, because they have no meaningful job prospects, because their neighborhoods are devastated, and because they have few recreational opportunities and little safe space to hang out in. They may have been mistreated or abused in a number of ways. For many, their everyday lives and concerns are simply ignored or devalued by the adults around them.

We know that well-paying and challenging jobs, good educational opportunities, and recreational programs work better than prisons to decrease violence and bring young men back into the community. "Discipline" and "Punishment" are the cries of those who want to throw away some of the young men in our community, usually because they are young men of color, are from poor and working-class families, or are challenging traditional community practices that perpetuate injustice and violence. Punitive discipline attacks the boy as the problem rather than looking to see if there is a problem to be dealt with. The result is that the problem is covered over and the boy is lost in the process.

Older youth need our loving support for problem-solving. They need to know what the limits are for certain kinds of behavior. They should be included in the discussion about what those limits are in your house or classroom or neighborhood. Setting limits for acceptable behavior without their participation or setting unrealistic limits dramatically increases the probability that they will find a way to challenge or subvert the limits. Meting out harsh punishment when they rebel against those limits doesn't work in our families and doesn't work in our society. Locking young men up, expelling them from school, subjecting them to punitive curfews and strict police surveillance doesn't produce the behavior we want. Instead these policies breed anger, resentment, manipulation, repression of feelings, and low self-esteem. They produce young men with little to lose from further violence. Yes, we have problems. But the problems are not young men. The problem may be the school, the lack of jobs and recreational programs, violence in the home, or devastation in the community. Young men need to be part of the solution to these problems.

Many schools in our local school districts here in California have long had extremely high suspension rates because administrators thought that the best way to deal with young men who were causing problems was to kick them out. In other words, the young men were labeled the problem and then eliminated. Parents, particularly African American and Latino/a parents, noticed the high rates of suspension and realized that the schools were unresponsive to the educational needs of their children and then were punishing the students for causing problems. Many of the schools were run down, lacked adequate supplies such as textbooks, and were filled with teachers who didn't think their students could succeed. The curriculum itself was outdated, inaccurate, and uninspiring.

The first thing that parents and other community activists did was to research the suspension rates by school and teacher, compiling a gender and racial breakdown of who was suspended. Then they studied alternative ways of dealing with unruly behavior with an aim of making the schools more responsive to students' needs. They found that suspensions had ceased to have much impact on student behavior or academic performance because students were glad to get out of school.

The group put pressure on the school board by publicizing their findings, talking with school board members, and organizing protests. The school board passed a resolution requiring schools to dramatically lower their suspension rates, to develop alternative, in-school ways to deal with problem behavior, and to make the schools places where students wanted to come to learn.

I recently talked with the dean at one high school whose goal was to make school so exciting that the young men developed the self-discipline to stay because they wanted to be there. His school had become a magnet school, offering special courses in a number of subject areas. It had developed more business and community partnerships to offer students a variety of opportunities to become involved in community service and job-training activities. Teachers and administrators were constantly looking for new resources to respond to the needs that students brought to them.

The dean I talked with told me that students wanted to participate in events at the school and did not want to miss any class time or student activities. They now rarely missed classes and there was a dramatic decline in "discipline problems." Students were being given an opportunity to be in an educational environment that responded to their needs — and their behavior had changed in response. What had been labeled discipline problems of the boys were now properly seen as educational responsibilities of the school.

We can learn a lot from examples like this one. Rather than seeing young men as the problem and locking them up in increasing numbers for longer and longer sentences, we need to address the problems they face, knowing that their aggressive or destructive behavior is just a response to their lack of other opportunities. If we invested more money in schools, recreation programs, and youth culture, we could dramatically reduce the violence in our communities, reduce our expenses for police and prisons, and welcome our sons back into our communities.

The democratic and cooperative values we are trying to practice in our families need to be reinforced at school — but often they are not. As the school described above demonstrates, we can make the educational system responsive to boys so that it plays a vital role in our efforts to raise our sons for courage, caring, and community.

10 From Competition to Cooperation: Democracy in the Classroom

To many of us, the school system seems to be working directly counter to many of the values we are trying to teach our sons. We may be practicing democracy, nonviolent parenting, and cooperative learning and problem solving at home, but without support from the schools we face an uphill battle. If schools reinforce the message that our sons should get ahead for themselves, they will have a more difficult time getting together with others.

SORTING AND TRAINING THE WORKFORCE

The original purpose of public schools in America was to train and educate the workforce — to prepare workers for the demands of work in an increasingly industrialized society. Some of the demands of factory work (or at least the demands of the foremen and factory owners in charge) were (and still are) that workers be on time, that they follow the rules, that they work hard, and that they do what their bosses tell them to do.

Factory owners, industrialists, and others at the top of the economic pyramid did not want, nor did they intend to create, a highly educated populace that was trained to think critically and would expect to participate democratically in the workings of government and the economy. Their goals were to give boys (white males — they were not thinking of the education of girls or children of color at all) the literacy skills, job training, and self-discipline necessary to become efficient workers. The curriculum and classroom practice that developed to meet these goals teaches children to obey, be on time, hide their feelings, repeat information without question, be quiet, perform on demand, and, perhaps most destructive of all, see every other student as a competitor for a limited number of rewards.

As people fought to extend access to education for girls, the children of ex-slaves, new immigrants, and others, the economic system continued to structure the educational system into a sorting mechanism that was not based on merit or democratic values but on economic status. The broadest division is between students who can afford to go to private schools and those who are limited to public schools, which separates the children of the wealthy from the children of the rest of us. Within the public school system, differential funding and support separates those children who live in well-off white suburbs from children who live in poorer rural and urban areas (which are often communities of color). Within particular schools, teachers and counselors decide which students are college bound and which are not, based on each student's economic background, race, gender, and previous performance, pushing some students towards college and careers, others towards jobs, and others right out of school and into our criminal justice system.

Schools still primarily serve the purpose of sorting and preparing people for their future economic roles. Even today, most discussions of education bemoan graduating students' lack of preparation to take their place in the workforce. The solutions offered by critics are limited to demands for better access to a system that is fundamentally undemocratic and anti-youth, with a main goal that remains the production of good workers and quiescent citizens so that the ruling class can continue to accrue profits unchallenged.

Schools are able to meet this goal in two ways: by channeling students towards their future place in society and by feeding them (in authoritarian classrooms) misrepresentations of history and democracy. The result is a vast number of students driven out of school or turned off learning because they are bored, are discriminated against, feel unsafe in school, or simply find what is taught irrelevant to their lives. Other students get high marks as they move through the system, but often they become seriously misinformed, more individualistic, more isolated from the majority of students, and increasingly passive participants in their own education. They learn facts and perform well on tests but develop little ability to think critically about what they have learned, and their ability to care about others is diminished.

Many groups of parents, teachers, and community activists are trying to make their local schools more responsive to the needs of young people. At both national and local levels, people are organizing for increased and more equitable funding, more relevant and accurate curriculums, a more diverse and better trained teaching staff, and democratic school and classroom practices with a cooperative learning and social justice emphasis. All of these are essential components of an education that promotes social responsibility and community caring in our youth.

A Parent's Dilemma

As parents, we often face a dilemma when dealing with our son's education. We want to help him succeed in school because getting good grades and moving from grade to grade towards college is still the ticket to better paying jobs, more status, and higher standards of living. We want to challenge the schools to be more democratic, relevant, and effective as a learning environment. We want education to reinforce what we nurture at home — our son's ability to get out of the "Act Like a Man" Box, to think critically, to connect to nature, to care about others, and to participate in a democratic and cooperative group process.

I assume everyone wants our sons to succeed in getting an adequate education. But what if they do so at the expense of the girls in the class? What if they do so at the expense of the other boys in the class? What if they do so while learning to be competitive, arrogant about their own achievements, and dismissive of women's accomplishments? What if they get called on because teachers favor aggressive boys? What if they succeed because the funding for their schools is two or five or eight times greater than the funding for schools on the other side of town?

These are tough questions to answer. I don't think academic success is enough. For many of us, it is certainly an achievement to have nurtured our sons through school and towards college. But it's not an achievement if it's gained because of undemocratic, irrelevant, and oppressive classroom practices that need to be challenged. We have to question the value of a system in which so few can achieve — one which pressures young men who don't or can't succeed in traditional avenues to become more aggressive in illegal, antisocial, or simply abusive ways. Young men from poor and working-class backgrounds, and many young men of color, have to rely on school because an education may be the only way out of poverty and into a more secure financial future. But they face more discrimination in schools and, because of severe discrimination in the job market, they also have fewer job opportunities than their white, middle-class counterparts, even if they have comparable educational achievements. This double discrimination sets them up for failure in a system that makes the false promise that succeeding in school will allow them to get ahead.

Even our attempts to encourage and support individuals from these groups that face the greatest structural barriers can exacerbate the inequalities. Successful boys from these groups are held up as examples with which we berate those who haven't succeeded, accusing them of lacking motivation or inner discipline or other personal failings.

All young men need to know that our hierarchical society only allows a certain percentage of young men to be successful, condemning the rest to unemployment, lack of education, few skills, and fewer opportunities for success. Because there is great pressure on boys to succeed, they often blame themselves and feel stupid if they don't. If they succeed in school they will likely succumb to the values that schools foster — becoming competitive, isolated, and insensitive. Without an understanding of the purposes and limits of the educational system they will be unable to participate in struggles to change that system.

There is no contradiction between being successful at school and being a critical consumer of education. Even as our sons get an education, they can also be taught to understand the role that education plays in stratifying citizens by class, race, and gender. For example, my oldest son recently brought home information about tutoring programs for students taking the Scholastic Aptitude Test (SAT). We had a discussion about the contradiction of paying a tutor to increase your test score when the test is supposed to measure something called intelligence that theoretically can't be changed by academic preparation. We talked about how you could spend fifteen dollars on a book, forty dollars on a computer program, or hundreds of dollars on tutoring — all based on the assumption that you could increase your score by spending more. If this assumption is true, students who had more money to spend on preparation would have substantial advantages. We talked about other advantages that might contribute to one's score. We also talked about the test's biases against girls and people of color because of the cultural experience assumed in the questions that are asked and in the nature of the test itself.

My son took the test and did as well as he could because he knew what was at stake in terms of college admissions. But he also realized the limits of testing and IQ tests, and, because of our discussion, is less likely to be arrogant or condescending towards those who score less well or to feel inferior to those who scored higher.

Our sons can be taught to analyze classroom dynamics, their curriculum, and the teaching practices they are subjected to. In fact, to be advocates for them in the school system we need to do this kind of critical analysis ourselves. The first step might be to pose some questions for ourselves and our children to investigate.

Questions to ask ourselves and our children

In your school (or the school your son attends), who, by race and by gender, gets called upon in class?
How much does the curriculum reflect the social participation and achievements of women and of men and women of color?
Are students divided into tracks which direct some towards college, some towards vocational training, and which give up on others?
Which groups of students gets tracked where?
Is there sexual harassment? How does it affect the girls and the boys in the school?
Is there equal opportunity for girls in the science program, in sports, in technical classes?
How does the school compare to others in the area in terms of funding, buildings, equipment, extracurricular activities, and levels of violence?
Does the teaching in the classroom involve a variety of activities, pacing, materials, and approaches that address the different learning styles of young people?

SCHOOLS AND SOCIAL EQUITY

Besides economics, gender and race play a big role in who succeeds in the school system. It is well-documented that boys receive considerably more attention in the classroom than girls. They are called on more often, receive more useful feedback, and participate in a curriculum that gives them male role models and heroes to emulate.

Schools are often segregated by race because of housing patterns — which are determined by white flight, biased real estate lending policies, real estate covenants, urban development, and deindustrialization. To understand racial differences in educational opportunity we need to look at area-wide patterns of discrimination. In integrated schools, the school itself is the relevant unit, whereas for gender discrimination the school and classroom are the places to look.

If you conduct a little research into your local school and school system you will have a better idea how these issues play out in practice. Examine the textbooks your son brings home; notice the gender and race of the authors he is assigned to write and comment on. Observe the classroom and note who is called on and what kind of feedback girls and boys receive for their comments, observe who dominates the halls and the playground. Look at the discipline policies and how they affect young people by race. Notice the funding and other forms of corporate and community support — within the school district by school, and within the area by school district. What is the ratio of spending on pupils in different areas? Ask your son questions like those listed above to sharpen his awareness of gender and racial bias and to provide you with more information.

When we say that most classrooms favor boys we need to qualify that statement and say that not all boys are favored. Our attempts to correct gender-based discrimination can exacerbate racial and economic inequality if we presume that all boys have more opportunity for success. Helping girls succeed can become a process of giving white, middle- and upper-middle-class girls the same opportunities as white, middle- and upper-middle-class boys. This doesn't challenge the systematic lack of opportunity that is experienced by most girls, and by many boys who are not white and/or economically well-off.

On the other hand, many of the kinds of school and classroom changes that would make education more accessible to girls would also make it more accessible to the rest of the boys in the room. More democratic, egalitarian, and cooperative learning activities and a multicultural curriculum would open the door to boys as well as girls, and there is considerable evidence that classrooms with these values foster the critical thinking and creativity of all students.[1]

Working with other parents and concerned teachers, we might be able to improve the education our children receive. If our children are involved, we will probably be more successful in our efforts. Across the country, young people have been in the forefront of struggles to end tracking in schools, to eliminate sexual harassment, and to develop multicultural curriculums. Some of our sons will want to become involved in issues of educational practice and justice, but participating in challenges to the school system can be risky for poor and working-class students or students of color because these students don't have other options or other family resources to fall back on. Other family members may be dependent on them financially, may have sacrificed a great deal to allow them an education, or may simply be counting on their success to lift the entire family's standard of living. When these boys protest conditions in the schools, they are quickly labeled troublemakers and moved out of the school system. Because of their vulnerability and lack of credibility, young people can only challenge the school system with support from parents and teachers and other community members.

When the community works together, extensive improvements are possible. In the

United States, Milwaukee's public school system has been responsive to community and teacher activism. The "K-12 Teaching and Learning Initiative" was an effort by activists to improve teaching and learning in Milwaukee public schools. Its aim was "to offer all children an equitable, multicultural education; and teach all children to think deeply, critically and creatively" (see below).[2] The K-12 Initiative involved thousands of teachers and hundreds of parents and community people working in a wide variety of educational areas over several years. Part of the Initiative was a district-wide set of teacher-led councils that helped organize and sustain the community efforts by focusing on progressive, inclusive classroom practices that could be taught and replicated throughout the district. The Milwaukee Initiative was funded by a tiny percent of the school district budget but it had wide-reaching effects. It dramatically changed the curriculum and the classroom practice of many teachers and inspired both students and teachers to take a more active role in the education process.

K-12 Reform Goals
(FROM MOVING FORWARD WITH K-12)

1. Students will project anti-racist, anti-biased attitudes through their participation in a multilingual, multi-ethnic, culturally diverse curriculum.

2. Students will participate and gain knowledge in all the arts (visual arts, dance, theater, literature, music), developing personal vehicles for self-expression reinforced in an integrated curriculum.

3. Students will demonstrate positive attitudes towards life, living, and learning, through an understanding and respect of self and others.

4. Students will make responsible decisions, solve problems, and think critically.

5. Students will demonstrate responsible citizenship and an understanding of global interdependence.

6. Students will use technological resources capably, actively, and responsibly.

7. Students will think logically and abstractly, applying mathematical and scientific principles of inquiry to solve problems, create new solutions, and communicate new ideas and relationships to real world experiences.

8. Students will communicate knowledge, ideas, thoughts, feelings, concepts, opinions, and needs effectively and creatively, using varied modes of expression.

9. Students will learn strategies to cope with the challenges of daily living and will establish practices which promote health, fitness, and safety.

10. Students will set short and long-term goals, will develop an awareness of career opportunities, and will be motivated to actualize their potential.

Unfortunately, in the last couple of years the Initiative has fallen victim to budget cuts, decentralization within the school district, a narrow school-to-work focus, and lack of visionary leadership at the top administrative levels, but such efforts to change the educational system do show what we need to create schools that teach our sons how to get ahead *and* get together. Introducing democracy and cooperative practices to the classroom will also help this process.

DEMOCRACY IN THE CLASSROOM

Most schools are structured hierarchically without any student participation in determining policy, practices, or curriculum. Within individual classrooms the teacher has absolute authority and students are supposed to do as they are told without question. Students are routinely punished for questioning any aspect of classroom practice. We might say that most schools offer an anti-democratic curriculum while extolling the values of democratic participation.

There is a growing literature on the value and practice of democratic process in the classroom. Researchers have found that the more students are able to participate in the decisions that affect their school life, the less need there is for discipline, punishment, threats, intimidation, rewards, protection, and other tasks that take up so much of teachers' and administrators' time.

Beyond this convenience to educators, however, a democratic classroom practice has the potential to enable students to work together to address common problems and begin to challenge arbitrary authority in any situation they encounter. They begin to expect to participate in matters that affect them. Just as with democracy at home, democracy at school builds young people's self-confidence and skill to make decisions and challenge authority both by themselves and as a member of a larger group.

A question to ask yourself

What kind of adult citizens would we produce if our young people expected to have a voice in the ways things were run and had direct experience participating in democratic processes?

It is possible to introduce concepts of democracy into teaching at any age level. Even young children can be active participants in setting classroom schedules, rules, discipline, and curricular activities when given adult guidance.

Teachers who are already involving students in classroom decision-making need the support of parents. In addition, we can share information about such practices with other teachers, encouraging them to introduce democratic practices into their classroom. We can also be advocates for such learning with school principals and other administrators. When we are involved in efforts to improve our schools we can make sure this issue is included on the agenda.

Teachers and other youth workers can begin by talking about democracy with their students. As the group develops agreements about participation and inclusion, it creates a vision of the kind of community it would like to create. A simple set of agreements such as that described in Chapter 9 for family meetings can serve as a foundation.[3] Just as in the family, the classroom process of deciding what kind of learning and social environment will work best and what kind of agreements or guidelines will support that environment are more important than the specific agreements themselves. In creating a democratic process, the key questions are who has power and who is excluded? Whether in a school or in another youth-serving institution, shared power and full inclusion are essential for ending competition and encouraging cooperation, for ending abuse of power and developing leadership skills. This will benefit both girls and boys, those who have previously done well and those who have been struggling.

Teachers' abilities to introduce these changes are constrained by administrators, school boards, and state agencies. We would begin to produce more educational activists if we demystified these constraints and helped young people understand how different factors influenced their education. Even with the constraints, however, it is still possible to give students a substantial role in deciding what the course work will look like during the semester.

Questions to ask yourself

The question for us as adults entrusted with the care of young people is, are we willing to give up some of our control and allow young people into the process?

If you are a teacher or youth worker, how could you share some of your power with young people by introducing more democracy into your programs or classes?

How might you introduce concepts of democracy into the stories, books, or curriculum you share with young people?

What would you have to change in your attitudes or practice?

What do you fear about giving more power to the young people you work with?

What would young people gain?

How might these changes produce skilled and thoughtful citizens?

Where can you turn for more resources about and support for making these changes?

© Kathy Sloane

DEMOCRACY IN THE CURRICULUM

Democracy is a curriculum issue as well as an issue of school and classroom practice. Most of the policies, laws, and decisions made by leaders have been in response to the actions of ordinary people. However, when these movements are covered in traditional textbooks, they focus on the leadership of exceptional individuals. As historian Howard Zinn points out, there needs to be room in the literature and history/social studies curriculum for study and understanding of the history of social movements to balance the traditional focus on politicians, generals, and exceptional leaders.[4]

What our sons need is an understanding of the role that ordinary people play in social change. For example, it is fine to talk about Harriet Tubman, but there was a network of thousands of people of color and white people in the United States and Canada who made difficult choices to participate in the underground railroad. Cesar Chavez and Dolores Huerta led the United Farmworkers, but the success of the movement was the result of thousands of actions by Mexican American, Central American, Filipino, and other Asian farmworkers, with support from white urban allies. Nelson Mandela and the African National Congress were successful in overturning apartheid because of the efforts of people throughout South Africa as well as of their allies in Africa, Europe, and North America. In all of these movements young people played active and courageous roles. Remember the children of Soweto and the active role of young people in the struggle to end apartheid in

South Africa. Remember the teenagers who sat in at lunch counters, integrated schools, and participated in marches and demonstrations during the civil rights movement in the United States. Young people need to know that active citizens, including many young people, have played a vital role in the history of their country so they can see themselves as such actors. We also need to supplement the curriculum with information about the role of women and women's struggles in history and literature and with materials about non-European cultures and their contributions to Western societies.

Cooperative Classrooms

It is one thing to introduce democratic processes and curriculum into a traditional classroom, but we can go a step farther and develop cooperative classrooms. More and more teachers are realizing that the highly competitive, individualistic atmosphere in traditional classrooms actually discourages learning for many students and encourages a focus on test performance, individual achievement, and antisocial behavior such as cheating.

Cooperative classrooms are not new. Research and experimentation in developing them began in the nineteenth century. They have been effectively implemented at all levels of education from preschool through university. In 1984, David and Roger Johnson, the sociologists of education, presented an overview of the results from 122 studies on cooperative learning between 1924 and 1980, which showed that, in addition to higher achievement, cooperative learning produces increased retention, greater use of higher levels of reasoning, increased ability to understand different points of view, greater intrinsic motivation, more positive heterogeneous relationships, better attitudes toward school, higher self-esteem, greater social support, and greater collaborative skills.[5]

These results are not surprising. Humans have always succeeded by working together. Interdependent networks have been mainstays of village and urban life, farming and manufacturing efforts, and many family, school, and recreational activities. But do we teach cooperation in the classroom?

John Slavin, a researcher at Johns Hopkins University, noted the contrast between what is needed and what is provided in schools.

> *Why have human beings been so successful as a species? We're intelligent — but an intelligent man or woman alone in the jungle or forest would not survive long. What has really made humans such successful animals is our ability to apply our intelligence to cooperation with others to accomplish group goals....Since schools socialize children to assume adult roles, we might expect them to emphasize cooperative activity. Yet schools are among the institutions in our society least characterized by cooperative activity.[6]*

Cooperative classrooms, which encourage young people to work together and care about each other's understanding and success, are an essential component for raising our sons for courage, caring, and community. They can't settle for getting ahead or getting by; they must consider how to get together for learning. As Sarah Pirtle describes it, "Cooperative learning has the potential to help students develop a sense of global citizenship and to foster environmental ethics and a sense of mutual responsibility."[7]

© Kathy Sloane

WHAT DO COOPERATIVE CLASSROOMS LOOK LIKE?

De-emphasizing achievement and emphasizing learning is at the core of a cooperative classroom. Answers are less important than questions. Students and teacher work together to explore the world and develop their responses to it. A variety of activities draws on different learning styles; the curriculum is relevant to the lives of students and the community; and students are encouraged to work together in pairs or small groups because it builds a sense of community. Everyone is a teacher and everyone is a student.

Some boys (and some girls) are uncomfortable in such a classroom at first. They want to know the rules, the assignments, and exactly what they have to know for the test. For most of the boys and girls, however, it is a tremendous relief to be able to focus on learning about the world rather than finding the right answers. Even students who are disoriented at first can learn to relax and let go of the need to please the teacher.

In the vast majority of classrooms students are required to learn a large number of isolated facts and demonstrate their mastery of these facts on tests. They are seldom asked to think about what those facts mean or to have discussions that would make them think about how those facts fit together. In a recent study, John Goodlad, an educational researcher, decided to look at how much time was spent teaching understanding and critical thinking rather than information. After observing classrooms in several schools he concluded that "not even one percent of the instructional time in high school was devoted to discussion that requires some kind of response involving reasoning or perhaps an opinion from students."[8]

In contrast, a cooperative classroom involves young people in making choices about their education. With the teacher's guidance they have some choice (not complete freedom) about the books they want to read, the subjects they want to write about, their partners on team projects, and the topics of their research papers. In exchange, they take more responsibility for their work, for accomplishing their projects, and for evaluating their achievements. Education becomes an interactive process in which students are active participants. There is more emphasis on learning through simulations, re-creations, role plays, critical analysis, and understanding than on memorizing and display of information. The goal is for students to become independent readers, writers, and speakers and to become part of a community of educated and active citizens.

I think there is substantial evidence that boredom, restlessness, and disruptive behavior that many boys display in traditional classrooms is seldom due to their different learning style, to attention deficit disorder, or to other psychological causes. These behaviors are, in general (though not without exceptions), a result of classroom teaching styles and curriculum content that are inappropriate to the needs of young people and to the needs of a democratic society. Cooperative classroom practices bring these boys back into the learning process as co-participants with other students and with the teacher.

Cooperative classrooms work. More students learn more, more quickly. They develop better self-discipline, their curiosity expands, and they are better able to work together and solve problems creatively.[9] However, such classrooms do not produce citizens who accept authority and workers who do as they are told. It is a bold act for any adult to establish a cooperative learning environment for young people in an institution like the school system, which discourages it. Parents can be supporting the teachers who are developing such practices and encouraging other educators to do so. Parents and teachers together can create learning environments in which our sons can thrive, learn, and practice teamwork and caring for others. Whatever the subject, the setting, or the style of a particular teacher, a cooperative classroom can provide an opportunity for our sons to learn caring about community.

11 Sports

Participation in sports is important for many of our sons but one that does not necessarily enhance the values of caring and community we want to encourage. Competition and aggression yield rewards for a few, while many boys go unrewarded.

> *Sports can amuse and relieve; they can pleasantly distract. They can make us laugh and shout. They can inject vigorous dramatic tension into otherwise routine lives. And of course they can break down social barriers; they can give us common ground; they can help us belong. On a more personal level, athletic challenges can be used to develop courage, endurance, and will; they help us push to our limits, and even beyond; they are a means towards personal fulfillment. They offer opportunities for physical expression in a technological world that threatens to deprive us of our sense of bodily strength and well-being.[1]*

Besides providing for the positive opportunities outlined here by writer Ray Raphael, sport is also, perhaps, the preeminent arena where preteen and early adolescent boys establish a respected male identity for themselves in most communities. It is the area that many families turn to when they are concerned about their son's masculinity, strength, sociability, or "feminine" interests. It is the training or proving ground for a boy's maleness. Participating in sports is an integral part of most boys' childhoods, and few escape the pressure to be part of a team or to excel at sports. The pressure leads many boys to feel less than adequate athletically at some point in their childhood.

How seriously and thoroughly a boy becomes involved in sports depends on many factors including his own skills and abilities, parental and other pressure, the role of sports in his community, and the availability of alternative activities that provide for validation and expression — in boys' language, "respect."

Our sons make choices about how much to participate and which sports to participate in. These choices are heavily influenced by the way they perceive their future options and how those options are foreclosed by race and class. For example, white boys tend to gain more from participating in organized sports than boys of color. These gains arise from several factors.

- White boys, especially those from the middle and upper-middle class, have a broader range of sports to choose from, many of which are less dangerous (such as tennis and golf) than the sports that boys of color have to choose from.

• White boys gain more from contacts made in sports because they are already in networks of guys who have or will have access to resources.

• White boys tend to move on from organized sports earlier (when less damage has been done to their bodies), choosing educational and career opportunities that are more attractive and less physically punishing than careers in sports.

Boys can gain many positive values from participating in sports. They will be more physically fit and pay more attention to their health and bodies. They can develop a sense of teamwork, greater self-confidence. They can learn new skills and make new friends. However, because sports is a social institution set up to train boys to become men in specific ways, participating in sports without caution may expose boys to mistreatment or manipulation by coaches who are intent on winning at all costs, or who pressure boys to become men by playing with pain, by hurting others on the field, and by putting down girls and nonathletic boys. Our sons may even end up being exploited by schools and community groups that are more interested in winning records and fundraising than in the well-being of the athletes. Some of the negative values may be reinforced by spending a lot of time as a spectator of sports. I encourage you to pay close attention to the extent to which our boys absorb the values and pressures of the athletics they are participating in and the professional sports they are watching on TV.

The highly competitive atmosphere surrounding many athletic programs trains our sons to see other teams and other schools as rivals and can lead to name calling, teasing, taunting, using ethnic and racial epithets, and fighting. It also encourages boys to base their self-esteem on their ability to be winners on winning teams. This level of team chauvinism carries over into spectator sports to the point where some young men become depressed or even abusive if their home team loses, or euphoric if it wins.

The pressure and pain encourage drug use, even at junior- and senior-high levels. Drugs are used to mask the physical pain of playing when hurt, to mask the emotional toll of constant competition and loss, and to increase one's physical and emotional strength and stamina to ensure one is a better competitor (e.g., steroids and speed).

Spending a lot of time participating in sports or watching sports on TV tends to crowd out time for thoughtful discussion, art, music, and building and creating things. It can also crowd out, and sap motivation for, reading, studying, and academic interests.

Most organized sports encourage boys to be stoical. Our sons are taught that to cry or to show their feelings is to be vulnerable, and if they do, they may be attacked by coaches or teammates, or labeled weak, girlish, or just too emotional to come through for the team. The message is to suck it in and never let on that anything affects them personally. This is the same dynamic set up by the "Act Like a Man" Box in which athletes are contrasted to other boys (fags, wimps, and sissies) and girls.

A boy's success in sports is usually contingent on conforming to expectations of male bonding against gays and against women, sometimes to the extent of having to be violent to prove one is acceptable, i.e., heterosexual. Part of the motivation used to goad boys into greater performance is to use the threat of their being labeled girls if they don't succeed. Separation from any "female" quality is extolled. At the same time, in the male-only space of the locker room, where boys' bodies are constantly on display, a rigid level of homophobia has to be enforced so that hints of homosexuality do not bring the manhood of the athlete into question.

One effect of this anti-women and anti-gay atmosphere is to encourage boys to have girlfriends and to have sex with girls to prove that they are neither girls themselves or homosexual. This can lead to inability to relate to girls or, more seriously, dating violence, sexual assault, or group rape. The pressure on young men to prove they are heterosexual is not unique to athletics, but some sports programs encourage this kind of behavior.

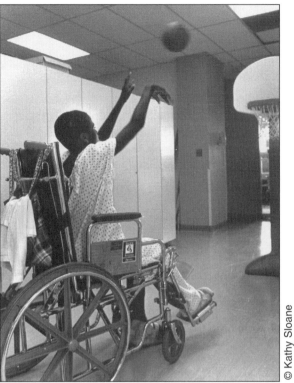

© Kathy Sloane

Sports also offer some promises that are attractive to boys. They offer proof of manhood (although this must be constantly demonstrated); acceptance by one's peers (at least as long as you perform well); safe, supported, and accessible extracurricular activities; and access to college and financial success. Some of these promised rewards are immediate, although often short-lived and not without costs. For example, for some boys participation in sports seems like a safer alternative than joining a gang for status and protection. Conversely, some sports such as hockey, boxing, football, and rugby become training for violence. Participation on some teams leads to violent competition, group violence against women or other men at parties, or fights between teammates.

Other rewards are only realized by the small minority of athletes who make it into professional sports. The total package of rewards, however unreachable, makes it hard for most boys to resist the allure of sports participation. Those who do resist, and even most of those who participate, end up feeling less than adequate because they can never live up to the images of success that are displayed constantly and in such detail by the media.

RESISTING THE PRESSURE

I want a society in which all children and adults get to play sports and other games with pleasure, without pressure, and with opportunities to learn about and take care of their bodies; develop skills, teamwork, and self-confidence; and learn more about themselves and others. This means valuing participation over winning, cooperation over competition, and public access over private control.

Every boy has to deal with the pressure to participate in and be successful at sports. On the one hand, we can help our sons find a response to this pressure that is based on realistic expectations and that works for them. At the same time, we can challenge the institutions of public and professional sports, particularly the corporate control and male dominance so prominent today. How do we help our sons make the best choices for themselves? First we must be clear about our own values.

Questions to ask yourself

What do you find valuable in sports?
What do you find of questionable value?
What do you think needs to be eliminated?
What sports did you participate in as a youth?
Which sports did you want to participate in?
Do you engage in sports now? If you do, what do you get from them?
Do you watch sports now? If you do, what do you like and what don't you like about the sports you watch?
What would you like to pass on to your sons about sports?

FAMILIES AND SPORTS

It is not necessary or inevitable that your son will participate in organized sports. It is a choice that you and your son make. Often a family will have to sacrifice time and money to buy equipment, transport athletes to and from practices and games, and watch games. Often it is the woman who does most of the support work to enable a son to participate, setting an example of the woman-behind-the-man syndrome that is so destructive of women's lives. In some families, support for a son's athletic participation can come at the expense of time and attention for a daughter's activities.

In addition, the relationship of many boys to their fathers is deeply contingent on their participation in sports. Most of the time I spent with my father while I was growing up centered around sports, either the games we listened to or watched together, the teams we rooted for, the games we attended, the sports we competed against each other in, and later the games I played that he watched.

If you are a woman you may have to acknowledge that sports is the main way your son will have a relationship with adult men, including his father. Acknowledging this does not mean you cannot challenge it. We can encourage men to widen their participation in boys' lives so that sports don't become the crucible through which a father's love is gained. If we are men we can examine our expectations for our sons, evaluate our leisure activities with them, and make sure we spend noncompetitive time with them.

Again, the challenge is to help boys think critically about the messages and training they are receiving. They should not have to participate in sports to gain our attention or recognition, to make us feel proud of them, or to increase the amount of time we spend with them. More important is to help them see that they do not have to participate in sports to prove they are men, to demonstrate they are one of the boys, or to give evidence of their heterosexuality.

I am not suggesting that you discourage or curtail your son's athletic participation. Boys are pressured to prove their masculinity in some arena or another. They will try to achieve their male credentials through professional accomplishment, high male-status activities such as driving fast or recklessly, accumulating money, consumption, violence, or high-risk activities such as drug use, if not in sports. Those with the most social privilege will have the most options regarding the arena in which to display their achievement.

The fact remains that many boys are judged by and judge themselves by their athletic ability. Boys who don't participate in sports are not allowed to opt out of their peer and parental evaluation system; they still get judged on the basis of their perceived worth in this area.

Pay attention to your son's athletic abilities and his sports interests. Look for opportunities to develop his skills in less competitive situations, and look for coaches who treat their athletes with respect and caring. Help your son find the competitive opportunities at school or in other sports programs but try not to be more aggressive or competitive than he is or to push him further than he wants to go. You can support your son's athletic success completely, without giving him the impression that it is his success you value about him. Because it can be difficult for boys to ignore the pressure to be aggressive, to tough it out, or to bond by putting down girls or other boys, encourage your son to talk about the pressure, to think about how he wants to respond. Support his choices regardless of your own disappointment or other feelings. You can share your observations, feelings, and thoughts about sports with him occasionally, but he needs a lot of time to think through for himself what role sports should have in his life.

One way you can diminish the hold that sports have on your sons' lives is to pay attention to, point out, and discuss specific incidents, comments, and responses you notice, whether they take place on the little league team or while watching an NBA game. Doing this can make a difference in how your son internalizes the messages he is receiving from organized sports. Over time you will find that, with your support, your son will become more insightful about the values he is being exposed to and better able to make choices that meet his own needs.

Questions to ask our sons

What did you think when the coach said, "Anyone who loses is a wimp"?

How do you feel when someone is carried off the football field on a stretcher?

How do you think he feels? How do you think his family feels?

Why do you think girls' sports aren't covered or supported as much as boys' sports are?

How important do you think it is to win?

What would help you learn more and develop your skills in playing on this team? What would make it more fun?

Have you been noticing all the athletes who have been involved in sexual assault or domestic violence cases recently? Why do you think that is?[2]

How healthy do you think it is to play when you're injured?

When message does that give to younger kids?

12 Ability and Disability

Sport is one area of life that challenges boys on issues of ability and disability. When we allow boys' culture to be so heavily focused on competitive sports — on how high they can jump, how fast they can run, how many baskets they can shoot, and how much pain they can endure — we give them little preparation for dealing with disability in their lives or in the lives of those around them.

The emphasis on highly competitive sports and the lack of resources devoted to other forms of physical activity dramatically affects the health, well-being, and self-confidence of most young people. Many boys, closed out of competition themselves, become spectators. Most boys will feel physically inadequate or not strong enough at some time in their childhood. Many will exercise to make themselves stronger. Some will turn their discomfort with their bodies into anger at others who have visible disabilities. They will judge themselves and each other by impossible standards of physical prowess.

When people are valued for what they can contribute rather than for who they are, a social system develops in which people who are "worth less" are vulnerable to violence. When some people are excluded from regular activities because of prejudice or lack of access, the message to others is that they are valued less and are inferior. In addition, people with disabilities are often the target of violence because they have less ability to take care of themselves. These dynamics have negative consequences for boys with or without disabilities.

Many boys feel the need to prove they are tough and so they verbally and physically attack boys with disabilities — or sexually assault girls with disabilities — because they can't defend or protect themselves. If we don't counter the social and media messages boys receive that say people with disabilities are acceptable targets for scorn, ridicule, and attack, we are encouraging their callousness, not their caring.

Because they have an increased vulnerability to violence, boys with disabilities need training in self-defense and.in child-abuse prevention. They also need support in speaking out on their own behalf and in asking for help when they need it. Because boys are often told that to ask for help is not okay, we ca reassure them that everyone needs help and it is appropriate to ask for it.

THE DOUBLE CHALLENGE OF DISABILITIES

Boys who are born with or develop physical disabilities face a double challenge. The external challenge is to deal with the teasing and put-downs by other guys, as well as the lack of physical access to full participation in society. The internal challenge is to learn to love their bodies, despite the social messages that tell them that their bodies are inferior and that physical independence is the mark of a real man.

The external challenges alone can be devastating for boys. They may face teasing and taunting from other kids or exclusion from male social circles and activities. They will probably have to deal with a series of adult teachers, counselors, and others who have little understanding of disability issues and who may seriously underestimate the mental abilities of a boy with a physical disability. Adults and other youth may feel so uncomfortable around a boy with a physical disability that they simply don't want him around and so do whatever they can to exclude him.

Disability rights' activists have challenged many traditional forms of segregation faced by people with disabilities, and in many places youth with disabilities are now mainstreamed in public schools. But there are still lots of ways that boys with disabilities are segregated socially and physically and they may have little access to extracurricular activities or to such basic things as exercise, games, and noncompetitive sports. These physical and institutional barriers are often accompanied by a lack of staff trained to work with children with disabilities.

Those of us with a son who has a disability face major battles. Rather than understanding that it is to the advantage of every boy to be exposed to and learn to value a wide range of physical abilities, many adults will resist your attempts to gain equal educational opportunity for your son and to counter the stereotypes and misinformation and abusive behavior he will face.

Our sons with physical disabilities also face a difficult inner challenge — maintaining their self-esteem and sense of pride even though they see few positive images of men who are not strong, independent, and physically able. If our sons have disabilities we can support their participation in a wide variety of activities and help them develop self-esteem separate from physical ability. We can also help them understand the ways they are systematically denied access to community resources as we advocate for and with them for equal access.

It is even more important for them than for other boys to understand the narrow range of male images presented by the "Act Like a Man" Box. We can provide them with information about men and women with disabilities who are public figures — for example, American president Franklin Delano Roosevelt and Helen Keller — though we may need to counter false information about these people. For example, although F.D.R. was in a wheelchair for most of his life after a case of childhood polio, he tried to hide his disability as much as possible and many people think that he was not disabled. Even recently there was a controversy over whether a statue of Roosevelt in Washington, DC, should show him in a wheelchair. Helen Keller was a lifetime human rights activist, socialist, and community organizer. However, most of the information about her more radical activities is excluded from public accounts of her life, which usually stress her disability and her relationship to her teacher, Anne Sullivan. It may be hard for you to find accounts of people with disabilities that give an honest description of their disabilities and a comprehensive representation of their life, though there are beginning to be more positive images not only of people with disabilities, but of the disability rights movements and its activists.

Boys with mental disabilities face similar challenges to those with physical disabilities. In addition, however, they often face teachers and classrooms ill-prepared to adapt the curriculum and classroom practice to their needs. Particularly in classrooms where the emphasis is on being first with the right answer and getting the highest score, supporting the needs of children with mental disabilities can be a challenge for a teacher. Cooperative classrooms, with their emphasis on learning as a process and on the interaction between students, offer a much more supportive environment for students with disabilities and are generally more effective for integrating children with a variety of mental and physical needs. Children with mental disabilities cannot always be in regular classrooms full time, but they have the right to an effective education and to be included in whatever classroom and extracurricular programs they are capable of participating in.

Boys with physical and mental disabilities need to understand how their access is limited by institutional practices that are not personal. They personally can educate other people, who have been fed stereotypes and misinformation about disabilities from an early age, and can defend themselves from abuse. More positively, they can connect with other people with disabilities and their allies to form support and resource networks and to challenge institutional practices that limit their access.

Our disabled sons also need information about the long history of struggle for disability rights — how people have fought and won major battles, gaining significant new rights in the last couple of decades. This is information that those without disabilities also need to have. Some schools include units on disability in multicultural, human rights, or anti-bias curricula. This should be standard practice throughout the country. Children who have contact with people with disabilities and who have

© Kathy Sloane

accurate information about these issues are easily able to integrate children with disabilities into classroom and social activities. These experiences actually provide all boys with much needed breathing room from the "Act Like a Man" Box's suffocating expectations that boys be physically fit, strong, tough, and independent. They also help to reduce verbal, physical, and sexual assault against those who have disabilities. They allow children with disabilities to take their rightful place as equal participants in the classroom and call on other students to stand with them, not out of sympathy or condescension, but with respect and a concern for justice.

As parents and teachers we can advocate for the inclusion of all our children, particularly those with special needs. You may find it difficult to advocate effectively for boys with special needs because of your own lack of knowledge, inexperience, or misconceptions about the needs of your child. Many parents, especially men, expect that their son will play little league baseball, go out for hockey, tennis, or football, and shoot hoops with them. If your son has a disability, you may have to deal with a feeling of profound disappointment. If your son was born with a disability you may blame yourself. Your disappointment and sense of betrayal may distance you from our son and possibly from the rest of the family. Even if you don't withdraw, it may be difficult to value your son fully because his body doesn't match your physical standards. Unless you are well-informed, you may wonder if he can succeed at all if he has a physical or mental disability. You also face sometimes daunting economic and physical demands for caring for boys with disabilities. There is little social support for doing so. But you don't have to do it all alone — you can't.

Reach out and get support. Your primary source of support will probably be other parents because they understand best how hard it is to raise children with disabilities in a society that doesn't support or value them. Other parents can share experiences dealing with various community institutions such as schools, hospitals, and government agencies. They can introduce you to local services that are available. Many of these families will have already dealt with some of the complex interactions that occur between parents, between parents and children, and between siblings when there is a child with disabilities in a family. Some of the books listed in the Resources section can also provide information on these issues.

Most areas of the country have support networks for the parents of children with disabilities. You can contact groups in your area through the Internet or through one of the agencies which provide services and advocacy for families with special needs in your area. Children with disabilities have many rights that you may not be aware of. Only by reaching out for support, information, and resources will you be an effective advocate for your son.

Including boys with disabilities into our community should not be the sole responsibility of their parents, or of specialists. If your own children do not have special needs it may be harder for you to see that we all have a responsibility for building an inclusive community where each person is cared for and supported. Each of us is dependent on others. This is most visible when we are a baby, when we are ill, perhaps when we are older, and for some of us who have disabilities. But no one is completely self-contained. Because of this we can try to build a caring network of family, friends, and community in which sometimes we are cared for and sometimes we care for others. In such a community, all members are valued for their uniqueness and intrinsic worth, not for their competitive edge, their muscles, their speed, or a particular kind of intelligence.

13 Violence

BETWEEN GUYS: GIVING IT AND TAKING IT

Our society promotes not only competition but also violence. Just as many of us still assume that boys are naturally aggressive and competitive, we may assume that they are naturally violent. We are so used to associating violence with boys that we may be overly quick to attribute their behavior to violent tendencies.

In general, young boys are neither violent nor aggressive. Labeling them as such reinforces expectations that "boys will be boys." When we label them, we either do not take their actions seriously or we come down on them harshly and begin to anticipate that they will act out abusively towards others.

Most young children (girls or boys), when they feel exuberant, will bump each other, grab things, push, and shove. They have a low tolerance for frustration and sometimes strike out when blocked. We need to give structure to children's play at times so that it is safe for them, and we need to give them tools for working out problems. However, if we quickly assume that our son or his playmate is violent, we will punish him rather than help him. In fact, punishment often rewards the behavior in question with attention (even if it's negative attention), which means it's more likely to be repeated in the future.

When boys are aggressive towards others we need to remember that such behavior is not unchangeable. There are many examples of adolescent and even adult men deciding to stop being abusive to others — making major changes in their lives. These examples suggest that the violent behavior of males is neither biologically determined nor unalterable. In fact, if violence was natural behavior it would not take so many years of training to turn boys into men who are controlling and abusive.

The false social message that boys are naturally violent can be particularly hard to disavow if our sons are African American or Latino. We receive such an overpowering cultural message that these boys are or will become violent that we may feel that we need to curb their behavior very aggressively. We may also fear for their safety if they are too exuberant or confident in situations of danger because often white people and cops of any color believe if a young man of color is confident, he has an "attitude" and is dangerous.

Some parents (often women) want their sons to stay safe at all costs. Others (often

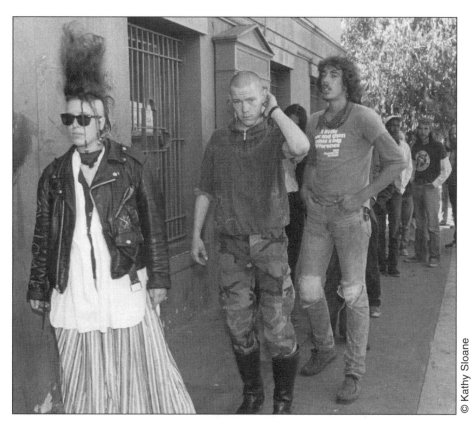

© Kathy Sloane

men) want them to maintain their honor at all costs. Neither is possible or desirable all the time. Unfortunately, in this society, boys have to constantly negotiate a balance between the two, depending upon the circumstances they face and the options they perceive. Because of our society's emphasis on being tough and not backing down, it can appear to boys that the safer you play it, the less self-respect you must have. You either challenge superior force or greater authority, or you feel as if you've failed to take care of business. Even if boys understand that safety and self-respect are not connected so simply, they still have to decide how to respond to threat, put-down, challenge, and abuse of authority.

Our sons will need to make decisions about how much they should be themselves in many different situations. The most important lesson we can teach them is to think before they act, to ask themselves, "What's going on here? How can I stay safe *and* maintain my integrity?"

Part of the problem is that we still often couch a boy's choice in a simplistic either/or framework — either court danger or play it safe. There are other ways to fight for ourselves and what we believe in than to clash head on with someone who has more power or authority. Only when we teach our sons to think strategically about what their options are will they be better able to take care of themselves.

For example, when a boy is threatened by another kid in elementary school he has to decide how to avoid a fight without getting picked on. He has a lot of possible strategies.

- He can stall until the bell rings.
- He can leave.
- He can joke about it and try to divert attention from the confrontation.
- He can call on other students to help him.
- He can look for an adult to intervene.
- He can try to settle things with words.
- He can try to find some common ground to work out a compromise.

Depending on his situation, any of these might be workable strategies.

If a teen male is disrespected by a teacher he also has to make decisions about how to respond. Just because he backs down does not mean he can't pursue the matter with his parents or with an administrator, by organizing other students, by writing a letter to the teacher asking for a parent/teacher/student conference, or by getting a transfer out of that class. Although he might decide to back down in a one-on-one conflict with that teacher, each of these responses gives the young man a sense of his self-respect as well as helping him to learn how to take care of himself in situations where he doesn't have a lot of power.

Aggressive actions — the tendency for boys to want to fight it out to "settle" things — need to be channeled into more productive responses. At the same time, natural energy and exuberance need to be encouraged and directed in appropriate directions. We should not panic over particular actions. One slap does not mean our son is a bully or will grow up to be violent. It's crucial to understand that our sons are in an ongoing, long-term development process and we need to remain patient. We won't see change overnight, but we should expect boys to develop more control over their behavior and awareness of the effects of their actions as they grow up. They should be developing into peacemakers, with increased skill to work out problems without violence. There are excellent programs in different parts of the country that teach children to be peace agents and conflict resolvers, and some of the books listed in the Resources section describe how our children can learn to be peacemakers. These are abilities every boy needs.

A peacemaker is not necessarily a pacifist. I am not a pacifist, for example, because I believe that violence, although largely avoidable in interpersonal situations, is sometimes necessary in self-defense and in liberation struggles. I don't think we can tell young men simply to turn the other cheek when the threat on the street is immediate and sometimes life-threatening. This would be a form of suicide for some of them.

Although few boys are voluntarily aggressive, most feel that they have to respond to aggression with force. Those who end up using violence talk about defending themselves, their reputations, their family, their respect, their turf, their homeboys. It becomes very tricky for parents who want to support a young man's right to defend himself without unintentionally promoting violence. This is particularly true in a world that justifies armed aggression in the defense of national interests, and where men routinely justify hitting their partners as a case of self-defense.

What we need to teach our sons to ask is, "When is 'self-defense' really an attack?" And "What is worth defending?" Because young men's self-esteem is often so fragile, and they are so acutely overprepared for affront, trivial incidents are perceived as attacks. This is partly because they are sitting on so many unexpressed feelings and so much anger that any frustration can ignite the fuse, and the anger quickly explodes into violence.

For too many of our sons, all they have is their self-respect. They are denied the jobs, skills, education, and training that would allow them to gain respect by this society's standards. It is not useful to tell them to let go of their self-respect and walk away from challenge. They cannot afford to give up all that they feel they have left. But we can talk with them about how they got to the point that all they had to protect was their self-respect.

Questions to ask our sons

How have different men, especially men from your cultural background, gained respect?
What do we respect them for?
Did they use force to get it?
What kind of a social system is it that doesn't automatically show respect for people?
Are you collaborating with that system by disrespecting others or by using force to gain self-respect?

STOPPING THE CYCLE OF VIOLENCE

I believe that our long-term strategy must be to organize with young men to challenge the injustice that leaves them with self-respect as their only claim to self-worth in a society that wants to throw them away or lock them up. In the short-term, we can teach them how to defuse these situations by expressing their feelings constructively, using alternative problem-solving skills and anger-management skills. We can also help our sons sort out what is worth defending.

When I work with groups of adolescent boys I explain how we create a cycle of violence. When violence is done to us, we carry around pain, anger, and frustration, and we often direct those feelings at people with less strength or power than we have — little kids, younger brothers and sisters, and girlfriends. I ask the boys a series of questions about whether they've ever been called names or yelled at, put down, threatened, intimidated, or hit by someone less physically strong than they. As we discuss why they were abusive, I can see them make the connection between being taught to "Act Like a Man" and to defend themselves and their inability to get out of the Box — which means they end up hurting others. This realization yields significant motivation for boys to get out of the Box, at least in those times when no one is attacking them.

Boys who step out of the Box, even a little, generally like it out there. There's more room to move around; it feels good. It is not hard to convince boys that it is better to be out of the Box. But it is hard for them to decide that it is safe enough for them to stay out for a while. Boys may be reluctant to let go of aggression because they have been taught by adults that if they are not aggressive they will not survive. In fact, many of us carry the following assumptions about the world.

- The world is a dangerous place.
- If you are not careful people will take advantage of you.
- If you don't stick up for yourself with force, you will be challenged again and again until you do.
- You can never let your guard down.
- Once you are branded a wimp you will gain a reputation as one and be victimized for ever. Therefore you have to defend yourself with force.

Questions to ask yourself

Are there any of these assumptions that you believe?
How do they influence what you teach your son?
What would change about your parenting if you adopted less defensive assumptions about the world such as the following?

- The world is occasionally a dangerous place but often it is not.
- If you keep your guard up people can't be close to you.
- It is possible to solve most problems without force.
- Every boy and many men are called wimps at some time in their lives. It is not the end of the world.
- Human development is based on people cooperating.

I think it is useful and important for boys and girls to learn self-defense skills, especially in classes where emphasis is placed on conflict resolution. Having these skills increases their self-esteem, provides alternatives to violence, and gives them courage and confidence to intervene when someone else is being attacked. Self-defense skills make young people less likely to be victimized.

These skills are also useful for adults to have. Learning some form of self-defense can help us resolve our own past victimization and make us more able to support our children. However, we still need to let them know that self-defense skills do not prevent violence. Running away is an important survival tactic. Sometimes being scared is the smart thing to be. There is nothing dishonorable in avoiding violence; often it takes more courage than fighting. With rare exceptions, the boys who get killed are not the ones who were trying to avoid violence, but the ones who were defending themselves using violence. Those who carry guns to defend their reputation, who refuse to back down or run away, play into the hands of the most aggressive. Even winning a fight does not prevent retaliation.

Some questions to ask yourself

If your son comes home from school scared that other guys are going
to beat him up, how would you feel?
How could you support him?
What could you do?
What support would you need?
If your son comes home from school having been in a fight,
how would you feel?
How could you support him?
What support would you need?
If your son comes home from school having been bullied,
how would you feel?
How could you support him?
What could you do?
What support would you need?
Do you think that boys need to fight to learn to take care of themselves?
Why or why not?
Who is your son most likely to get into a fight with
in your neighborhood?
If your son comes home from school having been in a fight to
protect someone else,
how would you feel?
How could you support him?
What kind of self-defense or problem-solving alternatives can you help your
son develop so that he is prepared for physical and verbal
confrontation from other guys?
How will you talk with him about the costs of violence?

VIOLENCE PREVENTION

Our sons are caught smack in the middle of the immediate, everyday reality of violence in America. We are their best allies when we can be fully present for them and help figure out what will work for them without judgment, second-guessing, or unasked-for advice, criticism, or blame.

We can also remind ourselves that although it is necessary to help them solve the problem of dealing with violence, this does not address the root of the violence problem. Very often I hear something that verges on nostalgia about the old days in which two boys could duke it out without worrying that one of them would pull a gun. This is a long-standing nostalgia. In *Harper's* in 1935, George Leighton and Richard Hellman wrote about a migratory worker "who has traveled back and forth across the country for 20 years [who] has described the comparatively recent appearance of firearms among the young bums." They quote him as saying, "In my day 'gats were almost unheard of...It's different now...you find high school kids armed."[1]

I don't want to underestimate the physical danger to our sons, especially those in inner-city areas. The escalation of violence, including the pervasive presence of guns, is real and we need to help our sons deal with the danger. But the root of the problem is not the guns but the social causes of violence, including poverty, inadequate schools, and the competitive, aggressive male thinking that fuels the fights.

It is not innocent, natural, inevitable, or trivial when two young boys duke it out because they know no other way to relate to each other, solve problems, or establish their self-esteem. They may not kill each other, but they are in training to live in the "Act Like a Man" Box and fill their slot in the economic pyramid just as surely and just as devastatingly as two adolescent men fighting it out with guns and gangs.

PROGRAMS FOR VIOLENCE PREVENTION

We can to a certain extent influence our son to become less likely to use violence for self-defense. But we can't change his peer culture unless we are working with boys in groups, helping them redefine peer norms and changing peer pressure into peer support. Even working with groups of boys is of limited effectiveness in a society where violence justified in the name of self-defense is the norm.

Many programs for boys in our schools and youth facilities begin and end with teaching boys anger management skills. Sometimes in our families we do the same thing. We are worried about the anger and want to make it less dangerous. This approach is rarely effective because boys do not adopt skills if they have no motivation for using them and no context for understanding the need for them.

There are five essential components that must be included in any programs dealing with young men's anger and violence.

1) Safety. Young men must be in a safe enough space that they can talk about what is happening in their life and what they are feeling, and where they can listen to what others are saying. Without safety the walls of the Box cannot come down and no change is possible.

2) A social framework for understanding their circumstances. The power chart and economic pyramid presented earlier in the book are models of one such framework. Boys need to be able to understand their individual situation within the context of the world around them.

3) An understanding of male role training. Boys particularly need to be aware of the pressures to be in the Box, in control, and abusive. They need to understand how the pressure they feel to be in control and abusive is meant to prepare them for the jobs of containment and enforcement they will fill in our society.

4) Motivation. They need to have paid some costs, suffered some pain, lost enough so that they have motivation to change. Most boys quickly come to

realize they have already paid more than enough to give them motivation if they are given a chance to reflect on what's happened to them and those around them.

5) New skills. The skills are important. If we don't give them new skills, we leave guys with the motivation and knowledge to change but without the ability to implement new choices. However, skills without safety, a framework, an understanding of male socialization, and personal motivation do not often produce a permanent change in behavior regardless of the initial level of commitment, enthusiasm, or desperation.

The "Young Men's Work" curriculum we developed at the Oakland Men's Project is an example of how these five components can create an effective program that allows young men to stop their violence, identify the problems they and their community face, and become part of the solution to those problems. On an individual level it has led to young men deciding to stop getting into fights, to stop abusing their girlfriends, and to challenge their peers when they put down women. On another level we have seen young men decide to support each other's attempts to get out of the Box, become less violent, and take leadership as peer conflict mediators. They have used the concepts in the curriculum to change peer pressure to peer support, building trust and intimacy with each other. Sometimes young men will decide to work with young women to make changes in their school or community.

When they are given alternatives, few boys want to be violent. Most have paid the costs and are looking for alternatives. If we get clear about our own assumptions and help our sons develop a wider range of choices when confronted with problems, they will not only be able to avoid most violence but will also be able to work with us to address the social roots of violence based on injustice and inequality.

GUNS

I cannot conclude a discussion of violence without a discussion of guns. Particularly in the United States, guns have become the symbol of male violence. Gunfire is expected to exceed automobile accidents as the leading cause of traumatic death in the United States in the next five years.[2]

I think some aspects of this situation are very clear:
- The presence of guns makes a situation unsafe.
- The purpose of most guns is to kill people.
- Some people are making a lot of money from the manufacture and sale of guns.
- Guns do not solve problems.

Until we eliminate violence we have to contend with the fact that over half of all American households have at least one gun. Adolescent boys are more likely to die from gunshot wounds than from all other causes combined. How can we deal with guns and violence so that our sons will survive their youth and not become violent as adults?

TOY GUNS

Boys are not naturally attracted to guns, but in a society in which they see so many images of men using guns to be powerful, they will naturally be attracted to and feel powerful using guns. This is a socialization process, and we can intervene to stop the process. For example, in my family's house we have always had a no guns/no shooting policy. There were brief times when our sons made guns out of Lego or sticks, but those were short-lived. From an early age we talked about guns and why we didn't want them around our house. This policy was not hard for our children to understand. Although occasionally they felt pulled to the glamor of guns, they had information about what guns do to people that helped them resist that attraction. At one point, when our youngest son was strongly pulled to make toy guns and shoot people, we told him he could turn it into a healing ray and go around and heal people. For a few days he went around asking people what was wrong with them and then healing all the physical problems they had. Soon after that he lost interest in guns.

Gun play not only desensitizes boys to violence and pain, but it sets them up as lone heroes against those who are delineated as the enemy — Indians, robbers, aliens, or people from other countries. It devalues difference and turns it into an excuse for attack. There is no way to play guns cooperatively. There is no way to play guns without diminishing one's capacity for empathy.

Boys need help to think about what they are doing, and they need tools for resisting peer and cultural pressure to be violent. Discussions and no-gun policies in the family provide them with these.

Is your son playing video games that involve constant shooting, or is he watching TV programs that contain great amounts of violence? If he is, then banning guns will not make much sense to him, nor will it have much effect. A no-guns policy must be consistent with the other activities your son engages in. Wanting to play with guns is a natural outgrowth of the glamorization of real violence. If we deglamorize violence, most boys will not find toy guns compelling.

A ban on guns is less important than exposure to alternative activities, an understanding of the use of guns, and cooperative thinking and problem-solving skills. In general, we want to keep the number of bans minimal, and to encourage our sons to consider the implications of their actions.

Questions to ask yourself

What kind of atmosphere do you want to create in your house?

Does the presence of toy guns support your efforts?

What kinds of activities does your son engage in that extol violence?

What limits do you want to set on these activities?

How do you want to talk with your son about the uses of guns
and the effects of violence?

When are you going to have that discussion?

REAL GUNS

Some of us have guns in our homes. We may not even know it, because the gun may belong to another member of our family who has not told us about it. Guns are dangerous — over 5,000 children under the age of nineteen die annually from firearm injuries in the United States. A gun in the home is 43 times more likely to kill a member of the household than to kill an intruder.[3] Even though we believe we'll only use a gun in self-defense, incident after incident shows that guns obtained for self-defense are involved in accidental killings, suicides, or spontaneous but intentional shootings. One of those guns might be the one in your house. There are some simple steps you can take to make a gun less likely to result in someone's death.

- Get rid of it safely.
- If you must have a gun, know how to use it.
- Keep it locked up.
- Make sure it has a trigger lock and loading indicator.
- Talk with your children about gun safety.

Even if you don't possess a gun, your children may well be exposed to guns at school, at a friend's house, or in the neighborhood. Many of our sons have seen a gun, handled one, or heard a gunshot. Many boys know how to procure a gun and most know someone who has one, possibly at school. With guns so prevalent, it is not surprising that young people are often fearful of gun violence.

The only safe thing to do in the presence of a gun is to leave. No matter how well-trained someone is, or how convinced that the gun is not loaded, in the heat of the moment guns tend to get used and people tend to get injured or killed. You cannot count on reasoning with a man who has a gun in his hand.

However, it might not be easy for a boy to walk away. He might be bullied or teased into staying. He might want to believe that it's not really loaded, especially if he finds it fascinating. He may be just too surprised to know what to do if he hasn't been challenged to think about it ahead of time.

Questions to ask your son

What would you do if a friend pulled out a gun?
What would you do if someone at school had a gun?
What would you do if you saw two people arguing on the street
and one pulled a gun?
What would you do if you heard gunshots outside the house?

For some of us these scenarios are all too real, maybe too real for us to talk about directly and easily. For others of us they may sound remote, unlikely. But there are over 50 million handguns in the United States, and 24,000 people, many of them boys and young men, are killed with them every year.[4]

If your partner has a gun, share with him or her information about the dangers guns pose to our children. Make sure the gun is properly locked away. Realize that regardless of the owner's original intent, in a family fight a gun can get pulled out and used. In many jurisdictions people convicted of domestic violence are prohibited from possessing a gun as a condition of probation because of the increased risk of violence in those situations (unfortunately this prohibition is not yet strongly enforced). In addition, suicide attempts with a gun are 91 percent successful and a home with a gun is five times more likely to be the scene of a suicide.[5] The use of alcohol or other drugs or the presence of family members prone to depression or mental illness are also risk factors that make it more likely death by gunshot will occur in a household with a gun.

All of that being said — you can't disarm your sons or partners if they want to have a gun. You can make the situation safer for yourself and those around you by providing them with accurate information about the danger of guns. You can challenge them to think about the consequences of gun ownership for them and for you. And you can set limits on the use and presence of guns around the house. Our sons will be less fascinated by guns and less tempted to use them when they are able to discuss the fears they have of being attacked, and when they can reflect on the dangers that possession of a gun imposes on everyone in the community.

We cannot stop the violence without organized social struggle to address its root causes. But eliminating easy access to guns and deglamorizing violence in our families will make it much safer for our sons and for the rest of us.

14 Drugs

Besides guns and violence, our sons will also be exposed to drugs. This is another issue where we must wade through an abundance of information and misinformation and decide on useful ways to approach the topic with the young men we care about.

Parents have long been concerned about drug use among young people. Generally, the public policy approach has been to blame young people for using drugs against adult advice and to punish them for doing so. Drugs, however, are an adult problem. Adults, particularly those in large legal corporations and large illegal organizations, grow, distribute, and profit from drugs. The two most deadly drugs, tobacco and alcohol, are officially sanctioned, legal, and part of the corporate economic system.

Because of the large-scale and legal production, distribution, and marketing of drugs, adults use drugs in tremendous quantities. In many of our families, drugs contribute to self-destructive behavior, domestic violence, inadequate parenting, and other problems. Young people see these drugs being used by adults who are admonishing them to just say no to drugs. It is not surprising that such simple homilies are generally ignored and dismissed as hypocrisy.

Drug use among young people is a symptom of several deep-seated social problems, not least of which is the pressure on boys to have money, to gain status, and to take risks to prove their masculinity. Drug use and involvement in the drug business are two ways for young men to gain money and status and to show they are willing to take risks — that they are real men. Drug use is also a way to numb the pain of not achieving any of these symbols of acceptance — to numb the pain of knowing that you won't make it.

Boys and young men also use drugs in other ways. When anger is too strong, excitement too great, or grief too unbearable, drugs provide a way to cover over and dampen those feelings so that they don't slip out of the "Act Like a Man" Box and appear vulnerable. Young men use drugs to lower their inhibitions to be violent towards other guys or towards women as well as to lower their inhibitions in social situations such as parties. Drugs are also used by young athletes to mask pain, to be able to play while injured, and to heighten performance. Drugs allow boys to feel less compunction or remorse about the use of violence. Drugs provide a cover, an excuse: "I didn't know what I was doing." Drugs are also a means of social control. When enough drugs are poured into a community they

© Kathy Sloane

deaden people, disrupt family life, and distract people from fighting against social injustice. Finally, drugs, like TV and other distractions, provide a temporary sense of pleasure and a release from the deadening effect of school, work, consumerism, personal abuse, and alienation many people feel today.

Especially for boys, for whom feelings are scary and socially taboo, being high permits both a deadening of the feelings and an excuse for having them. More intense expression of feelings is permitted when you are high, even if that is not actually a side effect of the drug, and this in itself is a powerful incentive for using it.

TALKING ABOUT DRUGS

All young people are exposed to drugs and most boys use them during their teen years. It is our sons' choice to use or not use drugs, but we can give them information and help them make that choice. We can give them information about the effects of using specific drugs as well as about the socioeconomic system that produces, distributes, and profits from them. (In some of our neighborhoods, both rich and poor, pushing drugs is an attractive financial option. This is a different issue than the use of drugs.)

Our sons need information about how the war on drugs is being used to wage a war on many of our communities. In particular, a very large police presence in most African American and Latino neighborhoods places the residents under constant and intense surveillance and leads to false or unjustified arrests, police brutality and other civil rights violations, and racially biased rates of arrests, prosecutions, and convictions in the criminal justice system.

Our sons need information on drugs themselves. They need to know what happens to their body when they use different drugs. What has happened to others around them? How are drugs connected to violence in their community and in communities across the country? On a more personal level, they need help figuring out what they are comfortable doing and what they are pressured to participate in. We can help them learn to ask these questions and others, and can support them as they find out the answers.

It may be difficult for us to put aside our own strong feelings about drug use so that we can talk with our sons about the realities they face. It might help to talk with friends about these issues first to clarify our own thoughts.

Questions to ask yourself

What drugs, if any, have you used?

Which, if any, do you use currently?

Why do you use them?

What are the dangers to you? What are the rewards?

What would you like to change about your use of drugs, if anything?

Are you well informed about the availability of drugs in your son's environment?

How might you find out more?

What is the one most important thing you want to convey to your

son about drug use?

How could you present that information to him so that he could best

hear it from you?

It may be useful to ask other parents and teachers for more information about what is happening in our community, but we should listen to them with a critical ear. Horror stories of lives ruined by drugs circulate widely and quickly, but their number is way out of proportion to actual incidents. We may be able to temper some of the aggressive anti-youth comments and misinformation we hear, or to challenge policies that are punitive or inappropriate. In any case, raising the issues with adults will balance the accounts we hear from young people and will allow us to find out what attitudes and beliefs young people face from other adults. This information can help us be better allies to young people.

As parents, our knowledge of particular drugs is probably not current and accurate. Scientists are constantly revising our knowledge about the effects of various drugs. It is difficult to keep up with the most recent information, and because we are bombarded with so much overdramatized and misleading information about drugs, we may find we're better equipped to warn our sons against using drugs at all, than we are to talk with them accurately about the effects of particular ones.

We also spend far too much time focused on less lethal drugs and not enough time providing information about tobacco and alcohol, the first and second most lethal drugs respectively in terms of the number of deaths and the amount of damage attributed to them. This is not to say we shouldn't worry about other drug use. Heroin, cocaine, amphetamines, and a host of designer drugs can be dangerous, are available in most schools and neighborhoods, and are tried by many of our sons.

Questions to ask your son

What drugs are available in his network of friends and at school?

What do they cost?

Who uses them?

What drugs has he been offered?

What drugs has he used?

What does he think the effects are on the people who use them?

Are there drugs at the parties he attends?

You should not be asking for this information so you can run to the school authorities but because you want to understand the environment your son is in. It is fine to express your concerns about particular drugs, but if you are accusatory or fearful your son will probably withhold information from you to protect himself or to protect you.

WHAT IF YOUR SON IS USING DRUGS?

If your son is using any drug heavily, he is not likely to tell you (he may well be in denial about it), but you will probably see evidence of his use and of its effect on his activities. If your son is dependent on drugs, you will need to get outside support for yourself to figure out how to respond and how to get him help. Remember that evidence your son is using drugs is not evidence that his life is disrupted by them. Don't take it lightly, but don't panic either.

It is not easy to decide how to respond to someone who is dependent on drugs, regardless of their age. With our children it is much more difficult because our emotional ties are so strong. These ties may lead us to deny or minimize our son's drug use, or to overreact.

We also have to take into consideration the effect of our son's drug use on other members of the family. We cannot support our sons at the expense of ourselves or other children. Young drug addicts are just as dangerous and out of control as adult addicts. We need professional guidance and peer support for handling a son who is addicted; uncritical support can become codependency.

Young men generally use drugs because they are available and there is pressure from other guys to experiment with them. Therefore, we can help our sons make good decisions about drug use by supporting their efforts to get out of the "Act Like a Man" Box and deal competently with peer pressure.

Young men also use drugs to make them less inhibited about using violence. This is a dangerous phenomenon because it allows young men to be more violent, and to be more vulnerable to peer pressure to be violent, than they would otherwise be. It may help to talk with them about why they are using drugs and what effect the drug has on their ability to avoid violence. However, if they are in a peer culture in which drugs are used to promote group solidarity and to encourage violence, we may have little influence.

Young men also learn from peer culture and from the media that it is okay to use drugs to lower a woman's inhibitions to having sex. This is a form of manipulation and abuse that is not acceptable, and young men need to know that it is rape to have sex without consent. A person cannot legally consent if they are intoxicated or high. Raising our sons to expect to have mutually consensual sexual relationships is discussed more fully in Chapter 17.

Some of our sons are themselves badly abused when high. Young men can be raped, beaten, or robbed if they are too high to protect themselves. There are people who will attempt to seduce them with drugs, just as they might be tempted to seduce women. Young men are trained to feel invincible to the dangers of drugs and violence, and warning them with scary stories about what might happen may only feed their sense of being an exception. However, they do need to have a chance to reflect on what it does to us and our community when people are preying on each other through the manipulative use of drugs.

Our sons are not equally vulnerable to the dangers of drug use. Young men of color are the targets of much more intense and systematic advertising for tobacco and alcohol than white youth. They are also likely to experience much greater surveillance, and therefore more danger of being hassled by police for using drugs, than white young men. There is greater drug use in the white community than in communities of color, but people of color are arrested in disproportionate numbers for drug offenses. The penalties they receive are harsher for equivalent use. At every level of the criminal justice system, young men of color are treated more harshly than white young men. Although young men of color know this through their experience, it helps them to have this information acknowledged so they can take it into account in their decisions about drug use.

In a society saturated with drugs, where adults and large corporations make tremendous profits from growing or manufacturing and selling addictive substances, we cannot leave our sons vulnerable with a simplistic message of "Just Say No" to drugs. They are under pressure from their peers and corporate-directed media campaigns to use drugs. Most do use drugs and some become addicted or otherwise seriously harmed by their use.

They need and deserve accurate information about the effects of specific drugs and the politics of their distribution, as well as encouragement to make thoughtful choices about whether, when, and where to use them. Rather than giving advice or warnings, I think it works best to ask them questions and encourage them to think about the choices they face and the consequences of those choices. Telling boys what to choose does not prepare them to take their place in a democratic society or to take responsibility for their life.

This section of the book has dealt with many of the issues boys must grapple with as they decide what they stand for. I have provided suggestions for helping them to create a strong sense of self, to develop skills for participating in cooperative and democratic processes, and to build a sense of responsibility for the world around them. In the next section I look at who they stand with — and *how* they stand with them, how they can reach outside the family to build full, equal, and intimate relationships with women and other men in the community.

PART 3

Relationships

15 Relationships with Women

Many of us raising boys in the 1970s and 1980s wanted our sons to treat their female friends, family members, and lovers (if they were heterosexual) with respect and without violence. We wanted them to do their share of the childraising, family work, cooking, and cleaning. In other words, we wanted women to be safe with them and we wanted them to be respectful of women's participation in all aspects of family, work, and community. These were admirable goals — we should certainly settle for no less. However, we can strive for more.

First of all, we often defined equality in instrumental terms, i.e., who does what, when. Women were asking why, when both parents had just come home from a long day at work, it was always the woman who was expected to start dinner and tend to the children? For women burdened with work and primary childcare and housekeeping responsibilities (the double shift for women that sociologist Arlie Hochschild has documented[1]), the desire for relief was paramount and having a man take on some of the housekeeping and childcare was a big step indeed, especially given most men's reluctance to do so. Although some single fathers and men from poor and working-class families had always been doing family chores, challenging the widely accepted stereotypes that men couldn't cook, clean, or change the diapers was a difficult task.

But in the long term, adding more tasks did not challenge men to become more expressive and nurturing, to respond to their children's and partners' emotional needs, and to give up some of the control they expected to have over family life.

A second major challenge to tradition male prerogatives within the family came from a change in attitude about male violence: men are now expected to refrain from hitting women or trying to control them. Thanks to the battered women's movement we have made tremendous progress in reaching a point where domestic violence is no longer socially or legally acceptable, but some men still do not accept this and we must continually fight for the safety of women within the family.

Good men share the chores and don't hit women. They respect women and are not abusive. But there is a further step in the process of boys becoming men who are fully human and active in the struggle for justice — a step that includes, but goes beyond, individual change and leads to social transformation. We need our sons to grow up to become advocates for women's rights and activists for gender equity.

Many women have expressed a need not only for men who do not hit them, but also for the elimination of violence against all women. They need help with childcare, but also widely available, inexpensive quality childcare. They need not only the end of sexual harassment and put-downs from a co-worker, but also equal pay for work of equal value and the elimination of job discrimination and glass ceilings. Women need affordable health care, control over their reproductive lives, inexpensive and safe public transportation, and the elimination of incest and date and marital rape. They are asking men to be their strong and effective allies in the struggles for these ends.

To give just one example, I think it is encouraging that many men now understand how their behavior was abusive and have made a commitment not to be violent toward or controlling of women. However, men still rape one out of every three women, one out of every four girls under the age of eighteen. Several million men batter their female partners every year. Women need men to work actively for an end to all male violence, not just to end their own abusive behavior. That is why we want our sons to understand the importance of taking action on issues of gender justice throughout their lives.

TREATING WOMEN AS EQUALS

Treating women as equals is still the single most difficult thing for most men to do. Men are taught systematically and thoroughly from an early age that men are important and women are not. Boys start receiving messages about women's place early. Segregated sports, same-gender play groups, gender-segregated classroom activities — all of these give boys the message that there is nothing wrong with a lack of participation by girls. The message is reinforced by textbooks that ignore the contributions of women, books and videos that have only male characters, and classroom dynamics that give boys the bulk of the attention.

Few men can escape or completely unlearn this conditioning. Men constantly focus their attention on other men as thinkers and doers and as the people who count and on women as sexual objects and caretakers for men and children. Recently we have seen large movements of men and public statements by prominent male leaders that reinforce the message that men are superior to women. The Promise Keepers, the Million Man March, various men-only retreats and initiation rites inspired by Robert Bly, Michael Mead, and others, all give boys the message that the company of men is what really counts. Such gatherings usually invoke a prior, happier time when men and women knew their place and men were responsible, in charge, and sat at the head of the table. The leaders of these events often blame mothers, wives, the women's movement, or just women in general for the deterioration of men's lives, which further fuels male anger towards women. Although these gatherings invite men to take responsibility for their own behavior and to end abuse towards women, they also give the message that when men get serious, or intimate, or deep, women should not be present.

Because men hold the power in our society, boys' activities will get more attention and resources and be more highly valued than girls' activities. You can see this on the playgrounds of most schools in the country, where some of the boys dominate the large open spaces with their games, and girls play on the sidelines in leftover space. You can see it in the classrooms, where some boys dominate the discussion and the activities unless such dominance is carefully monitored.

Beyond monitoring and changing such practices ourselves, we can give young people the tools to notice and intervene when they see inequality. For example, it is important for teachers to examine critically their teaching and classroom practices so they don't favor boys, discourage girls, or present a biased curriculum. The further step is to put issues of gender bias on the table with young people and help them recognize and make a commitment to fighting bias when it occurs. This kind of training at the elementary school level, when children have a tremendous commitment to fairness, leads to a lifelong practice of intervening when injustice is perceived. It also promotes critical thinking and democratic participation.

As a parent you can teach these skills to your son. The first step is to notice with him the absence of girls in the movies, games, books, and textbooks he encounters (as well as providing him with as many strong female characters and models as you can). Talk with him about why there are no female characters or why they are usually given certain kinds of roles. Discuss with him what effect this might have on girls. Ask them how accurate he thinks these depictions of girls are and whether he thinks they are fair. Your discussions may even influence him to get involved, write letters, or otherwise intervene in a situation if that is his inclination. You can certainly point out actions he can take and ask if there is anything he wants to do.

This process doesn't have to be coercive or heavy-handed. If you are aware of gender in all areas of your life, you will constantly notice and think about the difference that gender makes. It is easy to pass this concern along to your son in your comments, questions, and reactions. Although he may get tired of it at times, he will learn to notice these differences and he won't take them for granted. Nor do you need to pressure him to do something. His own sense of justice will lead him to intervene at such time as he is ready to do so. This might happen when he is a child or it might not occur until later in life. All you can do as a parent is to lay the groundwork of awareness that allows your son to build a foundation for community involvement as he gets older.

I am not suggesting that we raise boys who are passive, weak, or submissive to girls. Girls do not need boys to be disempowered or fearful of taking action for fear of making mistakes. Nor do we want boys to think they should control or protect girls. Girls needs boys who are strong and assertive and who will fight *with* them for social justice. We need to help our sons shift their focus from killing to repairing, from competition to cooperation, from goals to process, so they can be allies to girls and women, who reject traditional male prerogatives to be in control or in charge but who don't fall into being passive or afraid of making mistakes.

Boys and girls, women and men will not be able to have mutual relationships based on equality and respect until our very understanding of power is based on human interdependence and cooperation. What does it means to be powerful if we reject the standard definition of power as power over or control?

As the Power Chart in Chapter 2 conveys so clearly, those in more powerful groups have used power over others to exploit, harass and abuse those with less power. People in less powerful groups have used two kinds of power to resist and challenge power over them. The first kind of power is inner power — the strength, will, and understanding to get ahead despite discrimination, negative stereotypes, and lack of opportunity. The second kind of power is power with others, the ability to come together, work together, to develop common goals and to be part of a community challenge to inequality and violence.

Many boys are taught to have inner power — to develop the self-confidence, determination, and skill to succeed — without receiving support for developing the power with others that would enable them to care about others and work with others to make a difference in the world. There are many examples of men who have great inner power but who are isolated, competitive, uncaring, or abusive towards others. Inner power without power with others is as dangerous to our community as people who are getting ahead without getting together.

RELATIONSHIPS AT HOME

As we discovered when we analyzed the Power Chart, men are encouraged to blame women for the pain, frustration, confusion, and powerlessness they feel. Sometimes sons will bond with their fathers by teasing, harassing, and putting down women, particularly women in their family such as mothers and daughters or sisters. Such verbal and emotional harassment is terribly destructive to both the males and females in the family.

If you are a father, you need to realize that bonding with your son at the expense of the women in your family, or at the expense of women in general through the use of jokes, pornography, sexual harassment, or prostitutes, is devastating to women and completely undermines your own integrity. Trying to build up your self-esteem, to create ties with your son, or to hold up men as superior to women by teasing or telling jokes about women teaches your son that women are inferior, that they don't deserve your respect, and that it is okay to attack them. It conveys to your son that you have so little self-confidence that you are only secure when putting others down. It also prevents you from being closer to your son because you are talking about women rather than talking directly to each other.

When I was growing up I valued my father's attention and learned to connect with him and feel superior to my mother and, by extension, to my sister and other girls by laughing at his jokes and comments about my mother's incompetence and lack of intelligence. We never talked about women's bodies or sex in any way, but we did share a sense of superiority to women, and I felt included in a male brotherhood when I was around my father and other men. It was only years later, after my father had died, that I learned from my mother how devastating these comments and teasing had been to her self-esteem.

Male bonding does not have to have a sexual basis to be hurtful. If you bond over being more competent, smarter, more athletic, or more technologically or musically aware than women, it contributes to an anti-woman atmosphere that objectifies and degrades women. If your son learns from you that verbal or emotional attacks on women are okay and that women are not deserving of male respect, it reinforces messages he is exposed to from books, videos, music lyrics, and peers, and can lead to him being violent to women. It does a disservice to our sons and the women in our life to collude in this kind of bonding.

Questions to ask yourself
if you are a man

Do you make comments about women's bodies around your family?
Do you make comments about how much time women take getting ready for social events, or how much attention they pay to their appearance?
Do you tell jokes that make fun of women?
Do you tease your daughters about their appearance, their concerns, their talents, or abilities?
What effect does it have on your son when you are constantly making comments about women's bodies? Do you think he will learn to respect women?
Do you make comments about women being less athletic, less knowledgeable, less mechanically inclined, poorer drivers, less smart, or otherwise less competent than men?
If you engage in any of this kind of behavior, what effect do you think this has on the women in your family?
What messages does it convey to your son?
How does it reflect on your own attitudes towards women?
What steps can you take to encourage your son to be more respectful of women?

If you are a woman you know that it is not healthy for you or your daughters or sons to put up with this kind of banter, joking, teasing, or harassment. You will have to judge for yourself how safe it is to interrupt jokes or other put-downs of women. If you point out how hurtful it is to be told that you are stupid, ugly, overweight, incompetent, too emotional, unorganized, or any of the other judgments that some men think they have license to express, you might be able to stop the comments. Some possible responses to a man's comments are:

- You may not have intended to be hurtful but I am hurt by your comments.
- When you put down women you are putting me down as well.
- I don't want to be the brunt of your jokes.
- I feel disrespected when you make comments like that.
- If you care about me you won't want to hurt me with your jokes and comments.
- It is not a joke if it is at my expense.

You need not accept such excuses as "I was only teasing," "It's just a joke," or "Don't you have a sense of humor?" Boys (and men) need to learn that if girls or women feel a comment or action is hurtful or abusive, then that is how it is being experienced regardless of their intention. If they care about you they will change their behavior.

If direct confrontation has no effect or simply polarizes the situation, you may want to talk with your son about your concerns one-on-one. Sometimes when they are with older men, boys feel they have no choice except to go along with male bonding based on putting women down. They may be uncomfortable with the behavior but not feel able to interrupt it, perhaps because they fear becoming a target of negative attention themselves. They may also relish the special attention they receive from their father, stepfather, uncle, or other significant male and be unwilling to jeopardize it. Although I enjoyed the special attention I received from my father when I was a boy, I also know that I would have had an entirely different perspective if my mother had sat me down and explained how hurtful my father's actions were to her.

Even if there is no abusive behavior, a father who is in the "Act Like a Man" Box may rigidly enforce gender roles, leaving the woman (or women) to do the emotional work for the men in the family.

Questions to ask yourself

Who pays attention to the level of tension in the house and brings up problems that need to be addressed?
Who talks with the relatives and maintains those relationships?
Who arranges for social events with other families?
Who responds to the children when they are upset or struggling to deal with difficult issues?
Who cries, laughs, dances, yells with delight, or expresses other feelings in family settings?
Who holds family members when they need a hug?

A new male orientation towards women begins in the home with boys and men expressing their feelings, paying attention to other people's feelings, and nurturing the emotional life of the family. It is important that boys do not come to expect that there will be a woman available to do their emotional work for them. It is difficult for many mothers not to take emotional care of their sons (and the men in the house) because women have been trained to respond to men's needs, but this arrangement serves none of us well. If you are a woman, I hope you can resist the tendency to take care of boys and instead help them to take care of themselves. If you are a man, I hope you do your share of the emotional work in the family and encourage your son to share it with you.

When women take care of men's feelings and walk on eggshells around their anger, it teaches boys that male anger is powerful and they can use it to control others. In addition, they learn that they can remain in control by controlling their feelings and by withholding those feelings from the women around them. When a woman and man in a relationship focus all their attention on his needs and none on her equally legitimate ones, the woman ends up being exploited for her emotional labor. Furthermore, control shifts to the man as he can force the woman to spend her time and energy deciphering his unarticulated feelings. This kind of relationship is potentially very dangerous for the woman. She is under pressure to intuit and take care of all of the man's emotional needs. No matter how caring she is, there is clearly no way she can do that successfully. When she fails to take care of his feelings well enough, she will become the focus of his resentment. He may become angry at her failure or panic stricken if she leaves, withdraws, or refuses to carry the emotional burden. This panic is often the precursor to physical and emotional abuse of the woman and can lead to homicide, suicide, and other destructive behavior by the man.

Interrupting these patterns of control and abuse is not easy. Start when your son is young and teach him to be aware of and articulate about his own and other people's feelings. If he is older, or has already begun to be dependent on women for his emotional needs, or uses his expressed anger and unexpressed other feelings to gain control over women and to get female attention, you can still challenge these patterns and help him develop emotional skills. Whatever your son's age, you can help him develop a strong emotional foundation so that he can act responsibly towards others when he is at school or in other settings.

RELATIONSHIPS AT SCHOOL

We can see boys using the same patterns of withholding their other feelings and expressing their anger when they want to gain attention from teachers and female students at school. Boys have a complex range of feelings that they bring to school and additional feelings produced by being in school. They have fears and hopes, excitement, curiosity, doubts, enthusiasms, anger, and resentment. Many don't have the ability to express their thoughts and feelings about what is being done to them in the name of education. There is often little opportunity for them to express their feelings because of peer pressure and classroom policies. If no other outlet is offered, boys act out their feelings in various forms of resistance to the curriculum and the teacher. They may be aggressive or sullen, disruptive or apathetic. They may express their feelings through graffiti or vandalism, truancy or self-destructive activity. Many of them, nationally somewhere around 25 percent, simply drop out before completing high school.

At some point in their school careers, many boys take out their frustrations and their anger on the young women around them. Some develop a practice of proving to others that they are men by harassing women. Many times I have seen middle-school boys standing around the hall or playground, commenting on girls' bodies and teasing them. These same boys are often lost in the classroom, bored or frustrated by the curriculum. They have a lot of anger about the lack of opportunities in their lives and girls are a convenient target for their feelings. When I talk with them individually or in small groups they don't express a lot of anger at girls. They state that they harass the girls because they are there — vulnerable and easy targets. They express hostility and anger at teachers, school administrators, police, shopkeepers, and parents — none of whom they can confront directly.

Boys are also seriously vulnerable to abuse from other boys. In fact, much harassment of young women I have seen occurs because boys have been subjected to or are afraid of harassment being directed at them by other boys. Harassing girls not only lets them feel more powerful than they feel elsewhere in their lives, but it is also a way to divert other guys' attention from their own vulnerability. They gain status, acceptance, and a certain measure of safety based on how bold, outrageous, or aggressive their comments are towards girls or those boys picked out as vulnerable. They egg each other on, nod or voice their approval of harassment, and put each other down at any sign of weakness. One way to stay safe from harassment from other guys is to be the boldest harasser of girls. Such behavior "proves" that a boy is tough, aggressive, heterosexual, and not weak in any way.

No student is safe in an environment where boys and girls are subject to harassment. Everyone has a great deal to gain from a safe, harassment-free environment. It is, of course, the responsibility of the adults to create that safe environment and to involve young people in that process. The common, but usually inappropriate, response is for adults to punish a few boys who are most visibly acting out, without helping them identify what they are feeling or asking them to participate in creating a safer climate for everyone in the school. Often boys of lower socioeconomic status or boys of color will be identified as the ones who are being abusive. They will be disciplined individually, while similar abusive behavior by white or middle- and upper-class boys is often excused, minimized, or even tacitly encouraged. Often the problem is not with the behavior of particular young men, but with a climate in which such behavior is accepted as part of the culture, where women's safety is considered unimportant and where men's intimidation and control of women through emotional abuse remains unchallenged.

It is possible to create a school environment where boys and girls are safe from harassment, where boys are responsible for their behavior, and where boys gain emotional literacy skills along with girls.[2] It is only possible to create such an environment where the problem is understood as systemic rather than the fault of a few individuals, and where the approach to elimination of the problem deals with the complex gender, racial, and economic dynamics between students and within the school. I have visited schools where the halls and the classrooms were safe for all students, where students respected each other, worked together collaboratively, and were able to work out conflicts without fights. The halls and classrooms in these schools were just as loud and energetic as those where sexual harassment and male dominance are the norms. But the sense of safety and respect was palpable and boys were not pressured to gain some self-esteem at the expense of other students.

Many teachers, administrators, and parents are still resistant to efforts to eliminate sexual harassment and deny that harassment of boys is a problem, but recent research on the negative effects of harassment and, at least in the United States, new legal precedents holding schools and other institutions accountable for any harassment that they do not take steps to prevent or curtail, have begun to give us some tools for addressing this problem. To challenge such an environment, however, is to challenge deeply embedded social norms that grant males the right to dominate space, resources, and attention by harassing and blaming girls and women.

The Days of Respect program, adapted by Ralph Cantor from work developed at the Oakland Men's Project,[3] provides a blueprint for parents, students, and teachers to come together in a several-month process to put together a program for a day of respect at a middle school or high school. A parent/student/teacher team surveys the school to find out where and in what ways students feel unsafe based on gender, race, culture, sexual identity, or other areas of harassment. The team then facilitates a school-wide program where students can meet in small groups and talk about what they experience at school and what kind of atmosphere they want to create. There is room for musical and dramatic presentations from students about respect and a forum for students to make a commitment to changing the school environment so that everyone is treated with respect.

In one school the Day of Respect program included skits, rap songs, poetry reading, and a short video in addition to breakout groups and exercises. The day's events had a major impact on the school and became an annual event. Two immediate results from the program were that, in general, the levels of harassment and disrespect among students decreased throughout the school, and several of the young women who had been sexually harassed by one of the male teachers were able to talk to each other, identify their common problem, and then challenge the administration to address the teacher's behavior.

When coupled with conflict mediation training, multicultural awareness, and violence prevention education, such a program can have a significant impact on the environment at a school and make it safer for girls and boys. But it takes a community response — teachers, parents, and students working together — to bring about such a change.

Beyond Family and School

Boys don't innately think that women are inferior to men, are undeserving of respect, or are sexual objects. They think of them as friends, family members, classmates, and playmates deserving love, respect, and equal treatment. It takes years of training from family members, peers, the media, and school to instill in them the belief that women are less than men. As a result of this training, many reluctantly come to see women as different, other, sexual, powerful, and as adversaries. They learn so much about the differences between men and women that they don't realize that we are mostly the same and that the differences are largely, but not exclusively, socially constructed.

They have also been taught one of the most damaging of all lies about women — that there are good girls and bad girls. This division is expressed in different ways in our society, but basically boys (and girls, too) learn that there are some girls — such as mothers, sisters, possibly a wife or lover — who are good and deserving of respect, and there are lots of women who are bad and deserve whatever happens to them. These fallen women - — sluts, bitches, 'hos, feminists, feminazis, prostitutes, women on welfare, women who stand up to men, women who are battered, women who are raped, women who don't accept male limits on how they can dress or where they can go, women who challenge injustice, women who protest, women who are powerful, or women who do not accept male dominance — are considered to be stupid, defiant, manipulative, crazy, or dangerous. Once they are labeled as "bad" they have little protection from being harassed, mistreated, hit, raped, or murdered.

Although the definition of bad girls has shifted dramatically over the years, this centuries-old distinction between good girls and bad girls holds tremendous sway over our thinking about women. On a personal level, boys are encouraged to define entire categories of women as bad. Often these are groups of women that have little power in our society. At the same time, boys are encouraged to rate every girl or woman they encounter as a good girl or a bad girl.

At any time a young woman can slip from being a good girl to being a bad girl or bitch because the male she is with decides that she has said something or acted in a way that he regards as bad girl behavior. He then feels absolved from responsibility for anything he might do to her because anything that happens to her is "what she deserves." He may think that his only responsibility is to protect good girls like his mother, sister, or girlfriend (while she is in his good graces) from being treated like bad girls by other guys.

Since these are messages we all receive, there are probably categories of women or kinds of behavior that you, too, have grown accustomed to naming as bad and therefore as less deserving of respect and safety.

Questions to ask yourself

Which categories of women do you have less respect for?

Single women

Business women

Women on welfare

Teen-aged mothers

Immigrant women

Women in the sex industry

Women who use drugs

Women who dress provocatively

Women who demonstrate for equal rights

Women with disabilities

Lesbian and bisexual women

Women who have academic credentials

Women who are actors or movie stars

Women who are models

Women who have tattoos or body piercing

Women who are entertainers

Women who are athletes

© Cathy Cade

If you want your son to be an ally to women, you may have to rethink your own opinions and statements about certain categories of women. If you assume your son is heterosexual, do you worry that he won't marry or live with the right kind of woman, that he will find himself with a woman who is not well-off financially, not educated enough, not light-skinned enough, not polite enough, not deferential enough, not political enough? Do you tell him (or think) that he is too good for some women? Do you encourage him to value "pretty" women? Does he hear you blame some groups of women, such as women on welfare, for causing problems in your community?

Our sons need to hear from us that "good girl" and "bad girl" are artificial categories used by society to judge all women and justify violence against them. They need to hear from us that the existence of these categories makes things dangerous for their mothers, sisters, and daughters. It is dangerous for any woman to be cast out and thrown away. It is dangerous for men to judge women as saints or sinners. Because there are no saints, all women are in danger of being labeled sinners and treated accordingly. Bad girls, by whoever's label, are vulnerable to violence. In fact, men justify violence against women by saying those women are bad. Once a girl is trapped in this perception, she will receive little support or protection from men, from other women, or from the institutions that might protect her.

VIOLENCE AGAINST WOMEN

We commonly tell boys they should never hit a woman. This is part of a package of messages boys receive that tell them women are fragile, less intelligent, not strong, unable to protect themselves, and in need of men's protection and direction. At the same time boys receive extensive cultural messages from TV, cartoons, video games, advertisements, pornography, and movies that women are dangerous — that they are seductive, manipulating, entrapping, and dishonest.

Too often the conclusion boys draw from these conflicting messages is that men shouldn't hit women *except* when the woman is out of control, too emotional, going crazy, defiant, rebellious, manipulative, or just generally out of line, i.e., when she acts like a bad girl as men have been taught to define it. Men fear that if they let a women get out of control, or if they lose ultimate control of a relationship, the woman will take advantage of them or they will be abandoned.

Boys are also taught not to rape women. But the underlying and pervasive social messages boys receive is that women are sexual objects and that successful men are able to get sex from women. All men can buy pictures and videos of women's bodies, smooth-talking men can seduce women, rich men can buy access to women's bodies, and the rest have to use more force. Although extreme force is nominally condemned (but still rarely punished), the assumption that men should have access to sex from women when they want it is not generally challenged.

By the age of twelve, many boys have seen a woman being hit by a man in their family or at school, or have seen scenes in movies or on TV of a man hitting or sexually assaulting a woman. Whether in real life or in video, the results of such violence are rarely portrayed realistically. Boys often do not see the pain that results for the woman, nor do they see men taking responsibility for the violence. More often the violence is either glamorized or the woman is blamed for causing it. Many boys are left with the understanding that although men should not hit or sexually assault women in general, when they do so it is because she deserved it or asked for it or wanted it — in other words, because she was a bad girl. Some of the phrases boys hear and adopt themselves as acceptable rationales for physical or sexual assault are:

- She asked for it.
- She was dressed provocatively.
- She was acting seductively.
- She should not have been out at that time.
- She really wanted it.
- Why didn't she leave?
- She said no but she meant yes.

Because many boys have been hit, intimidated, threatened, or pushed around themselves, I have often found it effective to ask them what it feels like to be hit or threatened. After they describe their feelings, we can have a more realistic talk about whether girls really want or deserve or ask for violence. At this point some boys will raise questions like, "But what if she deserves it?" Then we can get into a discussion of why they think anyone deserves to be hit.

Men's violence against women is still so common in Western societies that we must begin discussions about this issue with boys with such basic statements as "No one deserves to be hit," and "No one asks to be raped." As they voice their objections, questions, and concerns, we can have a discussion that explores issues of equality, respect, and ways to build a community in which everyone is safe.

When we talk with our sons about violence against women we need to help them understand that the issue is a lot deeper and more complex than just whether a man hits or sexually assaults a woman. The key issue for men is control. To be in the "Act Like a Man" Box, boys are taught that they have to be in control in their relationships with women and should expect women to take care of them. These expectations *sometimes* lead to violence but *always* lead to disrespect, objectification, and attempts to control. The challenge for us is to help boys give up the expectation that they will be in control and that they should receive emotional or sexual services from women.

There are many ways to help your son resist these expectations of male privilege, most of which have been discussed in previous chapters. You can:

- Teach your son to take care of himself physically and emotionally and to develop intimacy with others.
- Help him learn to value his anger without taking it out on those around him.
- Teach him problem-solving and communication skills.
- Help him see girls and women as people who deserve his respect by exposing him to a diversity of women's writing, videos, achievements, and historical contributions.
- Talk with him about male violence and its effects on women, children, and men.

With this knowledge and set of skills as a basis, it is unlikely that your son will need to depend on women to take care of him or need to control them for his benefit. He will never have to rely on control or violence to get his needs met. He will be in touch with his own feelings, able to be intimate with others, and able to act as a strong and effective ally to women.

16 Relationships with Other Males

We live in an anti-gay, homosocial society. Heterosexual men are encouraged to socialize primarily with other men, but they have to be constantly vigilant so that they are not accused of being gay. This fear places strong limits on how close a man can get to other men. And since he is unable to receive nurturing from other men, he is forced to find a woman to take care of him emotionally. We can see the results of this social climate in relationships between young men. They are constantly testing each other and jockeying for position, looking for any sign of vulnerability. They will stand up for each other, perhaps, but many are too afraid to reveal their inner fears and hopes.

In many schools, elementary-level boys and girls are encouraged to play separately. Adults assume that boys want to play kickball and wall ball with each other, while girls prefer less aggressive activities. But there are always boys who don't like these competitive sports, and many others who would appreciate a mix of different kinds of activities. Adult assumptions that boys should play with other boys, but only in competitive, physically demanding activity, validate what boys are learning from other sources as well — guys should hang out with other guys, but not in ways that they might get too close.

Adults often see boys through an "Act Like a Man" lens and limit their opportunities. We may be well intentioned and think that we are catering to boys' needs when in reality we are catering to our preconceptions of what they need. Similarly, the competitive and aggressive atmosphere prevalent in many classrooms that challenges and occupies a few of the most verbal boys may be woefully inadequate for the rest, discouraging the sensitivity and ability of all boys to be close to each other. It is precisely because the Box discounts the vast diversity of boys' personalities and experiences that it is so destructive.

When we assume that boys will want to be separate from girls and that alternative and cooperative activities will not be of interest to them, we encourage them not to get along with each other. When we encourage, participate in, or tolerate the teasing, testing, and gay-baiting that goes on between boys we make it difficult for them to trust each other. Some of us encourage the highly competitive classroom environment in which every boy sees the others as opponents in the battle to get good grades or the teacher's approval.

© Kathy Sloane

Unfortunately, few of us teach boys the communication and cooperation skills that they need to be able to relate to each other, as well as to girls.

How do boys find ways to be close to each other without appearing to be gay or too vulnerable? They learn to relate to each other through competition, through sports, through computers, through shared interests in safe hobbies. They do find ways to relate, but inevitably these are unsatisfying for many of them because they are built on avoiding feelings and any kind of vulnerability. Many of these boys become men who are similarly unable or unwilling to be intimate with other men.

I think we can break this male/male dynamic only when we work with boys and young men in groups. Individually, no matter what their intention, boys are unable to sustain intimacy when faced with the reluctance and resistance of other boys. In a group situation it is possible to build safety, then trust, then intimacy over time. Once boys have an experience of intimacy with other boys, they often find ways to continue developing closeness in their lives. If we raise our sons to be close to others in isolation, without support from other boys, they will often make great allies for women but will have difficulty pursuing male/male closeness.

The way that boys come through for each other, even under very trying circumstances, is a testament to the possibilities for intimacy between boys. Some boys are incredibly loyal to their buddies. Often the only way they know how to show their caring is through the extraordinary actions they take to be there for someone in need.

We also need to realize that often a boy's deepest intimacy with another boy occurs in private, when they are off alone, out of earshot and free of censure from others. Walking in the woods or on the way to school, on a sleep-over after the lights are out, during a quiet moment between games — these are times of boy-boy intimacy we may not see but can certainly foster.

There are many ways for us to encourage our son's relationship with other boys. Sometimes it can simply be reminding him to call his friends or walk down the street to play with someone when he's sitting in front of the TV or computer. Helping him arrange overnight and extended visits with boy friends often leads to deeper connection and more quiet-time discussions. We can ask him questions about his friends and why he likes them, remind him that he cares about them, encourage him to talk with his friends when conflicts arise or when he is confronting a difficult challenge. It is also important to talk with him and his friends about how the male characters in movies or books show or don't show affection for each other, as well as to expose him to stories, books, and videos that portray boys and men being caring and close to one another.

At times your son may be confused about his feelings for a friend. Whether he is straight or gay he may become passionately attached to a boy friend (this may be more confusing for you than for him). He may find his desire to be close to his friend conflicts with the limits on showing affection between guys that he has been taught. He may wonder if he is gay. If your son becomes really close to another boy he needs you to acknowledge his feelings and support his relationship. You can help him do this by making non-judgmental statements like, "You seem to really like spending time with Dwayne these days." You can support his relationship by saying things such as, "I like seeing you and Charles play together because you are such good friends to each other."

If you have talked with your son about homophobia, given him contact with gay male friends (if you are not a gay male yourself), provided him with books and videos with positive gay male characters, you will have created an atmosphere that will support your son's exploring and deepening his relationship with other boys without his needing to fear your judgment or the possibility of social isolation when he pursues his feelings.

Your son needs to hear from you that it is important for him to develop close, loving friendships with other boys. At times, you may need to check homophobic fears and remind yourself that he cannot become too close to or be too caring about a male friend. If he is loving, if he spends a lot of his time with his friend, if they are affectionate together, he is gaining some experience in communicating with another person and creating intimacy. His closeness is not an indication of his sexual identity; it is a way for him to meet some of his natural human needs for closeness and affection. These are needs that many boys are discouraged from meeting or are taught to look only to women to fulfill.

Fostering cooperative family, school, and athletic environments in which teasing, put-downs, and gay-bashing are not acceptable also supports boys being closer to other boys. When a boy feels safe from name-calling and is not pressured to see other boys as competitors he is able to begin expressing a wider range of his feelings, which allows boy-boy friendships to deepen. He is able to step out of the Box without fear that other guys or the adults around him will shove him right back in by calling him gay, fag, queer, or sissy.

When his feelings are validated, he can explore some of those harder-to-express feelings that come from caring about others.

We need boys to grow into men who can be close to each other because male vs. male competition and the inability of men to be close to other men leads to fights, isolation, self-destructive behavior, and social divisiveness. It also puts tremendous pressure on women to take care of men's feelings. When we nurture our sons' ability to be close to other boys we are building a foundation for a community of men who can love and sustain one another and be full partners with the women in their lives.

17 Sexual Relationships

SAYING YES TO SEX

In a sexually repressive culture such as ours, it is difficult to teach our sons positive values around sexuality. On one hand, there is abundant sexual titillation at every turn, much of it aimed at young men. On the other hand, great restriction is placed on sexual discussion and expression. Boys' sexuality is often seen as dangerous and in need of control. It is not surprising that our sons are often misinformed and confused.

The easiest time to talk with boys about sex is when they are elementary school age, from six to ten, depending on the child. At that age they are curious, they have enough attention span, and they are not feeling personal pressure to be sexual. They will also listen to us and talk with us with less embarrassment than they will when they are older. There are many good books you can read with them that will answer some of their questions and raise topics for them to think about. (Some are listed in the Resources section.).

If he is older than six you can assume that your son is thinking about and noticing sexuality around him. He probably knows more than you think about your own sexual practice, if you have one. He notices sex in movies and on TV and has shared sexual jokes with his peers. He probably also has lots of confusion about sexuality if no one is talking about it candidly and honestly with him.

Although your inclination might be to begin by warning him about sex and pregnancy, or about AIDS and other sexually transmitted diseases, if you only give him warnings you are leaving him with a negative and one-sided view of sexuality. For many of us, sexuality is a positive and important part of our lives. We want to find ways to talk with our sons about sex that emphasize the value of sexual relationship. Unfortunately, most boys will receive very few sex-positive messages in our society. Rarely will they hear that sex is powerful, good, and life-enhancing when it occurs between two people who care about each other. Your son needs you to tell him what to watch out for, but he also needs to know about the positive aspects of sexuality.

At the same time, you can introduce your son to the range of sexual identities. He needs to know in general terms about the variety of ways that adults experience sexuality so he can learn to value and appreciate diversity without narrow-minded and prejudicial attitudes. This will also give him a sense of the possibilities for his own sexual expression so that he does not become confused, scared, or self-destructive if he discovers he is not heterosexual.

As he begins to ask questions and think about what he sees around him, your son needs to know that there are many different kinds of relationships. People form relationships casually and seriously, for a short term or a long term, monogamously or not. Each person has to come to terms with what works best for them and what kind of sexual practice they are most comfortable with.

Regardless of sexual identity or sexual practice, there are two underlying issues that demand our attention: How do we take care of our own sexual needs? How do we respect the needs of others? Your son should hear from you at an early age that his body is his and that no one should touch him or be sexual with him in any way until he is older. When he gets older, he gets to determine when, how, and by whom he wants to be touched and with whom he wants to be sexual. Many boys (current estimates say one in six) are sexually assaulted. Many others experience physical assault. It is important for your son to know that it is not right for someone to abuse him and that if it happens it is not his fault.

At the same time, you can let him know that it is okay to be sexual with himself, that masturbation is normal and healthy and feels good. There are some good resources listed in the bibliography that can help you when it comes time to talk with your son about these issues.[1] Often it is easier to read a book together and talk about the content then it is to bring up a subject without any context.

Because boys are pressured by their peers to be sexual at an early age and to direct their sexual attention towards girls, they need to know that other people have the same right to respect as they do. Talking about what consent means and what unwanted sexual attention means is a way to begin a lifelong dialogue about creating sexual intimacy.

Too much of boys' intrusive sexual attention towards girls goes uninterrupted by the adults around them. When boys in first or second grade make comments about the girls' bodies or touch them — whether it is sexual or not — they need to know that their behavior is disrespectful and will not be tolerated. If you notice boys harassing girls, making derogatory comments about them, or otherwise bothering them, think about how you can intervene in effective ways. Such intervention may include talking with the group about the interactions, restructuring the arrangements to encourage boy-girl play, or developing group agreements for respectful behavior.

You should not be trying to protect the girls from the boys' attention. That just gives both the girls and the boys the message that girls are fragile and need protection. If the girls are being harassed they need an opportunity to describe what the experience is like for them and how they want the boys' behavior to change. Both girls and boys need an opportunity to participate in a group process that takes every student's views and needs into account in order to create a safe environment.

If the boys and girls are playing separately it is more likely that the boys will harass the girls and not see them as peers. Boy-girl play and classroom activities help build inter-gender experience, trust, and respect and make it less likely that boys will see girls as sexual objects and more likely that the girls will be able to interrupt intrusive attention from the boys.

Sometimes adults overreact and suspend boys or treat them punitively. These adult responses give boys the message that there is something wrong with them or their curiosity about sex. What boys at this age need is information and an opportunity to talk about the difference between caring, respectful behavior and uncaring, disrespectful behavior. They also need to know clearly what behavior is considered abusive and will not be tolerated by the adults. As with all interactions between boys and adults, education and the setting of limits are more effective than punishment.

If you see boys harassing girls, rather than ignoring the situation or writing it off as "boys will be boys," understand the impact such behavior has on girls and boys and remind yourself that "boys will be men." They need our help in becoming the kind of men we want to live with in our communities.

PORNOGRAPHY

Some of our sons' confusion about their own sexual identity and about how to treat women comes from the stream of lies and misinformation about sex and sexuality that emanates from their peers and the media. A great deal of such misinformation may come from sexually explicit video games, music with women-hating lyrics, or pornography.

Boys have abundant access to pornography through magazines and pictures circulated at school, through pornography and video outlets, and through the Internet. They may be supplied with it directly by adult men, or they may find their way to it surreptitiously. What should you do when you find pornography under your son's bed or discover that he is logging on to a pornographic web site?

The first thing you might do is talk with another adult so you can clarify your feelings. You may be angry about pornography in general and about adult men who use it. Directing this anger at your son will not help him think about what he's doing. He needs to hear your anger about pornography and the way it exploits women without feeling that the anger is aimed at him. It is not easy to make this distinction unless you can talk with another adult to sort out your feelings and concerns before you talk with your son. Remember that your son is not a representative of the pornography industry and, in fact, is being exploited by it.

You may have ambivalent feelings about pornography. You may well have used it yourself (you may still be using it) and may not be sure about the harm it does. If you are concerned about issues of free speech, you may be confused about where pornography fits in. It is not surprising that an industry worth billions of dollars a year, which may be bigger than the record and movie industries combined, has developed many ways to justify its existence and insinuate itself into mainstream male culture. There are several books that describe in detail the harm pornography does to men as well as to women.[2] These books, listed in the bibliography, also contain descriptions of the pornography industry's efforts to suppress and disrupt people organizing against it.

Talking to another adult can also help you decide if this is a situation in which you want to forbid the presence of porn in your house or if you just want to make it clear to your son how you feel about pornography but will let him decide what to do with the

© Kathy Sloane

magazines or videos he has.

In either case, it is important to find out your son's thoughts about pornography. He may know little about the industry, its exploitation of women in the production of pornography, or the effects on women, men, and their relationships when men use it. It might be useful, if you have the stomach for it, to look through some of the material with him and talk about what you see.

Another option would be for all family members to discuss the issue and come to a family decision about the presence of pornography in your house. This process might raise other questions. For example, what if the women and girls in the household are offended by it and don't want it around, while the men and boys think it's a question of free speech and there's really no harm in it? What weight should the women's voices be given in this process? What responsibility do the men have to find out more about the effects of pornography and to respond to the issues of respect and safety that the presence of pornography raises? What if one woman in the household thinks it is not a big deal but another woman thinks it is? It is important to work through these questions either as a family or one-on-one with your son. Although your first impulse might be to say, "Throw the stuff out and never bring it in here again!" — all that conveys is that you have the authority to make the rules in the house. Your son will continue to use pornography and he'll end up thinking, "Just wait 'till I have a place of my own."

There are times, and this may be one of them, when you want to say, "There will be absolutely no (guns, disrespectful behavior, pornography, or fascist literature) in this house!" It is perfectly appropriate for adults to take moral stands about the kind of family environment they want to live in and maintain. My partner and I have set that policy with regard to toy and real guns and disrespectful language and behavior. On the other hand, I think that these unilateral decisions should be minimal. Whenever possible, family discussion and democratic decision-making should be the practice.

Whatever approach you decide to take, your son needs to know what the pornography industry is, how it affects our lives, and how you feel about it. Pornography is feeding your son misinformation about sex, about women, about people of color, and about his own body. You can help him unravel and correct it.

As well as pornography, advertising that uses images of women's bodies to sell everything from records to cars, from beer to computers has damaging repercussions on the ability of many men to interact with and appreciate real women. Boys are literally promised that if they have the right car or pants or beer or stereo or shaver, they will also have a young, thin, blond, blue-eyed, well-built woman to play with. This promise leads to false expectations about sex, unrealistic expectations about women's bodies, and a devaluation of women's intelligence.

If you talk with your sons about why companies use images of women to sell products, you can help them see how they are being manipulated and distracted by these images. Ask them what effect it might have on women to see images of themselves used in this way and how it might affect a man's expectation about how a woman should look. For young men of color, you may want to discuss whether this directs their attention towards white women, how it affects their standards of what is female beauty, and how this might affect women of color.

YOUNG MEN AND SEX

If we intervene at home and at school when our sons are young, we can counteract the information they may receive elsewhere that girls are around for boys' pleasure and amusement. We can also make them aware of the effects of their actions. However, a lot of boys do not receive this kind of loving support and become adolescents confused about sex, sexual identity, and the role of women in their life. Whatever their prior experience, young men are dealing with increased peer pressure to be sexually active and to see women solely as sex objects. Our challenge is to give them a sense of how to take care of themselves in sexual relationship and to teach them how to respect the sexual rights of others.

One tool I have found useful for helping young men look at these issues is the "Conditions for Sexual Intimacy" worksheet. It was designed to give young people who are ready for intimacy a way to decide what they want in a relationship. It can also serve as a good parent-son discussion starter. See worksheep on the next page.

Worksheet

CONDITIONS FOR SEXUAL INTIMACY [3]

These are my conditions for intimacy. I will respect myself and my partner by trying to make sure I am comfortable and ready to be sexual with another person.
(Add any conditions that are important for you. Cross out any that don't apply.)

- I need to feel good about myself.
- I need to feel good about my partner.
- I need to have reliable information about sex and birth control.
- We will have talked about birth control and safe sex.
- We will have agreed to use birth control and practice safe sex.
- There will be no pressure to do anything I am uncomfortable doing.
- I know my partner respects my feelings, my body, and my limits.
- I have the right to say no whenever I am uncomfortable — without retaliation. My partner also has this right.
- Neither of us will gossip to others about what is personal or intimate between us.
- If I am disrespected, put down, threatened, hit, or forced to have sex, I will leave or get help.
- I will not disrespect, put down, threaten, hit, or force my partner to have sex.
- I will not pressure my partner to have sex when he/she doesn't want to.

Of course these discussions can be complex, and our sons may come up with some sophisticated questions about mutuality and consent. But the basics are clear. If a person does not want to be touched, looked at, commented upon, or pressured to be sexual, then such behavior is unwanted, unwelcome, and disrespectful. If a person says no, it means no. If a person runs away, complains, or feels uncomfortable, it means the behavior or attention is unwanted.

As our sons become adolescents they will have to confront more complicated issues. For example, if someone is high or stoned or asleep, boys must recognize that that person is not able to give consent for sex. Getting someone high to have sex with them is abusive. Our sons must think about how they will respond if young men they are with act abusively. These are important issues to discuss with young men because so much sexual assault happens when guys get together in fraternities, sports teams, and gangs or at stag parties and other all-male gatherings. If one young man is willing to speak up, he can often stop a group of men from committing sexual assault. (Of course taking such a stand is not without risk, as the others may turn against the lone protester and attack him.) We can encourage young men to interrupt sexual assault by helping them think about such situations ahead of time.

The single greatest influence on our sons' adult sexual lives is their ability to talk with their partners about sex. If we talk with them early in their lives with ease and enthusiasm, it helps them become comfortable talking about sex with future partners. Talking about sex with one's partner not only prevents abusive behavior, but it also sets the stage for positive, mutual lovemaking.

MUTUALLY CONSENSUAL SEX

Young people have taken a dramatic step forward and are now beginning to talk about consent as a crucial part of sex. This is a major change from the old belief that the best we could hope for was a man sensitive enough to figure out what the woman wanted and who could please her and not take advantage of her — entirely without having to talk about sex. The new clarity helps both men and women feel safe in a sexual relationship. Men no longer need to try and guess what their partner is doing or saying. Their partners can take responsibility for saying "yes" to sexual pleasure or "no" to sexual contact without having to convey it nonverbally.

These developments are a healthy, important, and erotic step forward, one we need to prepare our sons for. Sex can be hot and passionate, deeply erotic — and mutual and respectful at the same time. In order to help our sons understand this, we have to challenge many of the old myths, such as the ones that say men are always ready for sex, that women want sex but can't say so, that women are turned on by male force, that resistance is sexy, and that there is such a deep separation between our bodies and our minds that we can't think about or talk about what we are doing and still have a good time.

These new attitudes towards sexual relationship are based on the assumptions that people are responsible for their feelings and can say what they want and that they are responsible for their actions and can communicate about sex. Obviously this is not always true. But assuming these things about people is certainly the most respectful approach. We honor our young people, especially our young men, by assuming they are capable of intelligent and respectful sexual relationships rather than assuming they are sexual beasts looking for prey. We honor our young people, especially our young women, by assuming they can communicate what they want rather than assuming they are confused and passive and inarticulate.

Beginning from these assumptions when you talk to your son about sexual responsibility and sexual communication will help you teach him that sex can be a positive, erotic, mutually enjoyable experience.

FIRST SEXUAL RELATIONSHIP

After all the years of preparing for it, there comes a time when your son is actually involved in a sexual relationship. What should you do if your son is sleeping with, or about to sleep with, someone?

I'll assume you've talked with him years ago about safe sex. Pick a relaxed time when you and he are hanging out together and ask him directly. "I see you and _____ are spending a lot of time together. Are you thinking of having sex?"

You might get one of several different responses. He might express embarrassment that you brought it up. That's okay; next time he'll be less embarrassed and, perhaps, more able to talk about it. He'll know you are there to talk with.

He might be angry or defensive and say it's none of your business. Your response could be a simple statement that you care about him and about his relationships and leave it at that.

He might answer you directly and tell you what's going on. Listen and support him without offering advice unless it is asked for.

He might not say anything at all. You can let him know you're always there to answer any questions he has.

Even before you think your son is about to have sex, buy some condoms, give him a few, and let him know where you keep the rest. Don't assume he is having sex with someone — but don't wait until you're sure he is sexually involved before you talk with him.

An excellent resource for our adolescent sons is *The Good Vibrations Guide to Sex: How to Have Safe, Fun Sex in the '90s*, which offers much information about sexuality in a positive tone.

Just because our sons become sexually active with a partner does not mean that they are free and clear or that we are off-duty. Although many of us attach great significance to a young man's first sexual experience (as he may himself), he will not be magically transformed into a sexually mature person as a result of it. He will still have questions and concerns and relationship problems; he will still be trying to figure out his values, needs, and identity. We can ask him about his relationship, talk with him about sexuality as we share movies, books, music, or cultural events, and generally be available to him. We will not like all, maybe even most, of his sexual partners. He will make mistakes in how he treats people and how he takes care of himself. He doesn't necessarily need advice (it may be hard not to give it), but he does need someone who can help him think reflectively about what he is going through. You may be able to be that person. If, through all this, we and our sons can remain in touch with the joys of intimacy and the pleasures of sexuality, we may yet be able to challenge those who would have us deny that pleasure and withhold that joy.

PART 4

Public Action

18 Consumerism

When our sons have a deep sense of relationship to others they will be able to get together to make a difference in the community. However there are many pressures in a capitalist economy urging them to substitute consumption of material goods and activities which create pseudo connections for real interaction with people. There are many products, whole industries in some cases, designed to sell almost exclusively to boys. Everything from guns and sporting equipment to athletic shoes, computers, video games, pornography, music, movies, and cars. Boys are trained to gain some of their self-worth through the accumulation of such toys and equipment, and some of their competitive edge and social status through their knowledge of the intricacies of these products. There are some characteristics of this consumption that I think are devastating for all of us.

- The production and sale of newer and flashier models garners outrageous profits for large corporations and is environmentally devastating.
- Many of these products and the activities connected to them cause young men to become focused on what they own or do rather than on what they think or feel.
- Although discussions about cars, computers, or movies produce limited bonding between guys, they generally undermine their ability to form intimate relationships.
- Most of these industries are built on the direct exploitation of women and of people of color both in North America and overseas.

There are so many opportunities to reflect on these issues that I want to suggest only a few areas and some questions that can start you off on your examination of consumption.

ADVERTISEMENTS AND OTHER MEDIA

The ability to decode advertisements and critically analyze publicity and marketing of any kind is essential to our sons' ability to withstand manipulation by corporations. Look at ads together, on TV or in print, comment on what you see, and ask your son what he sees going on. This stops the flow of images and allows time for him to really see what is presented and why. You can turn the sound off during TV commercials, which often makes the manipulation even clearer. Perhaps you and your son could make up parodies of commercials as you watch muted ones on TV. (Some teachers have developed study units on the media, but most young people don't get the chance to become media literate.)

As corporations buy sports equipment and space in gymnasiums and stadiums, and establish exclusive distribution arrangements with schools in order to reach young people more intensively, we need to be pointing out and organizing against such intrusions into our schools. More and more school districts are refusing to sell classroom time to corporations. Parents and teachers can provide boys with opportunities to reflect critically on this corporate dynamic and give them information about examples of protest. To inspire our sons to take an active role in resisting corporate encroachments into school and everyday life, you might tell them about the young man in an Atlanta school who wore a Pepsi logo on the day that the president of Coca Cola was coming to his school for a photo op. Another example of resistance to such corporate encroachment is UnPlug, a national campaign in the United States sponsored by the Center for the Promotion of Commercial Free Public Education to eliminate Channel One, a corporate-sponsored and -produced television news program that is filled with advertisements.

A more subtle form of propaganda is found in movies and TV programs. Our sons need to have critical thinking skills so that they choose what they want to see and analyze what they view. Teenage boys are one of the largest markets for mainstream movies. They are fed an unremitting stream of violent, sexist, high-tech fare that reinforces messages, such as:

- We live in a violent world.
- People who are different are the enemy.
- Force is always required to solve problems.
- Girls and women are peripheral to the real workings of the world.

If they don't have the skills to see through these messages, our sons will certainly be influenced by them.

I enjoy seeing movies with my children because we can talk about what we have seen together. When they were young we had short and fairly simple discussions about why various characters did what they did and what they might have done differently. We also discussed the lack of strong female characters and the portrayal of people of color, poor people, and working-class people in stereotyped and negative ways. As they grew older we've been able to have much more sophisticated discussions about relationships between characters within a film, the effect on the viewer of different special effects, the overall message that a movie is trying to convey, and the class, gender, and racial relationships depicted.

I don't think we've taken the joy out of watching movies by teaching our children to think critically about what they see. We have given them new appreciation of more complex and sophisticated films and raised their expectations about what they want from a video experience. They are also able to separate their video experience from the reality of the world and not confuse the two. This is a crucial skill for boys because movies feed their fears about the world and show them only men who are in the Box. While they grow up, steadily becoming more defensive in their daily lives, they become greater heroes in their dreams and resort to aggression more quickly to solve problems. In a parallel fashion, as they are exposed to more explicit sexual portrayals of women and see more graphic violence against them, they can easily become callous about the treatment of real women and expect women to be readily available to them sexually. Unless we challenge them to question their experience at the movies, we allow them to be exploited by the corporations that make money off them. They may eventually pass on that exploitation through aggression towards those around them.

CORPORATE EXPLOITATION

We can also focus on a particular company that sells products our son uses, and ask questions about how those products are made, who makes them, what they get paid, what their working conditions are, and who profits from them.

Serious consideration of these issues may lead them to question whether they want to wear brand names as walking advertisements for various products. Some boys may want to join efforts to put pressures on companies to change their policies. They may decide to write letters, join or organize boycotts, or develop other forms of activism. In recent years there have been major international boycotts of General Electric, Coors, Nike, Jessica McClintock, and Nestle's. There are also many smaller or regional boycotts to pay attention to. Many union magazines and newsletters, such as the United Autoworkers' magazine, *Solidarity*, have articles about and lists of current boycotts.

One company under intense scrutiny these days is Nike, which has been the subject of a national boycott. A great deal of information about the economics of this company's shoe production is available from such organizations as Global Exchange.[1] At first my own children were reluctant to boycott Nike because our local shoe stores carried so few alternative shoe selections. But we searched for other brands together. As they learned more about the exploitative labor practices of Nike they not only came to support the boycott wholeheartedly, but they also became critical of major sports figures who endorse Nike products and they began to look at Nike commercials with a more critical attitude.

Cars and computers are two other products designed to appeal to boys and young men. Both are part of the male consumer culture that focuses on so many products offering the illusion of speed, power, and control as a substitute for self-confidence, and the illusion of connection as a substitute for intimacy. They also rely on the rapid obsolescence of products, which requires significant amounts of cash outlay to stay current with the latest developments.

To counter our sons' tendency to be seduced by the manufacturers of expensive, environmentally destructive cars, we can give them more information about the role of cars in our society, information about alternative vehicles, the uses of public transportation, and the effects of car use on the environment.

Computers are a trickier case because we can't prepare our sons for the future without giving them basic computer skills and a certain level of comfort with technology. It's difficult for many of us to give our sons access to basic computer skills because we can't afford a computer at home and our schools are too poor to afford or maintain them. Those of us who do have computers at home have some control over what programs our boys use

and how much time they spend with them. I think it is important to set limits on how much time they spend at the computer or watching TV or doing any other noninteractive activity.

Micki and I still have to routinely remind our ten-year old son to turn off the computer and go outside. We tell him he can do anything except watch a screen. There are some good educational programs and there are several good artistic/design/creative programs, so we buy the software we want our son to use, and talk about the content of software he wants or hears about. We ask some of the same questions we might raise about TV shows or movies when we are discussing computer games.

The Internet is a very powerful tool. It offers wonderful opportunities for research, discussion, and accessing resources. There is also abundant pornography, much hate talk, and great amounts of misinformation. I think censorship works even less well in this area than in others. We cannot protect our sons, nor do I think we should try. They need to be prepared to make choices about what they do and how they use their time — and they need to learn how to take responsibility for those choices, but we can help them learn how to screen out what is useless or hurtful on the Internet.

If your son is gaining status or escaping teasing because of what he wears, what he owns, or what he knows about cars, computers, or other products, you may find it's a good time to talk with him about his values, the peer pressure or peer culture he participates in, and questions of male competition. You can help your son know about and use cars, computers, and other boy toys targeted at him without being seduced into a lifestyle dependent on them. In this process you can help him see the connections between their choices, the economic system, and the exploitation of others that make those choices possible. When young men realize how they are being exploited and how their purchases are tied to the exploitation of other people, many begin to question how the economic system works and who it works for. This may encourage them to take a more active role and join one of the many groups trying to transform the economic structure, and the consumerism it is based on by challenging the corporations that attempt to dominate our lives, program our minds, distort our values, and distract us from taking care of each other with ever new and more shiny goodies.

19 Public Policy

COMMUNITY SERVICE

When we help our sons develop strong and healthy relationships with others — girls and boys, men and women — they will naturally be concerned about the injustice that other people experience. If we raise our sons to be caring and courageous they will come to feel part of the community and committed to its struggles for social justice. They will know that they cannot just try to get ahead at other people's expense. They cannot just try to get by without their actions having an impact on others. Our sons will want to get together because they will feel part of the larger web of relationship connecting people and the natural environment into an interdependent whole. We can start nurturing this sense of connection and mutual responsibility from an early age by giving them opportunities to participate in activities that serve the community and promote a sense of our interconnectedness.

We now know that even very young children have the capacity to understand how others feel and the desire to help alleviate their distress. As one study from the National Institute of Mental Health concludes:

> Even children as young as two years old have (a) the cognitive capacity to interpret the physical and psychological states of others, (b) the emotional capacity to affectively experience the other's state, and (c) the behavioral repertoire that permits the possibility of trying to alleviate discomfort in others. These are the capabilities that, we believe, underlie children's caring behavior in the presence of another person's distress...there are signs that children feel responsible for (as well as connected to and dependent on) others at a very young age.[1]

When we offer our sons the opportunity to participate in community service projects we develop their sense of membership in and responsibility to a larger community. Even if they themselves don't have much materially, they will learn that they still have much to contribute. Boys needs to be able to make a contribution to the community in order to feel useful, valued, and connected outside of their immediate family network.

At elementary school age, most boys are fascinated by projects that take them out into the community to serve others. They may get to meet people from different age groups, different racial groups, and from different economic groups. They get to feel useful. They get to make friends outside of their immediate family/school/neighborhood circle. And it arouses their curiosity about why some people have less. Why are people hungry or homeless? Why aren't there better services? These are questions that lead naturally into discussion of social justice.

Take your son to help out at a homeless shelter, to feed the hungry, to clean up the local parks, to read to seniors, or to tell stories to little children. When there is a march or organized activities to demand better community services or to eliminate pollution, take him along. Encourage his sense of belonging to a community that cares about its members and works together on behalf of everyone.

All boys need this experience. For many young men who are isolated and in trouble, whether or not they have been caught in the criminal justice system, community service provides a way to reconnect with others, to feel positive about their contribution and therefore about themselves, and to reenter the community.

We have traditionally trained girls to get together, to nurture and support and work together with others in the community. Girls are given dolls and babies and pets to take care of. Girls are trained to do community service and jobs that provide social service. We need to bring boys into this system to prepare them to nurture and support others and to work with others for change.

In addition to taking our children to public actions and getting them involved in community service projects, Micki and I have tried to instill a sense of caring and compassion through their allowance. Not everyone believes in or can afford to give an allowance to their children. We decided that an allowance was something that we could afford and that provided important financial experience for the children. Since there are three things you can do with money — spend it, save it, or give it away — we began to give our children a three-part allowance when they turned eight. They received $1 to spend, $1 to save, and $1 to give away.[2] When their give-away money accumulated, they had to collect information about different community organizations and decide which to give money to. At first they were primarily concerned about saving endangered species, then they became involved in broader environmental causes. Now they tend to give to groups that are organizing on social justice issues important to them.

It is particularly important that community service — whether it is direct service or a financial contribution — not be seen as charity: something we do out of the goodness of our hearts for those less fortunate. In the traditional sense, charity implies the spiritual superiority of those who have and often produces shame in those who do not have. Community service should not be done because we are good or special people but because it is our responsibility as members of the community. We live in an interdependent web of connection and we need to do our part.

I prefer to use a term from my Jewish heritage, *Tikun Olam*, which means to repair the world. In our tradition, when injustice exists there is a tear in the fabric of the world. Things are out of balance. It is our responsibility to make things right, to heal the world, to bring justice into balance in the community. This concept moves our focus from "Aren't I a good person because I'm generous or charitable?" to "Is what I am doing effective in making things better?" It doesn't put personal blame on people for not having what they need; it does correctly identify that there are social forces limiting many people's options and that any one of us could need help in our lives.

Community service does not lead inevitably to work for social change but I think that, with guidance, boys can be encouraged to make connections between the plight of individuals in need and the socioeconomic framework that does not provide for those needs. They will then also start asking questions about who is in need and why primarily groups with less power in society end up in need. If we are fostering their critical thinking skills, they will begin to make these connections for themselves.

Introducing community service to our sons should not be just a parent's responsibility. Every school, youth group, and religious organization should provide young people with a chance to connect with others and to make a contribution. Many teachers and school administrators now understand the importance of community service projects and are building them into the educational program of their school.

As our sons participate in community service projects they develop critical thinking skills, they learn how to work together with and for others, and they become committed to taking action when it's called for. These are just two of the leadership skills they need to develop, which family, school, and community organizations can each play a part in helping them to do.

DEVELOPING YOUTH ACTIVISTS

There are many grassroots organizing efforts around the country that help young people develop leadership skills as they participate in community struggles for equity and opportunity. These community development projects take many different forms and cover a wide variety of issues. Many include job-training components, while others focus on youth-initiated small business. Some programs concentrate on environmental issues, violence prevention, community development, or on music, drama, or art. Finally, some youth programs are more directly political, providing youth with leadership and organizing skills as well as specific education about public policy issues.

These programs don't just provide services for youth, although more services are always needed. They also train young people to identify community problems and work with adults to plan and implement strategies for social change. These programs link education and training to community development, with a substantial focus on youth leadership. I want to describe a handful of these programs to remind us what young people are capable of and to show models of programs that help youth get together to build their community.[3]

Youth for Environmental Sanity is a youth-run environmental justice group based in Santa Cruz, California. Two high schoolers developed the idea that young people could empower others to stop environmental degradation by speaking out on conservation issues. They organized a tour of young speakers that has reached over 450,000 students in 72 cities in the United States as well as in Singapore and Taiwan. They present slide presentations, conduct workshops, run a series of environmental summer camp programs, and publish a newsletter and training manuals. Their work covers such issues as global warming, deforestation, toxic waste, environmental racism, and overpopulation. The staff of young people between the ages of fourteen and twenty-five engages young people in critical education and grassroots coalition-building that has resulted in the establishment of numerous school-based eco-clubs, regional organizing, letter-writing campaigns, and many other forms of activism on environmental issues.

Focused on a different area is Teens as Community Resources, a nonprofit agency in Boston. TCR makes grants of up to $5,000 to young people interested in initiating and organizing a community service project. Not only are the grant applications generated and carried out by teens, but the staff, administration, and policymaking board have teen participation. Young people establish funding criteria, conduct site visits, provide technical assistance, interview applicants, and evaluate proposals, giving them opportunities to develop their own skills while building a vital community resource.

Another economic-based project is the Youth Credit Union in Springfield, Massachusetts, started in 1988 as a project of the D.E. Wells Federal Credit Union. On the first day, 73 children signed up for membership, depositing $1,200. The board of directors consists of one representative from each of four age groups: seven to nine, ten to twelve, thirteen to fifteen, and sixteen to seventeen. The youth, with adult advisors, set policies on lending practices and serve as the organization's loan officers, clerks, managers, and on the credit committee. The credit union teaches the participants financial, work, and leadership skills, but it also has become a youth center, providing training, a safe place, peer and adult support, and an opportunity to participate in community development.

In the Highbridge area of the South Bronx in New York City, seven organizations came together to start the Take Charge/Be Somebody! Youth Network. In order to ensure diverse participation from the young people in the area they established a youth council as a policy-making board. A Youth Network was also created where teens could meet and discuss urban issues important to them. Some of the projects that young people have initiated are an AIDS/HIV information pamphlet, training programs to prepare young people for jobs, an assessment of teen employment opportunities in the area, a peer-led video production project to document the community's improvement efforts, and a monthly newsletter. The Youth Council and Network have become places for young people to come together, identify their problems, learn new skills, and plan and implement projects which benefit the entire community.

Finally, YouthBuild USA was started in 1988 and now has chapters in major cities throughout the United States. Participants learn practical trade skills while rebuilding their communities. Projects include creating community centers in church basements and vacant studio space, rehabilitating abandoned buildings for homeless housing, establishing transitional housing, and developing a neighborhood park. But YouthBuild is more than a job-training program. Young people are involved in running the programs and in developing other projects such as crime prevention patrols, a coalition to create youth employment programs, and other teen advocacy issues. The YouthBuild policy committee consists largely of young people and participates in staff hiring, program design, yearly

budget reviews, events planning, and overall decision-making in the program.

Each of the programs described above, and many others not mentioned here, provide young people with opportunities to contribute to community development efforts while learning job skills, critical thinking skills, and the organizational and interpersonal skills required to mobilize people and get together with others to make social change. They demonstrate the ability that many young people have to learn, grow, take charge, and become leaders.

Whether initiated by adults or by young people, these programs welcome our sons and our daughters into our ongoing efforts to create a better society. They provide some or all of the following: safe havens, peer leadership activities, role models, a youth voice in decision-making, jobs and job training, multigenerational connections, training in social issues and organizing skills, and meaningful community involvement. They provide youth with adult support in taking responsibility for themselves, each other, and the larger neighborhood or city that they are a part of. These efforts are a natural extension of the values and skills I have talked about establishing in our families and schools, giving young people a chance to apply what they have learned to challenges faced by the larger community.

Throughout the world young people are taking the lead in community development projects addressing our most pressing issues. There are probably programs near you that you could support and become involved in. The fact that we don't hear about these programs reflects the cynical and sensational character of the media and the common practice of blaming youth for our social problems. Rather than being the problem, young people are part of the solution. In many communities young people are often ready for much more involvement than the adults around them are willing to let them have. This means that as their allies, we must often focus some of our efforts on educating other adults.

CHALLENGING ADULTS

In general, adults are not used to listening to young people as peers, not used to treating their opinions with respect, and not used to including them in decision-making. Over and over again at meetings and other public events I have seen adults interrupt young people, disrespect them, make comments on their appearance and style, and ignore what they say. As adult allies of young people we have a responsibility to speak up and interrupt the abuse in these situations. We can gently but firmly challenge other adults on their attitude or behavior, and we can create space for the young people to speak out on their own. Since these adults may be our colleagues, co-workers, friends, or fellow community members, we may be hesitant to speak up for fear of alienating them. However, if we bring young people to the table and then other adults silence them, we have achieved little except a change in appearances. We need to help our youth retain their voices so that we can learn from their insight.

Organizations go through several stages when trying to increase youth participation.[4] In many organizations, including youth-serving agencies, young people have no say in the decisions that affect them. In other organizations, a small group of selected youth are allowed to participate. In still others, a broader cross section of young people participate, but the organization is still run by adults. Occasionally at this stage of organization young people have a decision-making voice and are able, for example, to vote along with adults at meetings. Finally, some organizations actually have adults and youth working together to reach decisions. These organizations foster a high degree of youth leadership and participation and are the most responsive to youth needs.

Questions to ask yourself

What is one organization, project, religious program, or activity you are involved in that could have young people participating at a much higher level of leadership?
What stands in the way of their doing so?
What steps could you take to create a place at the decision-making table for them?
Which adults will support your efforts?
Which adults might resist your efforts to increase youth involvement?
What is one thing you will do in the near future to start this process going?

PUBLIC POLICY

We can be advocates for our young people not only in the organizations we are involved with, but also in the larger area of public policy issues that have such a dramatic effect on the lives of our sons.

Any society that spends more on prisons than on schools is not building a positive future for its young people. How money is accumulated and distributed says a good deal about where a society's values lie. Those of us who care about young people need to be much more involved in setting public priorities for how our money is spent if we hope to reverse the devastating impact current public policy has on youth.

Many people would rather scapegoat and punish youth as a substitute for critical thinking and action on social problems. For example, many adults blame young people for using guns, but adults manufacture guns, promote and distribute them, and profit enormously from their sale. Young people are blamed for using drugs, but adults grow, distribute, and profit enormously from the trade in drugs. Adults blame young people for having babies and practicing unsafe sex, but adults sexually assault young people, deny them information about sexuality, and limit their access to health care.

We, the adult community, need to take responsibility for providing young people with the skills, resources, and information they need to succeed in their lives. Young people need each of us to become a public policy advocate for them. We can work with them to create policies that encourage young people to participate actively in our society.

One of our challenges as adults is to see through a youth lens and evaluate what impact public policy issues have on young people. Legislation that eliminates welfare funding for adults throws the children of these adults into poverty. Budget decisions that put money into building prisons often take money away from schools and other youth programs. The defeat of public transportation bills limits the opportunities of young people to get to jobs and recreational programs. Decisions like these were made in the United States, Canada, Great Britain, and other countries in the 1980s and 1990s and have had a long-term negative impact on the youth of those countries.

When there is legislation that directly affects young people and purports to benefit youth, we have to ask the question, "Which youth?" Are the benefits going to poor youth as well as better-off ones, to youth of color as well as to white youth, to programs serving girls as well as to those serving boys?

We can also examine public policy debates to see if they are actually addressing the roots of the problem. For instance, we know that affirmative action programs work and that they have opened the door of opportunity for hundreds of thousands of white women, working-class men, and men and women of color. But the University of California had 9,000 qualified high-school applicants for 4,000 slots in 1998. Of course we want every qualified candidate to have an equal opportunity to get into that school. But why are there not enough places in our universities for all the qualified students? Why are there not enough jobs for everyone who can work? Why aren't there enough recreational, sports, and arts programs for every young person who wants to participate? We need to ask the larger questions of social justice and not just fight over the crumbs thrown to those of us at the bottom of the economic pyramid.

Questions to ask yourself

List three or four current public policy issues and describe their impact on the lives of young people. How does the formulation of these issues implicitly or explicitly blame young people?

Pick one of the issues you listed above. How does (will) it affect young people? Which groups of young people?

Which groups and individuals are actually supporting young people by their actions, policies, or stances on this issue?

Which groups and individuals are working against the best interests of young people on this issue?

How are young people involved in responding to this issue?

What is one step you can take to become a better ally to young people on this issue?

What are local issues in your area that affect young people?

How are young people, or certain groups of young people, being punished, monitored, or harassed in your area?

What youth funding has been cut back?

What has funding for youth been spent on?

What would you like to see changed about this picture?

Which groups or individuals can you get support from?

What are you going to do about it?

AFFIRMATIVE INVESTMENT

More than affirmative action, we need affirmative investment in our communities for adults and youth alike. We need to redistribute wealth from the top of the pyramid to meet the needs of the rest of us. Every public policy discussion should include the demand that money be reinvested in our communities and in our youth.

Young people maintain that they need resources and support in three primary areas: meaningful and well-paying jobs, good quality education, and a variety of cultural and recreational programs. They also need accessible health care, safe housing as an alternative to abusive family situations, and opportunities for creative expression and cultural events. We can each be an advocate for funding for these needs.

Questions to ask yourself

What are the needs that young people have identified in your community?
If you don't know, how can you find out?
What kinds of programming exist for young people in your community?
What is the state of the schools? Are some young people served better by them than others? Which young people?
What kinds of jobs are available? How much do they pay? Do they provide a foundation for better jobs in the future?
What kinds of art and recreational programs are available?
Who are they available for?
Have young people and their adult allies organized in any way in your community for better programs for young people?
What response did they receive?
In what ways could you be involved?

KIDS FIRST FUNDING

One way that several U.S. cities have addressed these needs and increased funding for youth has been to pass Kids First measures that set aside a certain percentage of the city's budget for youth programs. Often this percentage is around 2.5 percent of the budget.

San Francisco was the first American city to implement such an initiative, and young people were involved from the start, winning substantial new funding for young people in the city. Oakland, California, followed with its own version a few years later. Although both cities had many indirect services for youth run by the police department, libraries, and other city services and funded through these agencies' budgets, there were few programs directly serving youth, and no youth participated in decisions about how money should be spent.

In Oakland, young people and adults surveyed the city's youth to determine their needs and mapped out a strategy to get the Kids First measure on the ballot in a city election. Young people collected the necessary signatures on petitions for the ballot measure by canvassing voters at grocery stores and other community sites. The measure passed and now Oakland allocates 2.5 percent of its general budget for youth programming. A twenty-one-member board, which includes nine young people under the age of twenty-one, directs where that money is spent, and there is an increased public awareness of the need for youth-focused funding.

YOUTH LEADERSHIP

Public policy is not just the province of adults. Young people have always taken the lead in the public arena despite attempts to keep them uninvolved. Remember the children who integrated schools in the south and the teens who sat in at lunch counters. Remember the protests against the Vietnam war. Remember the young women in the women's liberation movement. Remember all the young activists, gay and straight, youth of color and whites, those with disabilities and those without, those who were educated and those who were not, who have been active participants in our struggles to extend democracy, increase equity, decrease violence, and build a stronger and more caring community based on justice for all.

More recently we have seen young people take the lead in the struggle to maintain affirmative action and in the fight to protect immigrant rights, in efforts to prevent violence, and in challenges to unequal opportunity and poor quality education in schools.

There are many different ways we can support our sons' participation in the community. Taking action ourselves is a powerful message to them that involvement makes a difference. I hope that this book has given you many ideas about how to shift your attention and actions to bring boys into the community instead of pushing them out. Whether in our family, schools, or community organizations, we can help boys get out of the "Act Like a Man" Box and become allies to those around them.

Our sons have much to offer us and we have much to gain from their participation. They are part of the solution to our social problems. Our sons might or might not be leaders. But they will have to decide what kind of participants they will be in our current struggles for social justice.

The future of our society depends on the leadership of our sons and daughters. If we are strong and powerful allies to our youth, we will be in good hands. But that requires us to be advocates for public policies that invest in young people, that build schools and not prisons, that create well-paying jobs with opportunity and not minimum-wage dead-ends, and that provide for hope, not despair.

We need our sons and daughters to take strong and active roles in the struggle to bring caring and justice to our communities. What the National Commission on Resources for Youth wrote in 1974 is still true today.

> *Young people are impatient. When they see a problem, and they get an idea about how to cope with it, they want action. Often their enthusiasm can carry them over obstacles that would discourage adults. And their optimism seems to accelerate their ability to develop skills necessary for dealing with problems. Added to enthusiasm and optimism are physical and mental energy and a remarkable capacity for single-minded dedication to something they feel is truly important. With support from the school and community [and I would add family], young people can develop and learn to use the problem-solving skills so desperately needed for coping with current and future social problems.*[5]

In the introduction I mentioned the 2,000 young people who marched on the Concord police station. They have continued to organize, educate, and keep public attention on the needs of young people. These are some of our future leaders. Are you preparing your son to take his place beside them?

© Kathy Sloane

201

Conclusion

When I ask people at a workshop to name some of the wonderful qualities of young men they throw out words like:

- energetic
- challenging
- curious
- intelligent
- caring
- rebellious
- creative
- artistic
- expressive
- dramatic

- pushing the limits
- wild
- passionate
- loving
- clever
- ambitious
- tender
- hardworking
- experimental

Today, when young men, are blamed for being violent, drugged out, underachieving, sexual predators and the cause of many of our social problems, it is easy to forget the wonderful qualities of boys and young men. However, if we stay grounded in our love, caring, and high expectations for our sons, we can help them stay safe, develop strong and caring relationships, and achieve their most creative and visionary dreams. We can welcome them into a community to participate with us in creating a society where everyone, without exception, is nurtured, supported, challenged, and connected. We can raise them so that they will know how to get by and get ahead but will also know how to get together. We can raise them so that when we ask them, "What do you stand for? And who do you stand with?" they will give us answers we will be proud of, answers that will strengthen and transform our community.

Endnotes

Where full citation is not given below, see Resources section under topic heading, as indicated by square brackets following title — e.g., *Boys Will Be Boys* [Violence]

Introduction

1. I have found the following books to be some of the best: Miedzian, Myriam, *Boys Will Be Boys: Breaking the Link Between Masculinity and Violence* [Violence]; Pollack, William, *Real Boys: Rescuing Our Sons from the Myths of Boyhood* [Male Socialization]; Reddy, Maureen T., ed., *Everyday Acts against Racism: Raising Children in a Multiracial World* [Racism]; Silverstein, Olga & Beth Rashbaum, *The Courage to Raise Good Men: You don't have to sever the bond with your son to help him become a man* [Parenting]; and Wells, Jess, ed., *Lesbians Raising Sons: An Anthology.* Alyson, 1997.

2. My account draws on conversations with participants and an article covering the rally: Elizabeth Martinez, "High School Students In the Lead," *Z magazine*, June 1998, pp. 41-45.

3. I use the term "people of color" as a shorthand way to refer to Native Americans, African Americans, Latino/as, Asian Americans, and Arab Americans. I am aware that this term is problematic and covers over many important complexities.

4. See Ehrenreich, Barbara, and Deirdre English, *For Her Own Good: 150 Years of the Experts' Advice to Women.* Doubleday, 1989.

Chapter 1

1. See Pogrebin, Letty Cottin, *Growing Up Free: Raising Your Child in the 80s*, pp. 8-29 and 123-130 [Male Socialization], and Greenberg, Selma, *Right from the Start: A Guide to Nonsexist Child Rearing*, Boston: Houghton Mifflin, 1979, pages 40-56. These books also include suggestions for alternative, nonsexist childraising.

2. The height difference between men and women has been diminishing over the last century and therefore even this "biological" difference might eventually turn out to be socially created (Lewontin, Richard C., et al., *Not In Our Genes: Biology, Ideology, and Human Nature.* New York: Pantheon Books, 1985).

3. None of these behaviors or abilities is a simple quality, which is another reason to be cautious of generalizations about gender differences.

4. See Coontz, Stephanie, *The Way We Never Were: American Families and the Nostalgia Trap*. New York: BasicBooks, 1992.

5. For further information about the minimal impact of biology on gender differences see Fausto-Sterling, Anne, *Myths of Gender: Biological Theories About Women and Men* [Gender], and Harding, Sandra and Jean F. O'Barr, eds., *Sex and Scientific Inquiry*. University of Chicago Press, 1987.

6. The name "Act Like a Man" Box is copyright the Oakland Men's Project.

Chapter 2

1. Lyrics from the book "We Who Believe in Freedom: Sweet Honey in the Rock...Still on the Journey." Bernice Johnson Reagon and *Sweet Honey in the Rock*. New York: Anchor Books, 1993. p. 21.

2. To say that women are vulnerable to sexual assault from men does not mean that every woman will be sexually assaulted or that every man is a rapist. It does mean that every woman has to deal with the possibility of being raped. Male violence is an everyday concern for most women, whereas few men worry about being assaulted by women.

3. Figures are adapted from Mishel, Lawrence, et al., *The State of Working America 1996-97*. Armonk, NY: M.E. Sharpe, 1997, and from Sklar, Holly, *Chaos or Community?: Seeking Solutions, Not Scapegoats for Bad Economics* [Power, Economics, and Class].

4. For more on the scapegoating of youth see Michael Males, *The Scapegoat Generation: America's War on Adolescents* [Public Action].

5. For an historical account of these struggles in the United States see Zinn, Howard, *A People's History of the United States* [History].

Chapter 3

1. Created by Allan Creighton of the Oakland Men's Project.

2. See Diana E.H. Russell, "The Incidence and Prevalence of Intrafamilial and Extrafamilial Sexual Abuse of Female Children," in *Handbook of Sexual Abuse of Children*, Walker, Lenore E.A., ed. New York: Springer Publishing, 1988.

3. Adapted from Allan Creighton of the Oakland Men's Project.

4. More details on this incident can be found in Kivel, Paul, *Men's Work: How to Stop the Violence that Tears Our Lives Apart* (rev.) pps 8-11 [Violence].

Chapter 4

1. I am defining homophobia as the fear and hatred of homosexuals including the fear of being or even appearing to be homosexual oneself.

2. For information about contacting Parents, Families, and Friends of Lesbians and Gays (PFLAG), see the Resources section.

3. Boys experience this pressure much earlier, often upon entering kindergarten or earlier. Girls are often given some latitude for tomboyish behavior until they reach preteens or early adolescence, at which time the pressure becomes intense to appear interested in boys and to act "feminine" enough to demonstrate heterosexual identity.

Chapter 5

1. For an assessment tool, see Kivel, Paul, *Uprooting Racism* [Racism].

2. See Daphne Muse, ed., *The New Press Guide to Multicultural Resources for Young Readers* [Multiculturalism].

3. This commonly used phrase may have originated from the title of the book by Gibbs, Jewelle T., ed., *Young, Black, and Male in America: An Endangered Species*. Auburn House, 1988.

4. The first attempt to desegregate buses in the South occurred in the early 1940s.

5. There is a wonderful essay describing the ways in which Rosa Parks' story is distorted in textbooks and other accounts. See Kohl, Herb, *Should We Burn Babar? Essays on Children's Literature and the Power of Stories* New York: New Press, 1995.

Chapter 8

1. Wayne Hearn, "Suffering in Silence: 'Real men don't get sick' attitude common," in the *Tucson Citizen*, February 16/17, 1993; Joseph H. Pleck, et al., "Problem Behaviors and Masculinity Ideology in Adolescent Males," *Journal of Social Issues* 49, no.3, (1993) pps 11-29.

Chapter 9

1. Kohn, Alfie, *Beyond Discipline: From Compliance to Community,* p. 33 [School].

2. Dreikurs, Rudolf, and Pearl Cassel, *Discipline Without Tears*. Dutton, 1990. See also Faber, Adele, & Elaine Mazlish, *How to Talk So Kids Can Learn: At Home and In School*, S & S, 1995, and Kohn, Alfie, *Beyond Discipline: From Compliance to Community* [School].

3. For an excellent, detailed analysis of the ineffectiveness of rewards and punishments see Kohn, Alfie, *Punished by Rewards: The Trouble with Gold Stars, Incentive Plans, A's, Praise, and Other Bribes* [Family Life].

Chapter 10

1. Some critics suggest that, because of boys' different learning styles, changing the classroom to support girls may disadvantage boys. However, there is no evidence that the needs of boys are anything more than a construct of the training they have received to act like a man.

2. This quote and much of the information about the mobilization in Milwaukee is taken from an article by Bob Peterson, a fifth grade teacher in Milwaukee: "Transforming Teaching," *Rethinking Schools* 13, no. 1 (fall 1998).

3. Sample sets of agreements are also found in Creighton, Allan and Paul Kivel, *Helping Teens Stop Violence* [Violence]; *Young Women's Lives, Young Men's Work* [Violence]; and *Making the Peace: A 15-Session Violence Prevention Curriculum for Young People* [Resources for Teachers]. Agreement posters are also available with the Making the Peace curriculum.

4. Howard Zinn, "Why Students Should Study History," in Levine, David, et al., *Rethinking Schools: An Agenda for Change*, p. 93 [School].

5. As quoted in Sarah Pirtle, "Cooperative Learning: Making the Transition," in Berman, Sheldon, and Phyllis La Farge, eds., *Promising Practices in Teaching Social Responsibility*, p.63 [Resources for Teachers].

6. Slavin, Robert, "Synthesis of Research on Cooperative Learning" as quoted in Pirtle, Sarah, "Cooperative Learning: Making the Transition," Berman, Sheldon, and Phyllis La Farge, eds., *Promising Practices in Teaching Social*

Responsibility, pp 50-51 [Resources for Teachers].

7. Sarah Pirtle, "Cooperative Learning: Making the Transition" in Berman, Sheldon, and Phyllis La Farge, eds., *Promising Practices in Teaching Social Responsibility*, p. 51 [Resources for Teachers].

8. John Goodlad, *A Place Called School*, quoted in Peterson, "What Should Children Learn?" in Levine, David, et al., *Rethinking Schools: An Agenda for Change*, page 85 [School].

9. The Child Development Project at the Developmental Studies Center has excellent resources on developing cooperative and democratic learning practices, class meetings, and models of curriculum in math and reading. See Resources section for contact information.

Chapter 11

1. Raphael, Ray, *The Men from the Boys: Rites of Passage in Male America*, Books on Demand, 1988, p. 137.

2. It is unclear whether athletes are involved in more incidents of violence against women than men in general, but because of their high public profile such incidents are good discussion points.

Chapter 13

1. Quoted by Alexander Cockburn in "Kids plus poverty equals violence" in the *Oakland Tribune*, May 24, 1996.

2. Osha Gray Davidson, author of "Under Fire: The NRA and the Battle for Gun Control," in *Rethinking Schools*, 13, no. 1 (fall 1998).

3. A. Kellerman and D. Reay, "Protection or peril? An analysis of firearm-related deaths in the home," *New England Journal of Medicine* 314 (1986) pp. 1557-1560.

4. *The HELP NETWORK — Coalition for Gun Control information packet*, 1996, and Murray L. Katcher, "Firearm injuries among children and adolescents: I. The facts," *Wisconsin Medical Journal* (October 1994) pp. 511-515.

5. Murray L. Katcher, "Firearm injuries among children and adolescents: I. The facts," *Wisconsin Medical Journal* (October 1994) pp. 511-515.

Chapter 15

1. Hochschild, Arlie, and Anne Machung, *The Second Shift*. New York: Avon, 1989.

2. See the resources available from the Stone Center at Wellesley, particularly Nan Stein and Lisa Sjostrom, *Flirting or Hurting? A Teacher's Guide on Student-to-Student Sexual Harassment in Schools* [Resources for Teachers]; Sjostrom, Lisa and Nan Stein, Bullyproof: A Teacher's Guide on Teasing and Bullying for Use with Fourth and Fifth Grade Students [Violence]; and Wheeler, Kathryn A., *How Schools Can Stop Shortchanging Girls (and Boys): Gender-Equity Strategies* [Resources for Teachers]. Also see *Healthy Relationships: A Violence-Prevention Curriculum* , 2nd edition. Halifax, Nova Scotia: Men for Change, 1992.

3. Cantor, Ralph, with Paul Kivel, Allan Creighton, and the Oakland Men's Project, *Days of Respect: Organizing a School-wide Violence Prevention Program*. Alameda, CA: Hunter House Publishers, 1997. Also see Kivel, Paul and Allan Creighton, *Making the Peace: A 15-Session Violence Prevention Curriculum for Young People*. [Resources for Teachers].

Chapter 17

1. Some of the resources include Sanchez, Gail Jones with Mary Gerbino, *Let's Talk about Sex and Loving*. Burlingame, CA: YES Press, 1983 (elementary school level); Blank, Joani, *A Kid's First Book about Sex*, Burlingame, CA: YES Press, 1983 (elementary school level); Madaras, Lynda, and Dane Saaveadra,*The What's Happening to My Body? Book for Boys: A Growing Up Guide for Parents and Sons*. (pre-adolescent and adolescent level) [Sexuality].

2. See Kimmel, Michael S., ed., *Men Confront Pornography*. [Sexuality]; Russell, Diana E.H., ed., *Making Violence Sexy: Feminist Views on Pornography*. Buckingham, England: Open University Press, 1993; and Dines, Gail, et al., *Pornography: The Production and Consumption of Inequality*. New York: Routledge, 1998.

3. *From Myhand*, M. Nell and Paul Kivel, *Young Women's Lives: Building Self-Awareness for Life*. Center City, MN: Hazelden, 1998. This exercise is also found in Creighton, Allan and Paul Kivel, Young Men's Work: Stopping Violence & Building Community [Violence].

Chapter 18

1. Contact information for Global Exchange is listed under Organizations in the Resources section. Thanks to public pressure, Nike has recently made some concessions about monitoring overseas working conditions. In spite of these changes, we need to continue to closely monitor the company's labor practices.

Chapter 19

1. As quoted in Kohn, Alfie, *Beyond Discipline: From Compliance to Community*, pp. 8-9 [School].

2. Nancy and Kimo Campbell originally shared this idea with us.

3. These and many other programs are described in more detail in Lakes, Richard D., *Youth Development and Critical Education: The Promise of Democratic Action*. [Public Action].

4. These stages are described more fully in Van Linden, Josephine A., and Carl I. Fertman, *Youth Leadership: A Guide to Understanding Leadership Development in Adolescents*, p. 144 [Public Action].

5. As quoted in Lakes, Richard D., *Youth Development and Critical Education*, pp. 135-6 [Public Action].

Resources

Below are some suggestions for further reading, some videos to watch with your sons, and books for boys to have read to them or to read themselves. These will provide starting places for rich, provocative discussions and will lead to other materials and other topics. Many of the organizations listed separately also provide additional materials for specialized topics.

For easy cross reference, the order of topics parallels the table of contents.

GENDER

Bornstein, Kate, *Gender Outlaw: On Men, Women, and the Rest of Us*. New York: Vintage Books, 1994.

Fausto-Sterling, Anne, *Myths of Gender: Biological Theories about Women and Men*. New York: Basic Books, 1985.

Kimmel, Michael and Michael A. Messner, eds., *Men's Lives*. New York: Macmillan, 1989.

Stoltenberg, John, *The End of Manhood: A Book for Men of Conscience*. New York: Dutton, 1993.

MALE SOCIALIZATION

Crawford, Susan Hoy, *Beyond Dolls & Guns: 101 Ways to Help Children Avoid Gender Bias*. Portsmouth, NH: Heinemann, 1996.

Gonzalez, Ray, ed., *Muy Macho: Latino Men Confront Their Manhood*. New York: Doubleday, 1996.

Majors, Richard and Janet Mancini Billson, *Cool Pose: The Dilemmas of Black Manhood in America*. New York: Touchstone, 1992.

Pogrebin, Letty Cottin, *Growing Up Free: Raising Your Child in the 80s*. San Francisco: McGraw-Hill, 1980.

Pollack, William, *Real Boys: Rescuing Our Sons from the Myths of Boyhood*. New York: Random House, 1998.

Videos for Boys

Free to Be You and Me (1974). Stories, songs and dances challenging gender stereotypes and emphasizing human potentialities for boys and girls.

Books for Boys

Barrett, Joyce Durham, *Willie's Not the Hugging Kind*. New York: HarperCollins, 1989.

DePaola, Tomie, *Oliver Button Is a Sissy*. New York: Harcourt Brace and Company, 1979.

Lichtman, Wendy, *The Boy Who Wanted a Baby*. Old Westbury, NY: Feminist Press, 1982.

Meyer, Carolyn, *Elliott and Win*. New York: McElderry, 1986.

Pogrebin, Letty Cottin, *Stories For Free Children*. New York: McGraw Hill, 1982.

Villasenor, Victor, *Macho*. Houston: Arte Publico Press, 1991.

ABOUT GIRLS

Videos for Boys about Girls

Bastard Out of Carolina (1997) Autobiography of a white girl who struggles out of poverty and childhood abuse in the South.

The Color Purple (1985) A poor black young woman fights for her self-esteem when she is separated from her sister and forced into a brutal marriage.

Girls Town (1995) Refreshing and painful look at the lives of three young women dealing with the impact of their friend's suicide after she was raped.

I Like it Like That (1994) Strong-willed black/Latina single mother in the Bronx trying to make it.

Island of the Blue Dolphins (1964) Docudrama of a young Native American woman stranded on an island and learning to survive.

Just Another Girl on the I.R.T. (1993) Powerful young woman in New York has a vision for herself that gets challenged by an unplanned pregnancy.

POWER, ECONOMICS, AND CLASS

Barlett, Donald L. and James B. Steele, *America: Who Really Pays the Taxes?* New York: Simon & Schuster, 1994.

Domhoff, G. William, *Who Rules America?: Power and Politics in the Year 2000*. Mountain View, CA: Mayfield Publishing Co., 1998.

McIntosh, Peggy, *White Privilege and Male Privilege: A Personal Account of Coming to See Correspondences Through Work in Women's Studies*. Wellesley, MA: the Wellesley Centers for Women, 1988.

Moraga, Cherrie and Gloria Anzaldua, eds., *This Bridge Called My Back: Writings by Radical Women of Color*. New York: Women of Color Press, 1981.

Sennett, Richard, and Jonathan Cobb, *The Hidden Injuries of Class*. New York: Random House, 1972.

Sklar, Holly, *Chaos or Community? Seeking Solutions, Not Scapegoats for Bad Economics*. Boston: South End Press, 1995.

Videos for Boys

Breaking Away (1979) Working class youth compete in bicycle racing against local college students while trying to figure out their futures.

Bulworth (1998) A politician begins to speak the truth about politics and money, sending shock waves through society.

Newsies (1992) Musical about the 1899 New York strike by newsboys against the publisher Joseph Pulitzer.

Norma Rae (1979) A poor, uneducated textile worker joins forces with a New York labor organizer to unionize the reluctant workers at a Southern mill.

Books for Boys

Castaneda, Omar S, *Imagining Isabel*. New York: Lodestar, 1994.

Cohn, Janice, *The Christmas Menorahs: How a Town Fought Hate*. Morton Grove, IL: A. Whitman, 1995.

Colman, Penny, *Mother Jones and the March of the Mill Children*. Brookfield, CT: Millbrook Press, 1994.

Seuss, Dr. (Theodor Seuss Geisel), *Yertle the Turtle and Other Stories*. New York: Random House, 1950.

Soto, Gary, *Taking Sides*. San Diego, CA.: Harcourt Brace and Company, 1991.

Woodson, Jacqueline, *Maizon at Blue Hill*. New York: Delacorte, 1994.

HISTORY

Bigelow, Bill and Bob Peterson, eds.,*Rethinking Columbus: The Next 500 Years*. Milwaukee, WI: Rethinking Schools, 1992.

Louis, Debbie, *And We Are Not Saved: A History of the Movement as People*. Columbia, MD: The Press at Water's Edge, 1970.

Lowen, James, *Lies My Teacher Told Me: Everything Your American History Textbook Got Wrong*. New York: New Press, 1995.

Piven, Frances Fox, and Richard A. Cloward, *Poor People's Movements: How They Succeed, Why They Fail*. New York: Vintage, 1979.

Reiser, Bob and Peter Seeger, *Carry It On!: A History in Song and Picture of America's Working Men and Women*. New York: Simon & Shuster, 1985.

Takaki, Ronald, *A Different Mirror: A History of Multicultural America*. Boston: Little, Brown and Company, 1993.

Zinn, Howard, *A People's History of the United States*. New York: Harper Colophon, 1980.

Videos

Amistad (1997) The story of a slave ship on which the slaves rebel and are brought to trial in the United States.

Autobiography of Miss Jane Pittman (1974) This film chronicles the life of a young Black girl in the south who lived from emancipation through the civil rights movement.

Matewan (1987) Coal miners organize and strike during the 1920s.

Books for Boys

Baillie, Allan, *Rebel*. New York: Ticknor and Fields, 1994.

Dash, Joan, *We Shall Not Be Moved: The Women's Factory Strike of 1909*. New York: Scholastic, 1998.

Goble, Paul, *Death of the Iron Horse*. New York: Simon & Schuster, 1987.

Hakim, Joy, *A History of US*, 10 Vols. New York: Oxford University Press, 1994.

Hamilton, Virginia, *Many Thousand Gone: African Americans From Slavery to Freedom*. New York: Alfred A. Knopf, 1995.

Johnson, Dolores, *Seminole Diary: Remembrances of a Slave*. New York: Macmillan Publishing Co., 1995.

Mochizuki, Ken, *Baseball Saved Us*. New York: Lee & Low, 1995.

Levine, Ellen, *Freedom's Children: Young Civil Rights Activists Tell Their Own Stories*. New York: G.P. Putnam, 1993.

Matas, Carol, *Lisa's War*. New York: Scholastic, 1991.

Meltzer, Milton, *Bread and Roses: The Struggle for American Labor*, 1865-1915. New York: Vintage, 1967.

Ringgold, Faith, *Dinner at Aunt Connie's House*. New York: Hyperion, 1993.

Telemaque, Eleanor Wong, *It's Crazy to Stay Chinese in Minnesota*. Nashville, TN: Thomas Nelson, 1978.

Yep, Lawrence, *Dragonwings*. New York: Harper Trophy, 1975.

PARENTING (also see Family Life)

Osherson, Samuel, *Finding Our Fathers: How a Man's Life is Shaped by His Relationship with His Father*. Columbine, New York: Fawcett, 1986.

Silverstein, Olga and Beth Rashbaum, *The Courage to Raise Good Men*. New York: Penguin, 1994.

Taylor, Dena, ed., *Feminist Parenting: Struggles, Triumphs and Comic Interludes*. Freedom, CA: Crossing Press, 1994.

Wipfler, Patty, *Supporting Adolescents*. Palo Alto, Calif: Parents Leadership Institute, 1995

Books for Boys

Boyd, Candy Dawson, *Daddy, Daddy Be There*. New York: Philomel, 1995.

Bunting, Eve, *The Wall*. New York: Clarion Books, 1990

Steptoe, Javaka, *In Daddy's Arms I AM TALL: African Americans Celebrating Fathers*. New York: Lee and Low, 1997.

HOMOPHOBIA

Bass, Ellen and Kate Kaufman, *free your mind: the Book for Gay, Lesbian and Bisexual Youth — and Their Allies*. New York: HarperPerennial, 1996.

Pharr, Suzanne, *Homophobia: A Weapon of Sexism*. Little Rock, Ark.: Chardon Press, 1998.

Pollack, Rachel and Cheryl Schwartz, *The Journey Out: A Guide for and about Lesbian, Gay, and Bisexual Teens*. New York: Puffin, 1995.

Videos for Boys

The Incredibly True Adventures of Two Girls in Love (1995) Story about a relationship between an African American and a white suburban high school young women and their families' attempt to come to grips with their relationship.

Longtime Companion (1990) A group of gay men and their friends dealing with the crisis of AIDS in their community in the 1980s.

Philadelphia (1993) A successful corporate attorney is fired because he has AIDS and then fights a legal battle for justice.

The Wedding Banquet (1993) Naturalized Chinese-American lives with his gay lover but agrees to marry a woman to appease his parents and get her a green card.

Books for Boys

Bauer, Marion Dane, *Am I Blue? Coming Out from the Silence*. New York: HarperCollins, 1994.

Block, Francesca Lia, *Weetzie Bat*. New York: Harper & Row, 1991. (and sequels)

Elwin, Rosamund and Michele Paulse, *Asha's Mums*. Toronto: Women's Press, 1990.

Heron, Ann, ed., *Two Teenagers in Twenty: Writings by Gay and Lesbian Youth*. Boston: Alyson, 1995.

Klein, Norma, *Now That I Know*. New York: Bantam, 1988.

Mastoon, Adam, *The Shared Heart: Portraits and Stories Celebrating Lesbian, Gay, and Bisexual Young People*. New York: William Morrow, 1997.

Murrow, Liza Ketchum, *Twelve Days in August*. New York: Holiday House, 1993.

Velasquez, Gloria, *Tommy Stands Alone*. Houston: Pinata Books, 1995.

Wilhoite, Michael, *Uncle What-Is-It Is Coming to Visit!!!* Boston: Alyson, 1993.

RACISM

Barndt, Joseph, *Dismantling Racism: The Continuing Challenge to White America*. Minneapolis: Augsburg, 1991.

Goodman, Mary Ellen, *Race Awareness in Young Children*. New York: Collier Books, 1964.

Golden, Marita, *Saving Our Sons: Raising Black Children in a Turbulent World*. New York: Doubleday, 1995.

Hopson, Dr. Darlene Powell and Dr. Derek S. Hopson, *Raising the Rainbow Generation: Teaching Your Children to Be Successful in a Multicultural Society*. New York: Simon & Shuster, 1993.

Kivel, Paul, *Uprooting Racism: How White People Can Work for Racial Justice*. Gabriola Island, B.C.: New Society, 1996.

Reddy, Maureen T., ed., *Everyday Acts against Racism: Raising Children in a Multiracial World*. Seattle: Seal Press, 1996.

Videos for Boys

A Family Thing (1996) Two brothers, one black, one white, discover each other's existence late in life and try to find common ground.

Ballad of Gregorio Cortez (1983) Because of a misunderstanding of language, a Mexican cowhand kills a white sheriff in self-defense and then tries to elude the law.

Follow Me Home (1997) Four young men of color set out from California to paint a mural on the White House.

Incident at Oglala: The Leonard Peltier Story (1992) A documentary about the murder of two FBI agents and the trial of Leonard Peltier in the context of recent United States' government/Oglala Nation history.

Jackie Robinson Story (1950) Jackie Robinson plays himself as he breaks the color bar in baseball.

Lone Star (1995) Stories of fathers and sons in a border town dealing with race, class, immigration, and family issues.

Mandela (1987) A focus on the struggle against Aparteid before Mandela's imprisonment in 1964.

Not in Our Town (1994) The story of the successful struggle of the citizens of

Billings, Montana to fight hate groups.

Rosewood (1997) The tragic story of a prosperous Black community trying to survive attacks by neighboring whites.

School Ties (1992) A story about what happens when private school classmates find out that the football star on campus is Jewish.

Zoot Suit (1981) A Mexican-American is falsely accused of a murder in the 1940s during a time of intense racial conflict.

Books for Boys

Adoff, Arnold, *All the Colors of the Race: Poems*. New York: Beech Tree, 1992.

Ashley, Bernard, *Cleversticks*. New York: Crown, 1992.

Chen, Barbara, *The Christmas Revolution*. New York: Dell, 1993.

Duvall, Lynn, *Respecting Our Differences: A Guide to Getting Along in a Changing World*. Minneapolis: Free Spirit, 1994.

McKissick, Patricia C., *Taking A Stand Against Racism and Racial Discrimination*. New York: Franklin Watts, 1990.

Meltzer, Milton, *Underground Man*. New York: Harcourt Brace & Company, 1990.

Miles, Betty, *All It Takes Is Practice*. New York: Alfred A. Knopf, 1976.

Muse, Daphne, ed., *Prejudice: Stories About Hate, Ignorance, Revelation, and Transformation*. New York: Hyperion, 1995.

Springer, Nancy, *They're All Named Wildfire*. New York: Atheneum, 1989.

Taylor, Mildred, *Roll of Thunder, Hear My Cry*. New York: Puffin, 1976.

Villaneuva, Marie, *Nene and the Horrible Math Monster*. New York: Polychrome, 1993.

MULTICULTURALISM

There is a multitude of good multicultural books representing many different cultures and experiences. The best single guide to this literature is:

Muse, Daphne, *The New Press Guide to Multicultural Resources for Young Readers*. New York: The New Press, 1997.

Anthologies

Atkin, S. Beth, *Voices from the Fields: Children of Migrant Farm Workers Tell Their Stories*. Boston: Little Brown & Co., 1993.

Cockburn, Victor and Judith Steinburg, *Where I Came From! Songs and Poems from Many Cultures*. Brookline, MA: Talking Stone Press, 1991.

Cofer, Judith Ortiz, *An Island Like You: Stories of the Barrio*. New York: Orchard, 1995.

Frosch, Mary, ed., *Coming of Age in America: A Multicultural Anthology*. New York: The New Press, 1994.

Hubbard, Jim, *Lives Turned Upside Down: Homeless Children in Their Own Words and Photographs*. New York: Simon & Shuster, 1996.

Hubbard, Jim, *Shooting Back From the Reservation*. New York: The New Press, 1994.

Izuki, Steven, *Believers in America: Poems about Americans of Asian & Pacific Island Descent*. San Francisco: Children's Press, 1994.

Wolf, Adolf Hungry and Beverly Hungry Wolf, eds., *Children of the Sun: Stories by and about Indian Kids*. New York: Morrow, 1987.

Yep, Lawrence, *American Dragons: 25 Asian American Voices*. New York: HarperCollins, 1995.

Adopted and Foster and Mixed Heritage People and Families

Kaeser, Gigi and Peggy Gillespie, *Of Many Colors: Portraits of Multiracial Families*. Amherst, MA: University of Massachusetts Press, 1994.

Lazarre, Jane, *Beyond the Whiteness of Whiteness: Memoir of a White Mother of Black Sons*. Durham, NC: University Press. 1996.

O'Hearn, Claudine Chiawei, ed., *Half + Half: Writers on Growing Up Biracial + Bicultural*. New York: Pantheon, 1998.

Root, Maria P., ed., *The Multiracial Experience: Racial Borders as the New Frontier*. Thousand Oaks, CA: Sage, 1996.

Wright, Marguerite A., *I'm Chocolate, You're Vanilla: Raising Healthy Black and Biracial Children in a Race-Conscious World — A Guide for Parents and Teachers*. San Francisco: Jossey-Bass, 1998.

Videos for Boys

Mississippi Masala (1992) A young Indian woman falls in love with an African American man and the couple deals with the cultural fallout from their interracial romance.

Books for Boys

Adler, C. S., *Youn Hee and Me*. New York: Harcourt Brace Janovich, 1995.

Adoff, Arnold, Black is Brown is Tan. New York: HarperCollins, 1992.

Girard, Linda Walvoord, We Adopted You, Benjamin Koo. New York: Albert Whitman, 1989.

Keeshig-Tobias, Lenore, *Bird Talk*. Toronto: Sister Vision, 1991.

Lacapa, Michael, and Kathleen Lacapa, Less Than Half, More Than Whole. Flagstaff, AZ: Northland, 1994.

Okimoto, Jean Davies, *Talent Night*. New York: Scholastic, 1995.

Wosmek, Frances, A Brown Bird Singing. New York: Lothrop, Lee and Shepard, 1993.

COMING OF AGE

Videos for Boys

Boyz N the Hood (1991) Four very different Black high school students try to survive L.A. gangs and bigotry.

Dance Me Outside (1995) Native Canadian teens, cut off from their more traditional parents, confront contemporary problems.

Powwow Highway (1989) A look at life on the reservation as two Cheyenne young men travel to New Mexico.

A Separate Peace (1973) Two young men deal with war and personal tragedy at a prep school during World War II.

This Boy's Life (1993) A young man tries to choose between prep school and hanging with his friends when he and his mother move to a town near Seattle.

Books for Boys

Bolden, Tonya, ed., *Rites of Passage: Stories About Growing Up by Black Writers From Around the World*. New York: Hyperion, 1994.

Bunting, Eve, *Smoky Night*. San Diego: Harcourt Brace Jovanovich, 1995.

Byars, Betsy C., *The Pinballs*. New York: HarperCollins, 1987.

Childress, Alice, *A Hero Ain't Nothing But a Sandwich*. New York: Bantam Doubleday Dell, 1989.

Davis, Ossie, *Just Like Martin*. New York: Simon & Schuster, 1992.

Greenfield, Eloise, *For the Love of the Game: Michael Jordan and Me*. New York: HarperCollins Children's Books, 1999

Greenfield, Eloise, *Nathaniel Talking*. Inglewood, CA: Black Butterfly Children's Books, 1988.

Grimes, Nikki, *Something on My Mind*. New York: Dial Books for Young Readers, 1990.

Herrera, Juan Felipe, *Calling the Doves*. San Francisco: Children's Book Press, 1995.

Hirsch, Karen D., ed., *Mind Riot: Coming of Age in Comix*. New York: Aladdin, 1997.

Koertge, Ron, *The Arizona Kid*. Boston, MA: Little, Brown and Co., 1989.

Martinez, Victor, *Parrot in the Oven: mi vida*. New York: Joanna Cotler Books, 1996.

Wolff, Tobias, *This Boy's Life: A Memoir*. New York: HarperCollins, 1989.

SPIRITUALITY

Fox, Matthew, *Creation Spirituality: Liberating Gifts for the People of the Earth*. San Francisco: HarperCollins, 1991.

Herman, Marina L., et al., *Teaching Kids to Love the Earth*. Duluth, MN: Pfeifer-Hamilton Publishers, 1991.

Peck, M. Scott, *The Road Less Traveled: A New Psychology of Love, Traditional Values and Spiritual Growth*. New York: Touchstone, 1978.

Books for Boys

Baylor, Byrd, *Everybody Needs a Rock*. New York: Charles Scribner's, 1974.

Boritzer, Etan, *What is God?* Willowdale, Ont: Firefly Books, 1990.

ENVIRONMENT

Videos for Boys

The Burning Season (1994) Brazilian peasants in the Amazon form a union to protect their land.

The China Syndrome (1979) An executive at a nuclear power plant discovers a concealed accident and tries to sound the alarm.

Gorillas in the Mist (1988) Story of animal rights' activist Dian Fossey's attempts to save the African Mountain Gorilla.

Milagro Beanfield War (1988) Members of a small New Mexico town organize to oppose land development and save their water rights.

Books for Boys

Baker, Jeannie, *Where the Forest Meets the Sea*. New York: Greenwillow, 1993.

Caduto, Michael J. and Joseph Bruchac, *Keepers of the Earth: Native American Stories and Environmental Activities for Children*. Golden, CO: Fulcrum, 1988.

Clifton, Lucille, *The Boy Who Didn't Believe in Spring*. New York: Dutton, 1988.

Kress, Stephen W. and Pete Salmansohn, *Project Puffin: How We Brought Puffins Back to Egg Rock*. Gardiner, ME: Tilbury House, 1997.

Miles, Betty, *Save the Earth: An Action Handbook for Kids*. New York: Alfred A. Knopf, 1991.

New Mexico People and Energy Collective, *Red Ribbons for Emma*. Berkeley, CA: New Seed Press, 1981.

Seuss, Dr. (Theodor Seuss Geisel), *The Lorax*. New York: Random House, 1971.

Terani, Hasan, *The Yellow Leaf*. Washington, DC: Mage Publishers, 1995.

FAMILY LIFE

Coontz, Stephanie, et al., eds., *American Families: A Multicultural Reader*. New York: Routledge, 1999.

Crary, Elizabeth, *Kids Can Cooperate: A Practical Guide to Teaching Problem Solving*. Seattle: Parenting Press, 1984.

Faber, Adele and Elaine Mazlich, *How to Talk So Kids Will Listen, and Listen So Kids Will Talk*. New York: Avon, 1980.

Gordon, Thomas, *P.E.T.: Parent Effectiveness Training*. New York: New American Library, 1970.

Kohl, Herb, *Growing with Your Children*. Boston: Little, Brown, 1978.

Kohn, Alfie, *Punished by Rewards: The Trouble with Gold Stars, Incentive Plans, A's, Praise, and Other Bribes*. Boston: Houghton Mifflin, 1993.

SCHOOL

Bigelow, Bill, et al., eds., *Rethinking Our Classrooms: Teaching for Equity and Justice*. Milwaukee, WI: Rethinking Schools, 1995.

Cahan, Susan and Zoya Kocur, *Contemporary Art and Multicultural Education*. New York: Routledge, 1996.

Faber, Adele and Elaine Maslic, *How to Talk So Kids Can Learn: At Home and In School*. New York: Rawson Associates, 1995.

Gatto, John Taylor, *Dumbing Us Down: The Hidden Curriculum of Compulsory Schooling*. Gabriola Island, BC: New Society, 1991.

Kohn, Alfie, *Beyond Discipline: From Compliance to Community*. Alexandria, VA: Association for Supervision and Curriculum Development, 1996.

Kozol, Jonathan, *Savage Inequalities: Children in America's Schools*. New York: HarperCollins, 1991.

Levine, David, et al., *Rethinking Schools: An Agenda for Change*. New York: New Press, 1995.

Sadker, Myra and David Sadker, *Failing at Fairness: How Our Schools Cheat Girls*. New York: Touchstone/Simon & Schuster, 1994.

Sehr, David T., *Education for Public Democracy*. Albany, NY: State University of New York Press, 1997.

Resources for Teachers

Berman, Sheldon and Phyllis LaFarge, eds., *Promising Practices in Teaching Social Responsibility*. Albany, NY: State University of New York Press, 1993.

Bigelow, Bill and Norm Diamond, *The Power in Our Hands: A Curriculum on the History of Work and Workers in the United States*. New York: Monthly Review Press, (n.d.).

Child Development Project, *Ways We Want Our Class to Be: Class Meetings that Build Commitment to Kindness and Learning*. Oakland, CA: Developmental Studies Center, 1996.

Derman-Sparks, Louise, *Anti-Bias Curriculum: Tools for Empowering Young Children*. Washington, D.C.: National Association for Education of Young Children, 1989.

Jenness, Aylette, *All About You: An Adventure of Self-Discovery*. New York: New Press, 1993.

Johnson, David W. et al., *Circles of Learning: Cooperation in the Classroom*. Edino, MN: Interaction Book Co., 1993.

Kivel, Paul and Allan Creighton, *Making the Peace: A 15 Session Violence Prevention Curriculum for Young People*. Alameda, CA: Hunter House, 1997.

Lee, Enid, *Beyond Heroes and Holidays*. Washington, DC: Network of Educators on the Americas, 1998.

Levin, Diane E., *Teaching Young Children in Violent Times: Building a Peaceable Classroom*. Cambridge, MA: Educators for Social Responsibility, 1994.

McCormick, Theresa Mickey, *Creating the Nonsexist Classroom: A Multicultural Approach*. New York: Teachers College Press, 1994.

Perry, Theresa and James W. Fraser, *Freedom's Plow: Teaching in the Multicultural Classroom*. New York: Routledge, 1993.

Sapon-Shevin, Mara, *Because We Can Change the World: A Practical Guide to Building Cooperative Inclusive Classroom Communities*. New York: Allyn & Bacon, 1999.

Schniedewind, Nancy, and Ellen Davidson, *Open Minds to Equality: A Sourcebook of Learning Activities to Promote Race, Sex, Class and Age Equity*. Englewood Cliffs, N.J.: Prentice-Hall, 1983, 1998.

Stein, Nan, and Lisa Sjostrom. *Flirting or Hurting? A Teacher's guide on Student-to-Student Sexual Harassment in Schools*. Wellesley, MA: Wellesley Centers for Research on Women, 1994.

Wheeler, Kathryn A., *How Schools Can Stop Shortchanging Girls (and Boys): Gender-Equity Strategies*. Wellesley, MA: Wellesley Centers for Research on Women, 1993.

SPORTS

Clifford, Craig and Randolf M. Freezell, *Coaching for Character*. Champaign, IL: Human Kinetics, 1997.

Fine, Gary Alan, *With the Boys: Little League Baseball and Preadolescent Culture*. Chicago: University of Chicago Press, 1987.

Kohn, Alfie, *No Contest: The Case Against Competition*. Boston: Houghton Mifflin, 1986.

Messner, Michael A. and Donald F. *Sabo, Sex, Violence & Power in Sports: Rethinking Masculinity*. Freedom, CA: The Crossing Press, 1994.

Murphy, Shane, *The Cheers and the Tears: A Healthy Alternative to the Dark Side of*

Youth Sports Today. San Fransisco: Jossey-Bass, 1999.

Orlick, Terry, *The Cooperative Sports and Games Book: Challenge Without Competition*. New York: Pantheon Books, 1978.

Videos for Boys

Hoop Dreams (1994) Documentary about two inner-city basketball stars' lives through high school.

North Dallas Forty (1979) Focuses on labor abuses in pro football.

Books for Boys

Hu, Evaleen, *A Level Playing Field: Sports and Race*. New York: Lerner, 1995.

Lord, Bette Bao, *In the Year of the Boar and Jackie Robinson*. New York: Harper & Row, 1984.

Myers, Walter Dean, *Hoops*. New York: Delacorte, 1983.

Say, Allen, *El Chino*. New York: Houghton Mifflin, 1990.

DISABILITY

Morris, Jenny, *Pride Against Prejudice: Transforming Attitudes to Disability*. Gabriola Island, BC: New Society Publishers, 1991.

Russell, Marta, *Beyond Ramps: Disability at the End of the Social Contract*. Monroe, ME: Common Courage Press, 1998.

Saxton, Marsha, and Florence Howe, eds., *With Wings: An Anthology of Literature by and About Women with Disabilities*. New York: The Feminist Press, 1987.

Shapiro, Joseph P., No Pity: *People with Disabilities Forging a New Civil Rights Movement*. New York: Random House, 1993.

Videos

Born on the 4th of July (1989) A paraplegic veteran returns from Vietnam and becomes an antiwar protester.

Coming Home (1978) A look at the life of a disabled Vietnam vet as he returns to civilian life.

My Left Foot (1989) The life of cerebral-palsy victim Christy Brown as he moves from an impoverished Irish community to success as a writer and painter using his left foot.

The Waterdance (1991) An autobiographical story of a man paralyzed in a hiking accident who has to deal with all facets of rehabilitation.

Books for Boys

Aseltine, Lorraine, *I'm Deaf, and It's OK*. New York: Albert Whitman, 1986.

Hansen, Joyce, *Yellow Bird and Me*. New York: Clarion, 1986.

Johnson, Anthony Godby, *A Rock and a Hard Place: One Boy's Triumphant Story*. New York: Dutton, 1994.

Krull, Kathleen, *Wilma Unlimited: How Wilma Rudolph Became the World's Fastest Woman*. New York: Harcourt Brace & Company, 1996.

Krementz, Jill, *How It Feels to Live With a Physical Disability*. New York: Simon & Schuster, 1992.

Rodgers, Frank, *The Drowning Boy*. New York: Doubleday, 1992.

Southall, Ivan, *Let the Balloon Go*. Reed Books, 1990.

VIOLENCE

Carlsson-Paige, Nancy, and Diane E. Levin, *Who's Calling the Shots: How to Respond Effectively to Children's Fascination with War Play and War Toys*. Gabriola Island, BC: New Society Publishers, 1990.

Cooney, Robert and Helen Michalowski, eds., *The Power of the People: Active Nonviolence in the United States*. Philadelphia: New Society, 1987.

Creighton, Allan, with Paul Kivel, *Helping Teens Stop Violence: A Practical Guide for Counselors, Educators, and Parents*. Alameda, Calif.: Hunter House, 1992.

Creighton, Allan and Paul Kivel, *Young Men's Work: Stopping Violence & Building Community*. Center City, MN: Hazelden, (Part 1) 1994, (Part 2) 1998.

Fitzell, Susan Gingras, *Free the Children: Conflict Education for Strong, Peaceful Minds*. Gabriola Island, BC: New Society, 1997.

Kivel, Paul, *Men's Work: How to Stop the Violence That Tears Our Lives Apart*. Center City, MN: Hazelden, 1992, 1998.

Miedzian, Myriam, *Boys Will Be Boys: Breaking the Link Between Masculinity and Violence*. New York: Doubleday, 1991.

McGinnis, Kathleen, and Barbara Oehlberg, *Starting Out Right: Nurturing Young Children as Peacemakers*. Santa Cruz, Calif: New Society Publishers, 1988.

Sjostrom, Lisa and Nan Stein, *Bullyproof: A Teacher's Guide on Teasing and Bulling for Use with Fourth and Fifth Grade Students*" Wellesley, MA: Wellesley Centers for Research on Women, 1996.

Tavris, Carol, *Anger: The Misunderstood Emotion*. New York: Simon & Schuster, 1982.

Videos for Boys

American Me (1992) The realities of gang wars and drug life on the streets of East L.A.

Blood In...Blood Out: Bound by Honor (1993) Violent portrayal of three youth in a L.A. gang and the choices they face.

Gandhi (1982) The story of Gandhi's life and India's struggle for liberation from England using tactics of passive resistance.

The Unforgiven (1992) A former desperado, now a farmer, goes out on a bounty hunt and finds that his past is still with him.

Books for Boys

Brody, Ed, et al., *Spinning Tales Weaving Hope: Stories of Peace, Justice & the Environment*. Gabriola Island, BC: New Society, 1992.

Durell Ann and Marilyn Sachs, eds., *The Big Book For Peace*. New York: Dutton, 1990.

Fitzhugh, Louise and Sandra Scoppettone, *Bang Bang You're Dead*. New York: Harper & Row, 1986.

Hamanaka, Sheila, *On the Wings of Peace*. New York: Clarion, 1995.

Leaf, Munro, *The Story of Ferdinand*. New York: Viking, 1938.

MacDonald, Margaret Read, *Peace Tales: World Folktales to Talk About*. Hamden, CT: Shoe String Press, 1992.

Mazer, Harry, ed., *Twelve Shots: Outstanding Short Stories about Guns*. New York:

Delacorte, 1997.

Paulsen, Gary, *The Rifle*. San Diego: Harcourt Brace & Co., 1995.

Seuss, Dr. (Theodor Seuss Geisel), *The Butter Battle Book*. New York: Random House Books for Young Readers, 1984.

Shea, Pegi Deitz, *The Whispering Cloth: A Refugee's Story*. New York: Boyds Mills, 1995.

Tsuchiya, Yukio, *Faithful Elephants: A True Story of Animals, People, and War*. New York: Houghton Mifflin, 1988.

CONSUMPTION, ADVERTISING, AND THE MEDIA

Durning, Alan Thein, *How Much is Enough: The Consumer Society and the Future of the Earth*. New York: W.W. Norton, 1992.

Greenfield, P. M., *Mind and Media: The Effects of Television, Video Games and Computers*. Cambridge, Mass.: Harvard University Press, 1984.

Vanderbilt, Tom, *The Sneaker Book*. New York: The New Press, 1998.

Winn, M., *Unplugging the Plug-in Drug*. New York: Penguin Books, 1987.

MEN'S RELATIONSHIPS WITH WOMEN

Eisler, Riane, *The Chalice and the Blade: Our History, Our Future*. New York: HarperCollins, 1987.

Kimmel, Michael S. and Thomas E. Mosmiller, eds., *Against the Tide: Profeminist Men in the United States 1776-1990*. Boston: Beacon Press, 1992.

Videos for Boys

Antonia's Line (1995) Multigenerational story of a non-conformist Dutch woman's life in her village.

Portrait of Teresa (1979) Cuban housewife has to balance motherhood, textile job, and cultural group activities without the cooperation of her husband. (Spanish with subtitles)

Wildrose (1985) A woman must assert herself among her all-male co-workers at a Minnesota strip mine.

Books for Boys

Childress, Alice, *Those Other People*. New York: Putnam Publishing, 1989.

Paterson, Katherine, *The King's Equal*. New York: Harper Collins, 1996.

MEN'S RELATIONSHIPS WITH MEN

Miller, Stuart, *Men and Friendship*. London: Gateway Books, 1983.

Videos for Boys

The Chosen (1981) Friendship between the son of a Hassidic rabbi and the son of a Zionist professor in 1940s Brooklyn.

Five Heartbeats (1991) Relationships between five Black singers and their success and failures as individuals and as a group.

The Full Monty (1997) A group of unemployed British miners confront vulnerability and intimacy when putting together a strip show to raise money.

Get On the Bus (1997) A bus load of Black men drive from LA. to Washington to be part of the Million Man March.

Books for Boys

Plain, Ferguson, *Eagle Feather, An Honour*. Winnipeg, MB: Pemmican, 1992.
Polacco, Patricia, *Pink and Say*. New York: Philomel, 1994.
Potok, Chaim, *The Chosen*. New York: Fawcett Crest,1967.
Raschka, Chris, *Yo! Yes?* New York: Orchard Books, 1993.

SEXUALITY

Abbott, Franklin, ed., *Men and Intimacy: Personal Accounts Exploring the Dilemmas of Modern Male Sexuality*. Freedom, Calif.: Crossing Press, 1990.
Eisler, Riane, *Sacred Pleasure: Sex, Myth and the Politics of the Body*. New York: HarperCollins, 1995.
Kimmel, Michael S., ed., *Men Confront Pornography*. New York: Crown, 1990.
Sanday, Peggy Reeves, *A Woman Scorned: Acquaintance Rape on Trial*. Berkeley, Calif.: University of California Press, 1996.
Woll, Pamela and Terence T. Gorski, *Worth Protecting: Women, Men, and Freedom From Sexual Aggression*. Independence, MO: Independence Press, 1995.
Zilbergeld, Bernie, *The New Male Sexuality*. New York: Bantam, 1992.

Books for Boys

Blank, Joani, *A Kid's First Book about Sex and Loving*. Burlingame, CA: YES Press, 1983.
Freeman, Lory, *It's My Body*. Seattle: Parenting Press, 1983.
Harris, Robie H., *It's Perfectly Normal: Changing Bodies, Growing Up, Sex & Sexual Health*. Cambridge, MA: Candlewick Press, 1994.
Madaras, Lynda, and Dane Saavedra, *The What's Happening to My Body? Book for Boys: A Growing Up Guide for Parents and Sons*. New York: Newmarket Press, 1991.
Winks, Cathy and Anne Semans, *The Good Vibrations Guide to Sex: How to Have Safe, Fun Sex in the '90s*. San Francisco: Cleis Press, 1994.

PUBLIC ACTION

Berman, Sheldon, *Children's Social Consciousness and the Development of Social Responsibility*. Albany, NY: State University of New York Press, 1997.
Dass, Ram, and Paul Gorman, *How Can I Help? Stories and Reflections on Service*. New York: Alfred A. Knopf, 1985.
Lakes, Richard D., *Youth Development and Critical Education: The Promise of Democratic Action*. Albany, NY: State University of New York Press, 1996.
Males, Mike A., *The Scapegoat Generation: America's War on Adolescents*. Monroe, ME: Common Courage Press, 1996.
Van Linden, Josephine A. and Carl I. Fertman, *Youth Leadership: A Guide to Understanding Leadership Development in Adolescents*. San Francisco: Jossey-Bass, 1998.
Wade, Rahima, *Community Service Learning: A Guide to Including Service in the Public School Curriculum*. Albany, NY: State University of New York Press, 1997.

Books for Boys

Dingerson, Leigh and Sarah H. Hay, *The CO/MOTION Guide to Youth-Led Social Change*. Washington, DC: Alliance for Justice, 1998.

Fleisler, Paul, *Changing Our World: A Handbook for Young Activists*. Tucson, AZ: Zephyr, 1993.

Lesko, Wendy Schaetzel, *No Kidding Around! America's Young Activists Are Changing Our World & You Can, Too*. Kensington, MD: Information USA, 1992.

Levine, Arthur, *Pearl Moskowitz's Last Stand*. New York: Tambourine Books, 1993.

Lewis, Barbara, *Kids with Courage: True Stories about Young People Making a Difference*. Minneapolis: Free Spirit, 1992.

Salzman, Marian and Teresa Reisgies, *150 Ways Teens Can Make a Difference*. New York: Peterson's Guides, 1991.

Velasquez, Gloria, *Juanita Fights the School Board*. Houston: Arte Publico, 1994.

ORGANIZATIONS

AFL-CIO Organizing Institute, Youth Programs (youth leadership programs) 202-639-6200, 815 16th St. NW, Washington, DC 20006 organizers@aol.com www.aflcio.org/orginst/

Alliance for Justice (resources, trainings) 202-822-6070 2000 P Street NW, #712, Washington, DC 20036 comotion@afj.org www.afj.org

American Association of University Women (AAUW) (magazine, catalog, programs) 800-326-AAUW 1111 16th St. NW, Washington, DC 20036-4873   info@aauw.org www.aauw.org

Anti-Defamation League (catalog, books) 212-490-2525 823 United Nations Plaza, New York, NY 10017   webmaster@adl.org www.adl.org

American-Arab Anti-Discrimination Committee (resources) 202-244-2990 4201 Connecticut Ave. NW, #300, Washington, DC 20008   ADC@adc.org www.adc.org

Asian American Curriculum Project (catalog, curriculum resources) 800-874-2242 PO Box 1587, 234 Main St., San Mateo, CA 94401   www.best.com/~aacp/

Asian Americans United (resources, advocacy) 215-925-1539 801 Arch St., Philadelphia, PA 19107   asianau@libertynet.org www.libertynet.org/~asianau

Association of MultiEthnic Americans PO Box 191726, San Francisco, CA 94119 www.ameasite.org

Bilingual Publications Company (resources) 212-431-3500 270 Layfayette St. #705, New York, NY 10012   lindagoodman@juno.com

Black Student Leadership Network (training, resources) 202-628-8787 25 E St. NW, Washington, DC 20001   cdfinfo@childrensdefense.org www.childrensdefense.org

Bread and Roses (posters) 800-666-1728

PO Box 1154, Eatontown, NJ 07724

California Newsreel (catalog, films) 415-621-6196
149 Ninth St., #420, San Francisco, CA 94103   www.newsreel.org

Campaign to End Homophobia (catalog, resources) 617-864-4528
PO Box 438316, Chicago, IL 60643-8316

Canadian Ministry of Citizenship, Ontario Anti-Racism Secretariat
(resources, training) 77 Bloor St. West, 16th Fl., Toronto, Ontario M7A 2R9

Center for Campus Organizing (catalog, newspaper, resources) 617-725-2886
16 Raven St. #1, Boston, MA 02142   cco@igc.org   www.cco.org

The Center for Commercial-Free Public Education/Unplug (newsletter, youth
programming) 800-UNPLUG1
1714 Franklin St., #100-306, Oakland, CA 94612   unplug@igc.org
www.commercialfree.org

Center for Research on Women (catalog, resources, training) 617-283-2500
Wellesley College, 106 Central St., Wellesley, MA 02181
www.wellesley.edu/WCW

Center for the Study of Sport in Society (newsletter, programming)
617-373-4025
Northeastern University, 360 Huntington Ave., Suite #161CP, Boston, MA
02115   www.sportinsociety.org

Child Development Project of the Developmental Studies Center (training,
resources) 510-533-0213
2000 Embarcadero #305, Oakland, CA 94606-7270   info@devstu.org
www.devstu.org

Children Now (advocacy, resources) 510-763-2444
1212 Broadway, 5th Floor, Oakland, CA 94612   children@childrennow.org
www.childrennow.org

Children's Creative Responses to Violence (CCRC) (training) 914-353
PO Box 271, Nyack, NY 10960   ccrcnyack@aol.com

Children's Defense Fund (resources, advocacy) 202-628-8787
25 E St. NW, Washington, DC 20001   www.childrensdefense.org

City Kids Foundation (training, youth programs) 212-925-3320
57 Leonard St., New York, NY 10013   www.citykids.com

Coalition of Essential Schools (information, resources for schools)510-433-1451
1814 Franklin St., #700, Oakland, CA 94612   www.esentialschools.org

Coleman Advocates for Children and Youth (training, youth programming,
advocacy) 800-4-A-Youth
459 Vienna St., San Francisco, CA 94112   coleman@sirius.com
www.colemanadvocates.org

Credit Union for Teens (information, resources) 413-732-0519
D.E. Wells Federal Credit Union-Youth Programs, 864 State St., Springfield,
MA 01109

Data Center (information and reports) 800-735-3741

1904 Franklin St., #900, Oakland, CA 94612   datacenter@datacenter.org
www.igc.org/datacenter/

Donnelly/Colt (catalog, books, posters, T-shirts) 860-455-9621
Box 188, Hampton, CT 06247 donco@ncca.com www.donnellycolt.com

Educational Video Center (catalog, films) 212-725-3534
55 East 25th St.#407, New York, NY 10010 www.evc.org

Educators for Social Responsibility (catalog, books, training) 800-370-2515
23 Garden St., Cambridge, MA 02138 www.esrnational.org

Fairness and Accuracy in Reporting (FAIR) (information, reports) 212-633-6700
130 W. 25th St., New York, NY 10001 fair@fair.org www.fair.org

Family Diversity Projects, Inc. (photo-text exhibits) 413-256-0502
PO Box 1209, Amherst, MA 01004-1209 famphoto@aol.com,
wwwfamilydiv.org.

Family Pastimes (catalog, games) 613-267-4819
RR #4, Perth, Ontario, Canada, K7H 3C6 fp@superaje.com
www.familypastimes.com

Global Exchange (information, resources, programs) 415-255-7296
2017 Mission St., #303, San Francisco, CA 94110 infor@globalexchange.org
www.globalexchange.org

Highsmith Multicultural Bookstore (catalog, books) 800-558-2110
W. 5527 Hiway 106, Fort Atkinson, WI 53538 bids@highsmith.com
www.highsmith.com

Indian House (information, resources) 505-471-2651
2501 Perrillos Rd., Santa Fe, NM 87505

Institute for Peace and Justice (information, training) 314-533-4445
4144 Lindell Blvd., H124, St. Louis, MO 63108
www.members.aol.com/ppjn

Institute for Community Economics (training, information) 413-746-8660
57 School St., Springfield, MA 01105 iceconomic@aol.com

Kids Meeting Kids (resources, connections) 212-662-2327
380 Riverside Dr., Box 8H, New York, NY 10025 kidsmtgkids@igc.apc.com

LA Youth (newspaper)323-938-9194
5967 W. 3rd St., #301, Los Angeles, CA 90036 layouth@worldsite.net
www.layouth.com

The Mentoring Center (information, resources) 510-891-0427
1221 Preservation Park Way #200, Oakland, CA 94612 www.mentor.org

NAACP Youth Section (leadership program, resources) 410-358-1607
4805 Mt. Hope Dr., Baltimore, MD 21215 www.naacp.org/youthcollege/

National Association for Multicultural Education (NAME) (magazine, conference, resources) 202-628-NAME
733 15th St. NW, #430, Washington DC 20005 nameorg.@crols.com
www.umd.edu/name

National Center for Immigrant Studies (information, resources) 800-441-7192

100 Boylston St., #737, Boston, MA 02116-4610

National Coalition of Educational Activists (conference, advocacy)
914-876-4580
PO Box 679, Rhinebeck, NY 12572   rfbs@aol.com
www.members.aol.com/ncea.web

National Conference for Community and Justice (youth programming,
resources) 212-545-1300
475 Park Ave. S., 19th Floor, New York, NY 10016   www.nccj.org

National Council of La Raza (training, resources) 202-785-1670
1111 19th St. NW #1000., Washington, DC 20036   info@nclr.org
www.nclr.org

National Film Board of Canada (catalog, films)
16th Floor 1251 Avenue of the Americas, New York, NY 10020

National Indian Youth Leadership Project (youth programs) 505-722-9176
814 South Boardsman St., Gallup, NM 87301   niylp@cia-g.com
www.niylp.org

National Institute for Gay, Lesbian, Bisexual, and Transgender Concerns in
Education (information, advocacy)
55 Glen St., Malden, MA 02148

National Service-Learning Clearinghouse (resources, information)
800-808-7378
University of Minnesota, Vocational and Technical Education Bldg., 1954
Buford Ave., #R460, St. Paul, MN 55108   serve@tc.umn.edu
www.nicsl.coled.umn.edu

National Student Campaign Against Hunger and Homelessness (resources,
training) 800-NO-HUNGER
11965 Venice Blvd. #408, Los Angeles, CA 90066   nscah@aol.com
www.pirg.org/nscahh

National Women's History Project (catalog, books, posters) 707-838-6000
7738 Bell Rd., Windsor, CA 95492   nwhp@aol.com   www.nwhp.org

National Youth Leadership Council (training, resources) 651-631-3672
1910 West County Rd., St. Paul, MN 55113   www.nylc.org

Network of Educators of the Americas (catalog, books, posters, curricula) 202-
238-2379
PO Box 73038, Washington, DC 20056   necadc@aol.com
www.cldc.howard.edu/~neca

New Designs for Youth Development (newsletter) 202-783-7949 ext. 303
c/o National Network for Youth,1319 F St. NW, #401, Washington, DC
20004   editor@newdesigns.org   www.newdesigns.org

New Mexico Center for Dispute Resolution (catalog, books, training, youth
programming) 800-249-6884
800 Park Avenue SW, Albuquerque, NM 87102   nmcdr@igc.apc.org
www.nmcdr.org

Northern California Coalition for Immigrant and Refugee Rights (informa-

tion, newsletter, advocacy) 415-243-8215
995 Market St., #1108, San Francisco, CA 94103

Northern Sun (catalog, books, posters, T-shirts) 800-258-8579
2916 E. Lake St., Minneapolis, MN 55406   nsm@scc.net   www.northernsun.com

Parenting Press (catalog, books) 800-992-6657
PO Box 75267, Seattle, WA 98125   fcrary@parentingpress.com   www.parent-ingpress.com

Parents, Families, and Friends of Lesbians and Gays (P-FLAG) (resources, newsletter) 202-638-4200
1101 14th St. NW, #1030, Washington, DC 20005   info@pflag.org
www.pflag.org

Peace Education Foundation (catalog, training, books) 305-576-5075
1900 Biscayne Blvd., Miami, FL 33132   www.peace-ed.org

Peacework (resources) 617-661-6130
American Friends Service Committee (AFSC), 2161 Massachusetts Ave.,
Cambridge, MA 02140   afscnero@igc.org   www.pwork@igc.org

Project 21 — Gay and Lesbian Alliance Against Defamation (classroom resources) 415-861-2244
1360 Mission St., #200, San Francisco, CA 94103   glaad@glaad.org
www.glaad.org

Puerto Rican Organization Program (youth programming) 860-423-8476
738 Main St.,2nd Fl., Willimantic, CT 06226

Resolving Conflict Creatively (training, resources, youth programming)
212-509-0022
40 Exchange Pl. #1111, New York, NY 10005   www.esrnational.org

Rethinking Schools (catalog, magazine, books) 800-669-4192
1001 E. Keefe Ave., Milwaukee, WI 53212   RSBusiness@aol.com
www.rethinkingschools.org

Skipping Stones (magazine)   541-342-4956
PO Box 3939, Eugene, OR 97403   skipping@efn.org
www.nonviolence.org/skipping

Social and Public Art Resource Center (youth programming)
685 Venice Blvd., Venice, CA 90291   sparc@sparcmurals.org
www.sparcmurals.org

Southern Organizing Committee for Economic and Social Justice (resources, information) 404-755-2855
PO Box 10518, Atlanta, GA 30310   socejp@igc.apc.org

Southwest Network for Environmental and Economic Justice (resources, advocacy, youth programs) 505-242-0416
PO Box 7399, Albuquerque, NM 87194   sneej@flash.net

Southwest Organizing Project (training, youth programming, newsletter, resources) 505-247-8832
211 10th St. SW, Albuquerque, NM 87102-2919   swop@swop.net
www.swop.net

Student Environmental Action Coalition (resources, training) 215-222-4711

PO Box 31909, Philadelphia, PA 19104   seac@seac.org,   www.seac.org

Student Pugwash U.S.A. (youth programming) 202-393-6555
1638 R St. NW, #32, Washington, DC 20009

Syracuse Cultural Workers (catalog, posters, cards, calendar) 315-474-1132
PO Box 6367, Syracuse, NY 13217   scw@syrculturalworkers.org   www.syr-culturalworkers.org

Take Charge/Be Somebody (youth programming)
1375 Nelson Ave., Bronx, NY 10452

Teaching Tolerance (magazine) 334-264-7310(fax)
400 Washington Ave., Montgomery, AL 36104   www.teachingtolerance.org

Who Cares: the Tool Kit for Social Change (newsletter) 202-588-8920
1436 U St. NW, #201, Washington, DC 20009   info@whocares.org
www.whocares.org

Women's Educational Equity Act (WEEA) Resource Center (resources, books, articles) 617-969-7100
55 Chapel St., Newton, MA 02158-1060   weeactr@edc.org
www.edc.org/womensequity

Working Group (videos) 510-268-9675
1611 Telegraph Ave., #1550, Oakland, CA 94612   info@livelyhood.org
www.livelyhood.org

YO! (Youth Outlook) (newspaper) 415-438-4755
Pacific News Service, 660 Market St., #210, San Francisco, CA 94104
yo@pacificnews.org   www.pacificnews.org/yo/

Young Leaders Tomorrow — Volunteer Canada (youth volunteer opportunities) 613-231-4371
430 Gilmore St., Ottawa, Ontario, Canada K2P 0R8   volunteer@sympatico.ca
www.volunteer.ca

Youth Action Network (training, resources) 416-368-2277
67 Richmong St. West, #410, Toronto, Ontario M5H 1Z5   yan@web.apc.org
www.pathcom.com/~yan

YouthBuild U.S.A. (youth programming) 617-623-9900
58 Day St., PO Box 440322, Somerville, MA 02144
webmaster@youthbuild.org   www.youthbuild.org

Youth for Environmental Sanity (youth programming, advocacy) 877-293-7226
420 Bronco Rd., Soquel, CA 95073   camps@yesworld.org
www.yesworld.org

Youth Service America (training, advocacy, resources) 202-296-2992
1101 15th St. NW, #200, Washington, DC 20005-5002   info@ysa.org
www.servenet.org

Youth Today (newsmagazine) 202-785-0764
American Youth Work Center, 1200 17th St. NW, 4th Fl, Washington, DC
20036   www.youthtoday.org

Z magazine (magazine, tapes, on-line resources) 508-548-9063
18 Millfield St., Woods Hole, MA 02543   sysop@zmag.org   www.zmag.org
and www.lbbs.org/ZNET

Index

Numbers following the letter "n" refer to endnotes, with chapters identified in superscript.

discipline and authority issues, 104-105, 110-112, 192
  setting limits, 104-106, 110, 111, 114
drug issues, 156-157, 157
fostering activism, 105, 192-196
gender issues, 55-61
goals and childraising styles, 51-53, 81, 105, 106-109, 112, 143
listening, 46-47, 48-49, 80, 89-90, 98-99
  about racial issues, 64, 67, 70, 74-76
  validating feelings, 40, 108-109, 176
male bonding in family, 163-164
male presence in son's life, 47-48, 50, 79-80, 97, 134-135
mothers issues, 37-43, 164-165
physical expression and behavior, 44, 50, 143-147, 148-149, 172
questions about, 43
racial issues in, 68, 74-75
resources about mixed race families, 216
role in education system, 120-122, 123, 125, 126, 130
for self-defense, 144-147
sexual issues, 55-61, 177-184, 209n1[17]
strength of role models, 42, 57, 59, 73
See also allies and advocates; boys needs; homophobia; resources
The Parents Leadership Institute, 51
Parks, Rosa, 72-73, 207n55
participation, *See under* choices; community; sports; youth
physical punishment, 112-116
  questions about, 113
Pirtle, Sara, 128
policy, *See* public policy
pornography, 179-181
power, *See* socioeconomic structure and power
pressure, 18, 92, 104, 109, 149, 166
  for drug use, 153, 156-157
  from social influences, 21, 38, 92
  in gender issues, 56, 59, 131, 132, 133, 135

on girls, 37-38, 40-41, 206n34
racial/cultural, 62, 70, 72, 74
for sport participation, 131, 133-135
to "act like a man," 38, 43, 45, 92, 132, 167-168
See also messages boys receive
principles one stands for, 3, 36, 57
public policy, 22, 82,
  affecting youth, 19, 26, 196-199
  financial, 3, 26, 197, 198-199
  questions about, 198, 199
  socioeconomic, 25-27, 28-31, 148-149, 188-190, 194, 198-199

Q
questions concerning,
  abusive behavior, 39, 46
  "acting like a man," 13, 45
  adults perceiving boys, 18, 19, 21
  allies and advocates, 36, 79
  background experiences, 38, 39, 40, 44
  boys in economic structure, 27, 34
  boys in your life, 18, 19, 21, 79
  community participation, 32, 196, 198, 199
  conflict resolution, 50, 146, 147
  critical thinking, 80
  democracy in classroom, 125
  discipline and guidelines, 113, 115-116
  drug use, 155, 156
  emotional issues, 13-14, 98, 99
  family culture, 87, 165
  friendships, 106
  gender differences, 10, 11
  homophobia, 55, 58, 60
  identity, 32, 55, 58, 60
  men and male culture, 33, 44, 47, 164, 165, 169
  parenting, 43
  public policy, 198, 199
  racism, 68
  respect, 145, 164
  school system, 122, 125, 126
  self-defense, 147
  sports issues, 134, 136
  violence and guns, 150, 151
  women and girls, 33, 39, 40, 41, 43,

46, 164, 169

youth, 89, 113, 196

R

racism, 62-76, 224, 225, 227, 228

allies and advocates in racial issues, 70, 71, 73-76, 207n55

anger about racism, 66, 67, 69-71

anti-racist strategies, 63, 64, 65-66, 67, 70-76

centers of attention and power, 63, 64, 66

choices in racial issues, 67-68, 69-70

emotional consequences of, 66-67, 69-71, 73, 75-76

historic efforts against, 27, 64, 67, 71, 72-73, 206n52, 207n55

institutionalization, 63-64, 65-66, 67, 68, 69-70, 71-72, 121

in drug issues, 154, 157

in sports, 131-132

listening about racial issues, 64, 67, 70, 74-76

male solidarity in, 62-76, 156-157

media images/stereotypes of racial groups, 62, 64, 71

messages boys receive about, 62-63, 64, 66, 67, 71

mixed race families, 74-75

questions about, 68

resources about racism, 214-215

support for parents in racial issues, 68, 74

violence and abuse in racial issues, 66, 68-69, 70, 71

in white upbringing, 62-63, 66

Raphael, Ray, 131

resources concerning, 210-229, 208n210, 209n117

adoption, 216

advertising, 222

coming of age, 216-217

consumerism, 222, 209n118

disability, 220-221

the environment, 217-218

family life, 213, 218

gender issues, 210

girls, 211

history, 212-213

homophobia, 213-214

male socialization, 210-211

the media, 222

mixed race families, 216

multiculturalism, 215-216

organizations, 224-229

parenting, 213

power, economics and class, 211-212

public action, 223-224

racism, 214-215

relationships among men, 222-223

relationships with women, 222

school, 218

sexuality, 223, 209n117

spirituality, 217

sports, 219-220

for teachers, 219

respect, 5, 9, 50, 52, 66-67, 86, 98, 168

among youth, 142-144

questions about, 145, 164

in sexual relationships, 178-179, 180-181

of women, 9, 46, 162, 163-165, 169, 172

responsibility, 9, 111, 128, 130, 150, 157, 167, 189

lack of, 169, 171

within community, 191, 196-200

role determination, 3, 8, 11-15

role models, historic, 67, 71, 72-73, 95, 127, 207n55

for disabled, 138-139

Roosevelt, Franklin Delano, 138

rules, *See* guidelines and rules

S

safety and well being, 91-92, 98, 142-143, 169

honor and self respect, 142-145, 148-149

questions about, 98

of women, 166, 167, 168-172

scapegoating, 35

of mothers, 41, 42

of racial groups, 63, 64, 66, 71

of youth, 27, 195, 206n42

school system, 119-130

challenge to, 121, 122-123, 130

community partnerships with, 117-

118

competitiveness, 119, 121, 126, 128, 173, 174

conditions in, 116-118, 120, 123, 148, 167-168, 197

critical thinking in, 119, 120, 124, 129

curriculum issues, 120, 122, 123, 125, 127-128, 208n2[15]

relevance of, 127-128, 129, 130

discrimination in, 30, 119, 120-125, 126, 207n1[10]

environment of harassment, 166-168, 208n2[15]

gender issues, 119, 121, 122-123, 207n1[10]

goals and values fostered by, 119-120, 121

The K 12 Teaching and Learning Initiative, 124, 207n2[10]

parents response to, 120-122, 123, 125, 126, 130

perception of boys in, 167-168, 173

questions about, 122, 125, 126

resources about, 218

students in, 120, 121, 122, 123, 166-168, 197

undemocratic nature of, 30, 119-120, 121, 122-125, 162

strategies to democratize, 120-122, 123-125, 168

violence and abuse in, 132-133, 167-168, 208n2[15]

See also socioeconomic structure and power

self-defense, 143-147

questions about, 147

self-esteem, 137-141

self sufficiency, 1, 49, 78, 91-98, 172,

emotional literacy, 50, 98-100, 165-166, 167, 176, 208n2[15]

setting limits, 104-106, 110, 111, 114, 188-189

sexuality,

choices and information about, 177, 178, 179, 182, 183

communication and values in relationships, 177-184

messages about, 177, 178, 179-181, 183

sexual identity, 34, 55, 57, 59, 177-

178, 206nn1,2[4]

strategies for discussion, 177, 178, 179-181, 183-184

worksheet on "Conditions for Sexual Intimacy," 181-182

Sitting Bull, 95

skills, 5

for communication, 174, 175, 195

conflict resolution, 144, 146, 148-149

for cooperation, 102, 128, 174

for democracy, 103-104, 106, 109, 120, 126, 195

emotional literacy, 45, 50, 98-100, 104, 107-109, 165-166, 172, 176

for leadership, 3-4, 193, 194, 195, 199-200, 225, 227, 205nIntro

for survival and expression, 49, 71, 91-98, 99, 100, 108, 146

Slavin, John, 128

social construction of gender differences, 7-11, 14, 15, 205nn 2,31, 206n5[1]

socialization of males, 7-15, 148-149, 191-193, 210-211

See also men and male culture

social justice, 2, 3-4, 67, 148-149, 154, 191, 192-193

activism and awareness, 1-3, 18-20, 138-139, 148-149, 154, 192-193, 205n2[Intro], 206n5[2]

historic movements, 72-73, 127, 207n5[5]

child's sense of justice, 102, 191, 193

organizations concerned with, 224, 226, 227, 228, 229

See also individual issues

socioeconomic structure and power, 1, 3, 14-15, 24 fig., 25-28, 26 fig., 226, 228

economic policies and consequences, 25-27, 28-31, 148-149, 188-190, 194, 198

expectations and strategies for, 26, 28, 34

power in, 14, 24 fig., 22-28, 45

in race issues, 63, 64, 66

resources about, 211, 212

role of drugs in system, 153-157

in school system, 30, 119-130

in racial issues, 66, 68-69, 70, 71

resources about violence, 221-222, 208n2[15]

in school and sports, 132-133

sexual, 23, 44, 178, 206n2[2], 206n2[3]

sources of, 39, 44, 45, 102, 142, 148-149, 152

against women, 23, 161, 168-169, 170-172, 206n2[2], 208n2[11]

W

women, 14, 40-41, 52, 161

abusive behavior toward, 23, 161, 167-168, 170-172, 208n2[15]

advertised images of, 45, 181, 186, 187, 188

anti-women bias, 9, 14, 46-47, 161, 162, 163-165, 168-170

background experiences, 37-41, 51

categorizing women, 168-170

consequences of male control, 22-23, 166

emotional support roles of, 1, 45, 94, 134, 165-166, 172, 176

exercises and questions concerning, 33, 39, 40, 41, 43, 46, 164, 169

expectations of girls, 37-38, 40-41

male expectations of, 45, 165-166, 168-72

men as allies, 47, 161, 172

messages boys receive about, 169, 178, 181

models for male treatment of, 46-47, 163-164, 168, 170, 171

organizations concerned with, 225, 226, 227, 228, 229

parenting role of, 43, 164-165

respect of, 9, 46, 162, 163-165, 172

safety issues, 166, 167, 168-170, 170-172

as scapegoats, 41, 42, 45

violence against, 160, 161, 166, 168-169, 170-172

worksheet on "Conditions for Sexual Intimacy," 181-182

Y

youth, 186-190, 198, 203

agreement issues, 104-105, 109-112, 207n3[10]

allies and advocates for, 18-20, 60-61, 79-80, 82, 100, 195-200

behavior issues, 106, 107, 108, 109, 115-118, 166-168

community participation, 2, 3, 4, 33, 191-196, 199-200, 203, 205n2[Intro]

culture issues, 88-89, 198

discipline issues, 105-106, 110, 111, 112-118, 207n39

discouragement from adults, 30-31, 33

friends and relationships, 106, 186

images and scapegoating of youth, 3, 27, 195, 206n42

job prospects and skills, 26, 30, 104-106, 116-118

leadership skills, 3-4, 193, 194, 195, 199-200, 225, 227, 205n[Intro]

organizations concerned with, 225, 226, 227, 228, 229

public policy affecting, 3, 19, 25-27, 82, 196-199

questions and exercises about, 89, 113, 196

safety and respect issues, 56, 142-144, 148-149

school conditions, 116-118, 166-168, 197, 198

YouthBuild USA, 194-195

Youth Council, 194

Youth Credit Union, 194

youth culture, questions about, 89

Youth for Environmental Sanity, 193-194

Z

Zinn, Howard, 127

If you have enjoyed *Boys Will Be Men* then you may also enjoy
the following title by the same author:

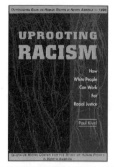

UPROOTING RACISM

How White People Can Work for Racial Justice

Paul Kivel

Uprooting Racism highlights the many ways in which concerned white people can play an active role in confronting
white racism, and helps the reader understand racism and explore
its manifestations in politics, work, community, and family life. It
moves beyond the definition and unlearning of racism to address
the many areas of privilege for white people and suggests ways for
individuals and groups to challenge the structures of racism.

Pb US$16.95 ISBN 0-86571-338-3 / CAN$19.95 ISBN 1-55092-277-7

Other related titles published by New Society Publishers:

DAUGHTERS OF THE MOON, SISTERS OF THE SUN

Young Women and Mentors on the Transition to Womanhood

K. Wind Hughes & Linda Wolf

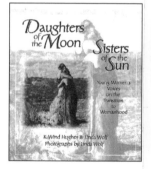

This book of compelling photos and autobiographical
stories from more than forty teenage girls who participated weekly in a two-year focus group provides validation,
support and vision for girls facing the transition to woman-
hood. By sharing themselves intimately on topics ranging
from bulimia to drugs, and from pregnancy through sui-
cide, these young women explore the process of discovery, healing, and self-esteem; they
are accompanied by interviews with accomplished women mentors — including Michele
Akers, Maya Angelou, Riane Eisler, Carol Gilligan, and the Indigo Girls.

Pb US$19.95 / CAN$24.95   ISBN 0-86571-377-4

*You may also want to check out NSP's Educational & Parenting Resources
which focus especially on conflict education and resolution.*

NEW SOCIETY PUBLISHERS

www.newsociety.com
800-567-6772